CONTROLLING FACTORS IN ECONOMIC DEVELOPMENT

THE BROOKINGS INSTITUTION

The Brookings Institution—Devoted to Public Service through Research and Training in the Social Sciences—was incorporated on December 8, 1927. Broadly stated, the Institution has two primary purposes: the first is to aid constructively in the development of sound national policies; and the second is to offer training of a supergraduate character to students of the social sciences.

The responsibility for the final determination of the Institution's policies and its program of work for the administration of its endowment is vested in a self-perpetuating board of trustees. It is the function of the trustees to make possible the conduct of scientific research under the most favorable conditions, and to safeguard the independence of the research staff in the pursuit of their studies and in the publication of the results of such studies. It is not a part of their function to determine, control, or influence the conduct of particular investigations or the conclusions reached, but only to approve the principal fields of investigation to which the available funds are to be allocated, and to satisfy themselves with reference to the intellectual competence and scientific integrity of the staff. Major responsibility for "formulating general policies and coordinating the activities of the Institution" is vested in the president. The by-laws provide also that "there shall be an advisory council selected by the president from among the scientific staff of the Institution."

Authors of studies published by the Institution have had the advice, criticism, and assistance both of an administrative officer and of a cooperating committee selected from the staff. In manuscript accepted for publication, the author has freedom to present his final interpretations and conclusions, although they may not necessarily be concurred in by some or all of those who cooperate with him or by other members of the staff. The Institution in publishing the work assumes the responsibility that it meets reasonable tests of scholarship and presents data and conclusions worthy of public consideration.

Controlling Factors *in* Economic Development

By
HAROLD G. MOULTON

Washington, D.C.
THE BROOKINGS INSTITUTION
1949

Set up and printed
Published June 1949

Printed in the United States of America
George Banta Publishing Company
Menasha, Wisconsin

To My Wife

Frances Rawlins Moulton

The study upon which this publication is based was made possible by funds granted by THE MAURICE AND LAURA FALK FOUNDATION of Pittsburgh. However, the FALK FOUNDATION is not the author, publisher, or proprietor of this publication and is not to be understood as approving or disapproving by virtue of its grant any of the statements and views expressed herein.

PREFACE

This volume is in the nature of a synthesis of the economic studies in which the author has participated during the last thirty years. Such an interpretative treatise was conceived as an ultimate objective at the time the Brookings Institution was established and its broad program of investigation was organized. Many of our inductive investigations of specific problems have contributed to its making, and it could not have been written in the absence of such studies.

I have chosen *Controlling Factors in Economic Development* as the title because of my view that this phrase best expresses the essence of the economic problem. It is concerned equally with the factors which impede and restrict, and those which generate and promote, economic advancement. The older textbooks on the "principles" or "laws" of economics were largely preoccupied with the factors which limit production and the laws which govern relative values and income shares. Later treatises were perhaps more concerned with the forces which maintain the economic system in a state of equilibrium. Scant attention was given to the dynamic factors which progressively offset the limitations of nature and open vast possibilities for economic development.

Part I looks backward and undertakes to appraise the forces and factors which accounted for the extraordinary, and unexpected, economic progress of the nineteenth and early twentieth centuries, and also the sources of maladjustment which restrained the rate of advancement. Part II looks forward. It indicates the economic potentialities of the century ahead and outlines the policies essential to their realization.

I take this occasion to express my deep appreciation to the scientific staff of the Brookings Institution, past and present, for their constructive aid in the development of this analysis. I am very especially indebted to Dr. Joseph Mayer for assistance in Part I and for much of the material presented in Chapter VII. Dr. Louis Marlio was of great aid in interpreting the significance of developments in the realm of physical science and engineering, and Russell S. McBride, editor of Chemical Engineering, performed a similar service in connection with the significance of chemistry. Karl T. Schlotterbeck collaborated on Chapters IX and X and served with numerous other staff members as critical reviewers. Louise Bebb prepared the charts and A. Evelyn Breck edited the manuscript.

Finally, I desire to express my particular indebtedness to The Maurice and Laura Falk Foundation of Pittsburgh, for having made possible this study, as well as numerous others which laid the foundations for it.

Harold G. Moulton,
President

The Brookings Institution
May 1949

CONTENTS

PART I. LOOKING BACKWARD

CHAPTER I

CHAPTER II

CHAPTER VI

CHAPTER VII

CHAPTER VIII

CHAPTER IX

CHAPTER X

CHAPTER XI

APPENDIX

PART I

LOOKING BACKWARD

CHAPTER I

SOURCES OF ECONOMIC DEVELOPMENT

The primary sources of economic growth and development may best be revealed by a study of the factors involved in the great economic expansion of modern times. The hundred-year period preceding 1930 was one of wholly unprecedented economic growth. If recorded history were reflected on the face of a clock, the period up to 1830 would represent the time from 12:00 midnight to approximately 11:40 in the morning, while the remaining 20 minutes until noon would represent the century from 1830 to 1930. The astounding fact is that during this 20 minutes economic progress—as measured in terms of the increase in output per man per hour—was as great as that in the entire 700 minutes of preceding time. What were the sources of this phenomenal development?

Before undertaking to appraise the forces responsible for this extraordinary economic growth, it will be interesting to note how the economic analysts of the preceding century foresaw the future. Beginning with Adam Smith, who published his *Wealth of Nations* in 1776, a succession of economic writers known as the classical school had formulated by the middle of the nineteenth century a systematic body of economic principles which set forth what they regarded as the controlling factors in economic development. The ultimate expression of this general system of economic thought is found in John Stuart Mill's *Principles of Political Economy*, published in 1848. These scholars, like their colleagues in the natural sciences, based their conclusions on fundamental physical factors which they believed to be of decisive importance.

I. THE DISMAL FORECAST A CENTURY AGO

The extraordinary economic expansion which was to occur was not expected by the classical school of economists. On the contrary, most of them forecast a relatively static situation in which there appeared to be little hope for improvement in the lot of the masses. Let us review briefly the arguments on which this somber outlook rested.

The dismal forecast was based on two related physical facts deemed of controlling importance.

The first physical fact which the early economists emphasized was the "niggardliness of nature." Land and other natural resources were none too productive at best; and the supply of the richer areas was very limited. *Scarcity* of resources was thus regarded as an inescapable limiting factor.

Coupled with the scarcity of resources was the law of *diminishing returns.* It was recognized that the yield of land might be materially increased through improved methods of tillage and more intensive cultivation; but it seemed obvious that there were very definite limits to the productive power of any given acre of ground. Moreover, it was noted that the point would soon be reached where the added yield would not be proportional to the added labor and other costs; that is, the *returns* would *diminish* in relation to the effort expended. Accordingly, as population increased, there could in due course be no escape from decreasing output per man hour. It would be necessary either to cultivate the more fertile areas under conditions of diminishing returns or to bring under cultivation poorer and still poorer land.

It was conceded that new highly productive agricultural areas might still be discovered or opened to settlement; but such possibilities were limited. It should be remembered that even at this time much of the great Middle West of America had already been penetrated by pioneer settlers, and that it did not appear probable that other virgin areas of comparable significance existed on the planet.

Thus the scarcity of rich land and the operation of the law of diminishing returns appeared to set definite limits to economic expansion. The same factors were regarded as equally operative with other natural resources —mineral, forest, and aquatic.

The second physical fact was the natural tendency for population to increase at a *geometric* rate. With productive resources increasing but slowly and subject to diminishing returns, there would inevitably be a continuous pressure of expanding population against limited productive resources.

Thus was laid the foundation for the *iron law of wages*, which held that actual living standards will always tend to be pressed down to the minimum of subsistence. While wars and pestilences might serve at times to reduce the excess population, there appeared little hope for any permanent improvement in living standards. The conditions of life in China, India, and other old civilizations afforded striking illustration of the permanent tendency of population growth to outrun the supply of productive natural resources.

The early writers did not attach much significance to capital development.

In analyzing the factors responsible for economic progress, the classical writers placed comparatively little emphasis upon the potential significance of capital. Such epoch-making inventions as the steam engine and the steamboat, the cotton gin and the spinning jenny, were of course extolled as having made possible the factory system in manufacturing enterprise; and there was frequent reference to general "improvements in the productive arts." The importance of thrift was also emphasized. Indeed, it was pointed out that savings and the creation of capital were indispensable to economic progress. But it nevertheless remains true that these writers attached no *decisive* importance to machinery and other capital instruments as means of increasing productive efficiency and raising living standards.

Adam Smith emphasized the increasing riches that would accrue to nations from: (1) the removal of restrictions on private enterprise; (2) the extension of the principle of division of labor; and (3) geographic specialization, facilitated by the elimination of barriers to international trade.

By *division of labor* was meant the breaking up of the production of a given commodity into a number of distinct stages. [The modern term for this principle would be specialization.] The principle of division of labor was made broad enough to cover both specialization by tasks and specialization by industries, trades, and occupations.

Smith illustrated the principle of specialization by reference to the making of pins. He pointed out that when one individual made an entire pin, a day or more of time was required, whereas, once the process of pin-making had been divided into a number of specialized acts in which "one man draws out the wire, another straights it, a third cuts it, a fourth points it, a fifth grinds it at the top for receiving the head," etc., a group of ten persons could make nearly 50,000 pins in a day.

Since Smith wrote before the industrial age, it was natural that he should attach little importance to capital instruments. Capital meant to him chiefly *stocks* of goods (inventories, in modern parlance), the materials which hand labor was engaged in processing. While Smith recognized that machines saved labor, they were discussed as a minor topic under *division of labor*.

The classical writers in general, while emphasizing the importance of the principle of division of labor, did not of course deem it capable of continuous extension. It could not offset for long the operation of diminishing returns resulting from the pressure of population against limited natural resources.

The advantages derived from *geographic specialization* were regarded as of great significance. Since geographic regions were highly diverse in character, much was to be gained from concentrating production in each area upon the things for which it was best adapted and exchanging products with other areas. This conception was the basis of Adam Smith's argument that the most effective means of promoting the wealth of each and every nation was to abandon the restrictive "mercantilist" philosophy and remove all barriers to free international exchange.

John Stuart Mill, writing in the middle of the nineteenth century, had of course witnessed the first stage of the industrial revolution. Yet he saw no great potentialities in capital instruments. Rather he concluded that: "It is questionable if all the mechanical inventions yet made have lightened the day's toil of any human being."[1] He was apparently impressed with the fact that the factory system had not as yet shortened appreciably the length of the working day or raised materially the level of real wages—which was constantly depressed by the rapid increase in urban population.

The possibilities of capital expansion appeared to be limited by basic natural laws.

Two lines of reasoning contributed to this pessimistic conclusion. On the one hand, it was noted that the amount of money set aside for capital investment depends upon the ability and also the disposition of the people to save. Saving of course involves sacrifices—a restriction of present consumption. But for a double reason the great majority of human beings could not be expected to save much. First, they were, in the main, regarded as shiftless and thriftless—almost wholly lacking in forethought; and, second, the existing plane of living was so meager that there was little if any margin out of which savings might be made. Hence large savings did not appear probable—however much the virtues of thrift might be extolled.

A second line of reasoning proceeded from the demand side. It was observed that the rate of interest that would be paid for savings funds depends upon the efficiency of the additional capital goods that might be created. It was pointed out that since additional capital goods must be used in conjunction with limited natural resources, subject to the law of diminishing returns, the output made possible by additional units of capital would in due course decrease; and hence the rate of interest that would be paid for its use would naturally decline. In consequence, the inducement to save would be lessened, and the flow of savings would be automatically reduced.

Thus even if the people should perchance for a time become more thrifty and be able and willing to increase their savings, the process would quickly become self-defeating.[2]

Mill held that the rate of return on capital in a country of large production and substantial savings "is habitually within, as it were, a hand's breadth of the minimum, and the country therefore on the very verge of the stationary state."[3] He noted, however, three factors which work to prevent interest and profits from reaching absolute zero. One was "the waste of capital in periods of over-trading and rash speculation, and in the commercial revulsions by which such times are always followed." Another was "the perpetual overflow of capital into colonies or foreign countries." A third was resulting "improvements in production" which by reducing costs extend the "field of employment." It will be observed that the virtue of the first two of these factors was found in the fact that they destroy or get rid of excess capital—thereby relieving the pressure. The emphasis placed upon these capital destroying factors indicates that the third or constructive factor was regarded as of very minor importance. At the most it was thought of as providing additional employment. It was not conceived as a creative force capable of easing the burden of toil and progressively raising the levels of living for all mankind.

That these factors could presumably only postpone

an ultimate static condition is indicated by the following concluding statement in Mill's analysis. Unlike many of his contemporaries, Mill was disposed to look upon the approaching stationary society as perhaps a blessing:

It must always have been seen, more or less distinctly, by political economists, that the increase of wealth is not boundless; that at the end of what they term the progressive state lies the stationary state, that all progress in wealth is but a postponement of this, and that each step in advance is an approach to it. . . .

This impossibility of ultimately avoiding the stationary state—this irresistible necessity that the stream of human industry should finally spread itself out into an apparently stagnant sea—must have been, to the political economists of the last two generations, an unpleasing and discouraging prospect; for the tone and tendency of their speculations go completely to identify all that is economically desirable with the progressive state, and with that alone.

I cannot regard the stationary state of capital and wealth with the unaffected aversion so generally manifested toward it by political economists of the old school. I am inclined to believe that it would be, on the whole, a very considerable improvement on our present condition. I confess that I am not charmed with the ideal of life held out by those who think that the normal state of human beings is that of struggling to get on; that the trampling, crushing, elbowing, and treading on each other's heels, which form the existing type of social life, are the most desirable lot of human kind, or anything but the disagreeable symptoms of one of the phases of industrial progress. . . .

The density of population necessary to enable mankind to obtain in the greatest degree, all the advantages both of cooperation and of social intercourse, has, in all the most populous countries, been attained. A population may be too crowded, though all be amply supplied with food and raiment. It is not good for man to be kept perforce at all times in the presence of his species. A world from which solitude is extirpated is a very poor ideal.

It is true that not all of the early English economic writers expressed equal pessimism about the future. Adam Smith was preoccupied with the immediate gains that might be obtained by removing hampering restrictions on enterprise and on trade, and he was not much concerned with the limiting long-run factors. Some writers attached more importance to the progress of the arts and to the perfectibility of human nature than did others. But it remains true that it was the somber conclusions, based on the limitations of nature and of man, which gave to political economy the appellation of "dismal science."

It should be added that there were a few early writers, outside the classical group, who were much more hopeful with respect to the future of economic trends. For example, an obscure Scottish writer, John Rae, foresaw unlimited possibilities flowing from "the progress of the inventive faculty"; and J. B. Say, a French economist with an industrial background, had a deep insight into the significance of mechanized industry. But they were looked upon as outsiders, and their studies were not even published in Great Britain.

It should be noted here also that as time passed economists in the classical tradition came gradually to attach great importance to industrial capital. Indeed, by the end of the nineteenth century thrift, saving, investment, and capital accumulation were being extolled as the sources of progress and rising living standards. Even so, as we shall see, the specter of diminishing returns had not been allayed. (See pages 36-37.)

II. FACTORS OVERLOOKED

It is obvious that there was something basically defective in the analysis of the early classical economists—

for instead of static conditions and perpetual poverty, we have had a highly dynamic society and an astounding improvement in the material well-being of all classes. Either their underlying assumptions were faulty, or important new factors which could not be foreseen entered the picture.

Two possible explanations immediately suggest themselves: (1) that the extent to which new agricultural resources might be discovered and opened for settlement had been greatly underestimated; and (2) that the influence of birth control in restraining the rate of population growth had been overlooked.

The progress since 1850 cannot be explained by the discovery of extensive new agricultural areas.

Some important agricultural areas were, to be sure, opened for settlement in the world after 1850; and the frontiers within the United States continued to be extended for another generation or so. But since the most rapid improvement in living standards has occurred since the disappearance of frontiers—that is, since about 1900—it is evident that the primary explanation is not to be found in the continued discovery of rich arable lands.

It is highly interesting to note that grave concern over food shortages and consequent progressive increases in food prices continued to be manifest throughout the nineteenth century. Among economic writers it was accepted doctrine that food prices must progressively rise. In a presidential address before the British Association for the Advancement of Science in 1898, Sir William Crooks, a distinguished physical scientist, confidently forecast the future as follows:[4]

England and all civilized nations stand in deadly peril of not having enough to eat. . . . Should all the wheat-growing countries add to their area to the utmost capacity, . . . [it] would give us only an addition of some 100,000,000 acres, supplying at the average world yield of 12.7 bushels to the acre, . . . just enough to supply the increase of population among the bread eaters until the year 1931. . . . Thirty years is but a day in the life of a nation. Those present who may attend the meeting of the British Association thirty years hence will judge how far my forecasts are justified.

Thirty years later the leading nations were consuming more and were troubled not with rising prices but with the phenomenon of market surpluses and persistently falling prices. By that time the "agricultural problem" had come to be conceived rather in terms of overproduction than of scarcity.[5]

The escape from poverty was not the result of a declining rate of population growth.

Notwithstanding a decreasing birth rate in certain social groups, we have had an extraordinary growth in aggregate population. In fact, during this century the population of the world as a whole increased at a much more rapid rate than during preceding centuries. The British population rose from 26.7 millions in 1840 to over 47 millions a hundred years later; while that of the United States increased from 17 to nearly 130 millions. In this period, however, per-capita income, both in England and the United States, rose some three- to fourfold. In Japan from 1870 to 1930 the population more than doubled; meanwhile the standard of living, instead of falling as was expected, rose well over 100 per cent.[6]

Several developments combined to produce the great era of economic progress.

One of these developments—science and technology—was fundamental in character, operating directly to increase productive power and to offset the limitations of nature. The others were improvements in economic organization, which facilitated the progress made possible by science and technological applications. Among the most important of these were: (1) the creation of the corporate form of business organization; (2) the evolution of bank credit; and (3) the maintenance of improved monetary and fiscal systems. The significance of such developments could not of course have been perceived a century ago.

It will be observed that in this list of factors no reference is made to "free enterprise." This is because the so-called system of free business enterprise did not come into being *during* the period under review. It had already been in existence for a half century at least, and its virtues rather than being overlooked were vigorously expounded by most of the economic writers whose dour conclusions are summarized above. (See Chap. VI.)

A. Science and Technology

The most fundamental of the several developments which combined to transform the economic world during the last century has been the phenomenal advance in science. Without scientific discoveries and their application through engineering to the processes of production, the limiting factors discussed by the early economists might well have operated to prevent any great improvement in living standards.

The economists of a century ago had witnessed only

the beginnings of the technological revolution. There had been numerous important inventions in the field of textile production, and a considerable range of small-scale manufacturing had developed. Of much greater potential significance was the beginning made in the use of steam power in manufacturing and in transportation. But most of the great scientific discoveries and inventions were yet to come. Engineering was still in the infancy stage, and the epoch-making developments in the fields of metallurgy, electricity, oil, and chemistry belonged to the future. While as events proved economic society was on the threshold of a technological revolution, observers of the time could scarcely be expected to perceive the economic significance of coming developments.

In every field of production—agriculture, mining, manufacturing, transportation, public utilities—the developments which have occurred have increased manyfold the productive power of the individual worker. Instead of diminishing returns from natural resources—agriculture and mining—we have witnessed constantly increasing returns. This outcome, as we shall see, is not so much a result of the discovery of *new* agricultural and mineral resources as of a more efficient use of *known* resources.

I. THE REVOLUTION IN AGRICULTURE

Until well into the nineteenth century there had been very little improvement in methods of agricultural production for many centuries. Indeed, in 1800 farmers were in the main employing the production techniques of 3,000 years earlier. The crude wooden plows were so antiquated that in many areas hand tools for preparing the soil were preferred. Small grains were broadcast by hand; hoes were used in planting cotton and corn; haying and harvesting were done with the scythe and the cradle, and threshing with the flail.[7]

The great era of technological progress in agriculture may be said to have begun in the second quarter of the nineteenth century. In the succeeding 100 years, two distinct types of development combined to revolutionize agricultural production methods. One was the introduction of labor-saving machinery—made possible by preceding developments in the field of manufacture. The other was the direct use of scientific knowledge in agricultural production—a development, in the main, since 1900.

The use of labor-saving machinery in agriculture has involved two stages: the first was the replacement of hand tools by machines—the mowing machine for the scythe, the reaper for the cradle, the cultivator for the hoe. The second stage came with the introduction of power-driven machinery during the last thirty years.

The significance of farm machinery is found in reduced labor requirements and net costs.

The increase in man-hour output resulting from the introduction of labor-saving machines was truly extraordinary, even before the advent of power machinery. For example, the Department of Agriculture estimates that around 1830 about 50 to 60 man-hours of labor were required to produce one acre (20 bushels) of wheat —with walking plow, brush for harrow, hand broadcast of seed, sickle, and flail; while in the nineties to produce 20 bushels of wheat on an acre with gang-plow, seeder, harrow, binder, thresher, wagon and horse, only

8 to 10 man-hours of labor were required. This represents a saving in labor amounting to as much as 85 per cent. The labor saving in corn production between 1850 and the nineties was roughly 50 per cent.[8] In a broad group of farm products—including grains, cotton, hay, and potatoes, the saving in labor time during the course of the nineteenth century averaged nearly 80 per cent.[9]

These savings in labor requirements were not offset by the added cost of the machines. In the group of farm products referred to above, the *dollar* costs of production decreased more than 50 per cent in fifty years—and this despite a four-fold increase in farm wage rates.[10]

Since 1900 the increasing variety of farm machines and the extensive use of mechanical power have brought large additional labor economies in agriculture. In wheat, for example, only 3 to 4 man-hours of labor were required in 1939 to produce one acre of wheat with three-bottom gang plow, tractor, ten-foot tandem disk harrow, twelve-foot combine, and trucks. In American agriculture as a whole the increase in output per worker between 1900 and 1939 was as much as 90 per cent.[11]

The primary significance of the development of farm machinery in the nineteenth century is found in its effect upon costs rather than upon yields per acre. With some crops the yield may have been increased somewhat as a result of the better tillage which machines make possible, but in other cases the output may have been adversely affected. In any case, the statistics of crop production reveal no important changes in the decades here under review—in contrast with the results achieved in the period of scientific agriculture which followed.

The significance of the direct use of science in agriculture lies in increased yields.

The scientific age in agriculture is the result of the scientific research fostered by the Department of Agriculture, agricultural colleges and experiment stations, and also by industries dependent upon agricultural markets. These scientific developments have been directed along the following principal lines:

(1) Better systems of crop rotation.

(2) Soil fertility improvement—by studies of the chemical requirements of plants; the development of fertilizer formulas for different soils and crops; the better placement of fertilizers in relation to plants; the various types of soil conservation.

(3) Plant disease control—by means of spraying and dusting, quarantines, and baits; the discovery and importation of "natural enemies"; and the wholesale destruction of infested plants.

(4) Plant breeding or genetics—for the double purpose of obtaining more productive plants and stronger disease-resistant organisms.

(5) Animal breeding—through the process of careful selection of the best specimens and the rapid elimination of poor producers—with special attention in recent years to the development of disease-resistant qualities.

(6) Control of animal diseases—such as hog cholera, the cattle tick, bovine tuberculosis, and the hoof and mouth disease.

(7) Animal nutrition, involving the use of scientific knowledge of food values and the requirements for balanced rations.

These developments have served directly to increase output per acre. They have also conserved and increased the food value of plants, and they have increased the productivity of livestock. It is only within the last 25 years, however, that the effects upon yields have become important. Future potentialities along these lines, discussed in Chapter VII, are very great.

As a result of the technological improvements thus briefly sketched, the percentage of the working population engaged in agricultural production steadily declined over the century under review, while at the same time per-capita consumption of foodstuffs steadily expanded. Whereas in 1830 as much as 70 per cent of the labor force was engaged in agriculture, by 1940 the figure had been reduced to less than 18 per cent.

2. THE REVOLUTION IN MINERAL PRODUCTION

During the century under review, mineral exploration and prospecting uncovered vast resources unknown to our forefathers. But important as these discoveries have been they are of less significance than the expansion of mineral resources that has resulted from improvements in the arts of mining and mineral processing.

Mineral technology has both increased resources and reduced costs of production.

The application of scientific knowledge in this field has brought improvements of many types. The more important of these may be briefly summarized as follows:[12]

Prospecting has been greatly facilitated by geology, aided by equipment devised in the laboratories of physicists and seismologists.

Deeper mining has been made possible by improved ventilation and air conditioning, which combat both high temperatures and high humidity.

The rotary drill and the development of superior steel alloys, and special cements adapted to high temperatures have made it possible to drill oil wells to great depths, thereby making available enormous additional reservoirs of oil, and uncovering huge new fuel resources in the form of natural gas. (See Chapter VII below.)

Blasting, by means of low freezing and low density explosives, has greatly decreased the cost of mining operations.

The development of the pneumatic rock drill has led, even within the last 25 years, to a three-fold increase in drilling speed.

Block caving methods have made it possible to mine economically much lower grade ores.

Power shovels for loading by compressed air, and electric locomotives have greatly reduced the cost of moving ores.

During this period there were developed: the cyanide process in gold and silver mining; the open-hearth method in steel production; froth flotation in copper mining; the electrolytic process in aluminum, copper, zinc, and lead refining; and the debismuthizing of lead by the addition of calcium and antimony. It has been said that: "At least once every generation technical advances in methods of treatment make new mines out of old dumps or revive abandoned mining districts."

These improvements in metallurgical methods have brought a great reduction in the amount of labor required to turn out a given quantity of product. In the mineral industry as a whole, one man in 1939 could turn out in an hour 3.67 times as much as in 1902; in the oil and gas division the increase in man-hour efficiency was nearly five-fold.[13] Since these progressive decreases in labor requirements were not matched by corresponding increases in capital requirements, there was a continuous decline in over-all costs of production.

Modern methods have improved the quality of minerals and also furnished additional metals.

There have been many improvements in the quality of minerals to meet specific consumption requirements. Washeries and cleaning plants installed at mines have reduced ash and sulphur content. Uniform sizing has increased efficiency in blast furnaces. The efficiency of fuel has been improved by better heating devices such as residential stokers. The development of large public utility power plants has reduced the amount of coal required to produce a kilowatt hour of electric power from over 7 pounds in 1899 to an average of 1.4 pounds in 1936. Special analyses have been made to determine the relative yield of gas, coke, and by-products for particular purposes.

Improved methods of production have also given us important additional by-product metals. For example, silenium is obtained from copper residues, palladium from electrolytic nickel production, and cadmium from lead refining.

Because of the vast importance of oil, an additional statement is desirable with respect to this mineral. The first American oil well was opened in 1859. In the next 60 years oil—because of its combined uses in lighting and heating and as lubricant and source of power—came to be regarded as indispensable to modern civilization. But exploitation of this rich mineral resource had been so rapid that by the end of World War I grave fears were expressed over its prospective early exhaustion. Twenty-eight billion barrels of oil had been produced in the United States between 1860 and 1920; and remaining reserves were estimated at only 7 billion barrels. By the end of 1943, however, 27 billion barrels of additional oil had been produced, and the proved reserves were then estimated at 20 billion barrels. As a leading oil geologist points out:

> The recoverable oil reserve is not a fixed quantity. . . . As time proceeds, more oil is discovered by existing techniques, new methods of discovery are devised, the areas of search are extended both regionally and vertically. The efficiency of recovery is raised, the effectiveness of processing and utilization is improved, and entirely new resources are created by chemical science through its ability to rearrange molecular structures. . . .[14]

Modern methods of oil processing have, moreover, greatly increased efficiency in the use of oil, thereby lessening the amount required for a given purpose. This is of course equivalent to an increased quantity of oil reserves.

In summary, the revolution in mining processes has furnished us abundant supplies of mineral products. Instead of expected shortages, we have had in many lines chronic surpluses. Thus the mineral foundations for an expanding economy proved altogether adequate.

3. CREATIVE CHEMISTRY

Perhaps the most remarkable scientific achievements of the last century have been those in the field of chemistry. Chemistry has not only given us many new products and increased the value of old ones; it underlies so many productive processes and industries that its influence ramifies throughout the economic system. Not the least of its contributions is found in its effects upon medical science and health.

Chemistry is creative because of its capacity to transform matter.

We have already noted that entirely new resources of oil have been created by the capacity of chemistry to rearrange molecular structures. It is of similar importance in the field of agriculture where knowledge of the chemical composition of soils and the requirements for plant growth produces phenomenal results. Scientific chemical processes have converted waste materials into useful products and also given us numerous new products and synthetic materials—often equal, if not superior, to natural products. Among these may be mentioned rayon, rubber, oil, leather, and plastics. Chemical science also played a role of vast significance in many phases of modern metallurgy. Finally, it discovered and developed the principle of catalysis, by which the presence of a small quantity of a given material permitted other materials to be fruitfully combined.

The significance of chemistry is manifest not only in the wealth of new and important products which it has created or made possible, but also in its competitive stimulus and in its effects upon productive efficiency in the varied industrial fields to which it contributes. By developing methods which reduce costs of production and improve quality, its economic effects are cumulative in character. Chemistry is truly the equivalent of a new fundamental productive factor—comparable in importance to the primary factors—land, labor, and capital.

4. NEW TYPES OF POWER

A century ago the economic importance of steam power was already apparent. The steam engine (1775) had made possible a small-scale factory system and to some extent had broadened market areas by expediting and cheapening transportation. But the electric motor and the gasoline engine belonged to the future.

Electric power development exerted a very great influence on nearly every phase of economic life. It not only conferred direct benefits of inestimable importance upon consumers, but it also increased productive efficiency, especially in the fields of mining, manufacturing, and transportation.

The significance of electric power lies in its transmissibility and its divisibility.

Electric energy possesses a supreme advantage over steam power in that electric current may be sent long distances from its source, and at low cost. Moreover, it can be divided into whatever sized power units may be needed for particular tasks. If 1,000 kilowatts are necessary per hour, that amount is furnished at whatever spot desired; if only 10 watts are needed, that amount is supplied. Within a factory it may be used for lighting, heating, and cooling purposes, or for propelling machinery—both heavy installations and small portable tools.

The very high temperatures generated in electric furnaces have brought extraordinary advances in metallurgy, especially in the development of alloys, making possible the high-speed, precision machine tools, which have so remarkably increased the efficiency of production in recent times. Electricity has also permitted the development of the electro-chemical industry, including aluminum and magnesium.

The production of electric power has not been subject to diminishing returns. That is, despite the fact that it is derived from natural resources (coal for steam power; falling water for hydroelectric power), the most productive of which would presumably have been utilized first, the cost of electric current has been progressively lowered. This has been made possible in the case of steam power by better mining techniques, and by vast improvements in power generating methods. In the case of hydroelectric power, decreased costs have been made possible both by the development of larger power works and equipment and the development of ever more efficient transmission systems.

Oil, and the internal combustion engine, introduced mobile power

The invention of the internal combustion engine, using a then inconsequential by-product of kerosene—gasoline—opened the way to a new revolution in transportation. The distinguishing feature of this new type of power lay in the fact that an individual could carry it with him—in whatever amounts suited his convenience. To a limited extent only had this been true of either steam or electricity.

This new type of power was of greatest significance in expediting and cheapening *local* transportation—within urban communities, between farm and town, and on the farm. In these areas gasoline power was replacing chiefly horsepower. Motor transport thus contributed enormously to the efficiency of production, particularly in farming and in local distribution. The importance of the automobile from the standpoint of personal enjoyment is of course another story.

The significance of the internal combustion engine has been most strikingly revealed by the developments of the Second World War. The speed and mobility of motor vehicles has radically altered the character of ground warfare, while the airplane has created a new operational dimension.

The economic consequences of the power revolution have been so far-reaching and pervasive that some writers have asserted that the development of modern power (like chemistry) has been the equivalent of the creation of a new basic factor in production. It is clear in any case that it has enormously increased the effectiveness with which labor and capital may be employed.

Future potentialities in these various fields will be discussed in Chapter VII.

5. THE INCREASING SIZE OF BUSINESS ENTERPRISES

A century ago factory production was still on a very small scale. Since transportation was too slow or costly to permit long-distance freight traffic, except in articles of relatively high value, most products were sold in local markets. The revolution in transportation made possible by the new forms of power, created both national markets and world markets for a wide range of commodities.

The widening of markets had two consequences of profound importance. First, the advantages of geographical specialization and exchange of products which the early economists had emphasized could for the first time be fully realized. Second, and more important, the size of the business establishment, or factory, hitherto limited by restricted sales outlets, could now be almost indefinitely expanded.

Large-scale enterprise resulted in an unprecedented increase in productive efficiency.

The second half of the nineteenth century witnessed a gigantic effort on the part of industries to expand the scale of operations, in order to take advantage of broad markets and to realize the economies inherent in volume production. This expansion in the scale of business operations in turn made possible the installation of machinery and equipment of ever-increasing size and efficiency. Meanwhile, continuing scientific discoveries and progress in engineering constantly accelerated the process.

6. THE FUNDAMENTAL SIGNIFICANCE OF CAPITAL

As was pointed out above, the early classical economists attached relatively little importance to capital as a means of offsetting the limitations of nature. In their conception, increasing capital meant chiefly adding more units of capital of the same kind and quality as existing units. It was this conception which led to their conclusion that since the added capital must be used in conjunction with natural resources subject to diminishing returns, the productivity of the additional units of capital would in due course inevitably decline. They did not foresee the rapidly increasing productiveness of machines and tools.

The ever-increasing efficiency of machines and tools has multiplied man-hour productivity.

The increasing productivity of capital instruments as measured by man-hour output has come from the invention of new types of materials and machines, from improvements in the quality of tools, from greater durability of materials, and from the increased size of plant, fixed installations, and movable equipment. Modern machine tools are incomparably superior in performance to those of only two decades ago. The Diesel engine has multiplied traction power. The efficiency of the present steam electric turbine is many times that of its prototype.

In consequence of developments such as these, a new machine may have an efficiency double or triple that of the one it replaces, although the dollar cost may be the same. Or, a larger machine, costing twice as much as its predecessor, may have a producing capacity five times as great. Adding better units of capital is a wholly different matter from adding like units, which was the assumption of earlier economists.

The increasing productivity of capital instruments, aided by improvements in the organization and layout of industrial establishments, has greatly increased man-hour output during the course of the last century. Between the Civil War and the end of the century, machine methods were introduced in a wide range of manufacturing industries. Perhaps the most striking advance in productivity accompanying the shift from hand to machine methods was that which occurred in the manufacture of shoes and textiles. At the end of the period as compared with the beginning, there could be produced in a given time about 8 times as many pairs of shoes, 74 times as many pounds of cotton thread, and 80 times as many yards of gingham. The accompanying reduction in the cost of labor per unit of output during these three and a half decades was equally dramatic. For shoes the reduction was from $4.60 a pair to 60 cents, for cotton thread from 87 cents a pound to 2 cents, and for gingham from 20 cents a yard to 1 cent.[15]

After 1900 improvements in machine technique were rapidly extended throughout the greater part of the economy. While precise data are not available for all the various lines of industry, it appears that for the economy as a whole output per man-hour during the first four decades of the twentieth century "doubled or more than doubled." In manufacturing as a whole the increase was at least threefold.[16]

In the fifteen-year period of rapid technological advance from 1923 to 1937, man-hour output in the major divisions of American industry increased as follows: in manufacturing, 50 per cent; in railroads, 43 per cent; in mining, 89 per cent; and in public utilities, 111 per cent.[17] This increase in efficiency was more or less continuous, occurring both in periods of prosperity and depression.

Improvements in the *quality* of capital instruments have been the cutting edge of economic progress.

B. Improvements in Economic Organization

Science and technology made possible vast increases in productive efficiency and provided the impetus for large-scale business enterprise. But the possibilities of large-scale enterprise could not be realized without certain accompanying developments in the realm of business organization, now to be considered.

1. THE CORPORATE FORM OF ORGANIZATION

Large-scale enterprise was dependent upon the assembling of great aggregations of capital funds. Since the amount of capital which could be brought into a working unit under either the individual or partnership form of organization was severely limited, a new device for raising capital was essential. This was found in the development of the corporation, which could enlist the financial co-operation of a large number of individuals and gather a multitude of small savings into large blocks of capital funds.

Adoption of the principle of limited liability was of crucial importance.

The early joint stock companies were found inadequate because each stockholder, like each member of a partnership, was liable for the capital of other contributors, as well as for his own. Large numbers of share owners could not be induced to purchase stock until the principle was adopted that the liability of each shareholder was limited to the amount of his individual contribution. The necessities of the situation finally led the British Parliament in 1856 to pass an act permitting the organization of corporations on this principle.

The limited liability corporation made possible the vast expansion in the size of business enterprise which has characterized the modern era. Without it the capital necessary for large-scale business organization could not be assembled. While the corporation also possessed advantages in the operation and conduct of business affairs, its greatest importance was as a capital-raising device.

2. THE EVOLUTION OF BANK CREDIT

The enormous economic expansion of the last century inevitably required a vast increase in the supply of money with which to operate. The gradual replacement of payments in kind by money wages greatly extended the role of money in economic life. Money came to be required not only in exchange and trading operations, but in the production stage as well. Every growing business had to have increasing quantities of liquid capital; every new business had to have funds with which to construct plant and equipment, purchase supplies and materials, and meet pay-roll requirements.

Between 1850 and 1930 the total money in use in the leading industrial countries of the world increased many fold. Moreover, it increased several times as much as the supply of gold and silver money. This multiplication of the currency supply was made possible chiefly by the evolution of what is known as bank credit money.

We cannot here enter into an exposition of the process by which bank credit money was created. It must suffice to say that in the course of the evolution of the commercial banking system a given quantity of foundation reserves of specie came to support an ever-expanding superstructure of credit currency—and this without abandonment of the principle of paying depositors in cash on demand. Only during occasional periods of crisis were difficulties encountered.

This bank credit expansion served the needs of agriculture as well as of manufacturing and trade. Moreover, it provided long-term as well as short-term capital funds, and thus facilitated the creation of plant and equipment as well as the manufacture and distribution of commodities.[18]

Bank credit extensions served to accelerate the pace of economic expansion.

At the beginning of the great era of development the demands for capital funds with which to expand productive operations were greatly in excess of the volume of available money savings. The economic significance of bank credit currency is found in the fact that it permitted economic expansion even when funds derived from savings were not available. Instead of having to wait upon the accumulation of investment money, businessmen, through the use of bank credit, could proceed at once to the construction of new plant and equipment. The resulting increase in productive efficiency served to accelerate the expansion of output of consumer goods and services. Had businessmen always had to wait until savings were available, the rate of our industrial progress would have been much slower. It will be observed that the resulting increase in production provided the money income by means of which the credits previously extended could in due course be liquidated.[19]

3. THE SIGNIFICANCE OF STABLE MONETARY AND FISCAL SYSTEMS

Prior to the nineteenth century, trading operations were handicapped by the fluctuating and uncertain value of currencies. For many centuries the principal difficulty had been the lack of uniformity of metallic currency. Defective methods of coinage encouraged both mutilation and counterfeiting, with the result that trade was hampered by uncertainty over the weight and the quality of the money offered in payment. More serious was the fact that it was profitable to use the light weight inferior coins in meeting money obligations, and to melt down or export the better coins. "Bad money drove out good." It was not until the seventeenth century that the perfection of coinage techniques reduced this evil to negligible proportions.

But a second difficulty remained. Both gold and silver were used as money, and they were coined into the monetary unit—dollar, franc, or pound—at stipulated weight ratios. The relative value of these metals, however, fluctuated with changes in the commercial markets for gold and silver bullion; hence gold was at times over-valued as coin and at other times under-valued—and similarly with silver. Moreover, these metals would sometimes be worth more in France than in England, or more in Germany than in the United States. Traders naturally sought to make a profit out of these variations in value; and the result was that now gold and again silver would disappear from the channels of circulation.

A recognized, definite, currency system was a prerequisite to extensive credit operations.

Large-scale business enterprise necessitated a vast expansion of credit or borrowing operations. Indeed the capitalistic economy that developed in the late nineteenth century is often referred to as a "credit economy." The sale of goods in world-wide markets involved the extension of commercial credits covering the period while goods were in transit and in process of sale. At the same time the rapid development of large-scale enterprise required a vast expansion of capital funds borrowed on a long-term basis. Moreover, new or backward countries could not improve their productive facilities without extensive loans from older and richer countries.

Such international credit operations involve very nearly prohibitive risks when the monetary standard is uncertain. The lapse of time before payment might easily result in monetary changes which would wipe out the entire margin of profit—even in the case of short-term commercial loans. Long-term credit extension, under such conditions, is virtually out of the question.

Great Britain took the lead in creating a definite, certain monetary system by the establishment of the single gold standard in 1816—the gold unit being a stated quantity of gold of a specified purity. Thereafter the pound sterling came to be recognized throughout the world as altogether reliable—"as good as gold" to use the descriptive phrase of the time. When one got paid in sterling he got paid in full. While the level of commodity prices might still fluctuate somewhat, the lender was no longer short-changed by receiving payment in a unit of different worth.

In the course of the nineteenth century the single gold standard was adopted by all the leading nations. By 1900 we had, in effect, an international monetary system based on gold.

Monetary stability could not be maintained without fiscal stability.

Unbalanced government budgets require borrowing operations. If the borrowing takes the form of an issue of paper money which is not redeemable in specie, doubt is created as to the value of such paper. Accordingly, only gold will be accepted in meeting international obligations; and in consequence, the gold supply is drained away—which still further undermines the position of the paper currency. This principle is well illustrated by American experience with the irredeemable greenback currency during and following the Civil War. When the government borrowing takes the form of bond issues, there is no direct or immediate deterioration of the monetary system. But if the borrowing is either extensive or long continued, confidence in the ultimate credit of the government is in due course impaired. It then becomes necessary to borrow from government-controlled banks.

Under such conditions investors, both in public securities and in private securities, become timid and seek safer havens by shifting their funds to other countries. This "flight of capital" dries up the supply of investment funds, depreciates the value of the nation's currency in the foreign exchange markets, and leads to commodity price inflation. This disastrous chain of consequences was strikingly illustrated by the experience of France in the middle 1930's.

During the nineteenth century there was progressive improvement in fiscal policies and in the financial position of governments. Every important nation was committed to the principle of fiscal stability, and nearly every important country succeeded—except in time of war—in raising sufficient revenues from taxation to keep the public debt within manageable proportions.

Fiscal and monetary stability was the foundation upon which the credit system rested. And as we have seen, credit extension, both for short-term commercial uses and for long-term investment purposes, was indispensable to the vast expansion of industry and trade which occurred during the great period under consideration.

In summary, a combination of factors had circumvented the law of diminishing returns.

The developments which we have been reviewing in this chapter served, in combination, to render inoperative the law of diminishing returns which appeared of such controlling importance to the early economists. During the ensuing century, instead of diminishing returns (rising costs) we had progressively increasing returns (decreasing costs). This was true in the extractive industries—agriculture and mining—scarcely less than in manufacturing and transportation.

The phenomenal increase in man-hour productivity which was occurring received tardy recognition by the successors of the early classical economists. Until very recently the universal sweep and significance of the forces making for increasing productive efficiency and decreasing costs per unit of output were only dimly perceived.

Alfred Marshall, near the end of the nineteenth century, recognized a law of *increasing* returns in industry, which he stated as follows: "An increase of labour and capital leads generally to improved organization, which increases the efficiency of the work of labour and capital." The important factor to Marshall appeared to be the improved organization made possible by the introduction of machinery and accompanying specialization of tasks rather than an increasing efficiency of constantly improving types of machinery and tools. Technological progress, as now conceived, had little place in his thinking. As he stated the problem:

> The two tendencies toward increasing return [in industry] and diminishing return [in agriculture, etc.] press constantly against one another. . . . If the people can for a time escape from the pressure of the law of diminishing return by importing food and other raw produce on easy terms . . . ; then every increase in their numbers is likely *for the time* to be accompanied by more than proportionate increase in their power of obtaining material goods.[20]

It is apparent from this passage that in his thinking the principle of increasing return in industry was of transient importance. Moreover, he stressed elsewhere that, as the supply of capital is expanded, the productivity of the added units inevitably declines.

F. W. Taussig, writing in 1921, placed much emphasis upon increasing returns in industry but gave little place to the principle elsewhere. "In agriculture though it [increasing return] sometimes appears, as a passing phase, it is not ordinarily found at all; and the same is true of systematic forestry."[21] On balance he adhered to the view that the productivity of capital declines as the supply is increased.

Even today the conception that the application of additional units of capital to natural resources yields progressively diminishing returns pervades the thinking of economists in the classical tradition. As we shall show in Chapter IV, this conception lies at the basis of the pessimism of John Maynard Keynes.[22]

It was just 100 years ago that two very influential works in the field of political economy appeared—John Stuart Mill's *Principles of Political Economy*, and the *Communist Manifesto* by Karl Marx and Friedrich Engels.[23] Mill's work, which was the culmination of classical thought, concluded, as we have seen, that the masses of the people must, because of the operation of certain controlling physical laws, continue to live at or near the margin of subsistence. Moreover, the rate of return to the capitalist class in the form of interest and profits would, in consequence of the law of diminishing returns, tend to a minimum approaching zero. In the not distant future, a stationary society appeared inescapable.

The basic shortcoming in Mill's analysis lay in his failure to foresee the significance of what has come to be known as technological progress. As we have seen, he regarded the employment of additional capital as inevitably attended by declining productivity. Hence no significant increase in national income could for long be generated for the benefit of either labor or capital.

Marx attached much more importance to capital than did his contemporary classical economists. But he held to the iron law of wages even more rigidly—labor could receive little if any more than the bare minimum required to sustain life. But since labor's production materially exceeded this minimum, large and increasing amounts of "surplus value" in the form of interest and profits were available to the capitalist exploiters of labor. Accordingly, the growth of capital would be continuously accelerated and the gulf between the proletariat and the capitalist classes would be constantly increased, until, in accordance with a universal law of conflict, the system would lead to its own destruction. The expropriated would eventually shake off their chains and in turn "expropriate their expropriators"—by means of bloody revolution.

Marx, like Mill, did not conceive that the position of the masses might be improved progressively as a result of technological developments and increasing productive efficiency. In his view, improvements in productive processes would only redound to the benefit of the capitalist class. The conclusions of both Mill and Marx were, as we have seen, completely belied by the great rise in living standards which occurred in all industrial countries in the ensuing century.

CHAPTER II

RECURRING BUSINESS DEPRESSIONS

The story of economic progress during the last century, as outlined in the preceding chapter, gives an impression of an economic system functioning with remarkable efficiency in producing ever-increasing quantities of goods for the benefit of all classes, and this at an ever-decreasing expenditure of human effort. It would almost seem that the social millennium so often conceived had at last been attained. The sobering fact must be faced, however, that despite the extraordinary economic achievements of the century as a whole, the path of progress was not an open highway permitting a smooth and uninterrupted advance. The forward movement was marked by frequent business recessions, which entailed enormous economic losses and untold human suffering and greatly retarded the rate of economic progress.

While there had long been occasional financial and commercial crises associated with speculative manias, it was not until the nineteenth century that the phenomenon of recurring financial and economic disorders emerged as a serious problem of economic organization under a capitalistic system. In modern times business depressions have attracted perhaps more attention than any other aspect of economic organization.

I. FREQUENCY AND DURATION

It is necessary to sketch briefly the history of business depressions during the last century in order to reveal the extent and significance of the problem here under consideration. The present purpose will be served by indicating merely the length of the depression phase of the numerous cyclical fluctuations which have occurred.

Between 1819-1938 American business was depressed nearly one third of the time.

As it is often difficult to determine *precisely* when a depression begins or ends, the duration figures given in the following summary are mere approximations. Some minor recessions are omitted; and it should be noted that during some of the major depressions there were short-lived recoveries. The summary starts with the first severe depression in the United States—that which began in the spring of 1819.[1]

1819-21—24 months	1882-85—36 months
1825-26—12 months	1890-91— 9 months
1833-34— 9 months	1893-97—48 months
1837-43—72 months	1907-08—12 months
1857-58—18 months	1913-14—20 months
1866-67—18 months	1920-21—18 months
1873-78—66 months	1929-33—42 months
	1937-38—10 months

Some of these depressions were much more acute than others, and there were also wide differences in the intensity of activity in the intervening prosperous periods. The most severe and protracted depressions, and consequently the ones which have been most discussed, were those which began respectively in 1819, 1837, 1873, 1893, and 1929. The depressions of 1907-08 and 1920-21, while very acute, proved of short duration. It is of interest to note that the depression of 1929-33 was exceeded in length by three others. The chief difference between this depression and those of the seventies and the nineties is found in the severity of the impact upon employment, in consequence of the greater degree of industrialization.

Over this period as a whole, American business was more or less depressed approximately 30 per cent of the time. If one takes account of minor recessions or periods of dullness, it would appear that business was genuinely prosperous only about two years out of three.

The depression pattern in other countries has been similar to that in the United States.

British depressions have in the main closely paralleled those in the United States. Sometimes they started a little earlier; at other times a little later. In some cases British recoveries preceded American recoveries; in other instances they followed. Moreover, there were some minor recessions in each country which did not occur in the other. But all of the acute depressions were similar as to time, duration, and severity.

Major French depressions have been closely articulated with those in Great Britain and the United States. The minor fluctuations, however, show a little greater variation in the matter of timing. The widespread impression that because of the well-balanced economy of France and the conservative thriftiness of the French people fluctuations of business have been much less violent there than elsewhere, is not supported by the facts. The number of depressed years in France has been about the same as in the United States and Great Britain, and the major depressions appear to have been of comparable severity.

In other European countries, the story is similar, especially in recent decades. All have shared to a greater or less extent in the major depressions. Moreover, such countries as Japan, Argentina, and Brazil show fluctuations surprisingly like those in Western Europe and North America—at least so far as the major depressions of recent times are concerned. Even India and China suffer *trade* disturbances somewhat akin to those in more highly developed capitalistic countries.

This similarity is of course a reflection of the extensive international commercial and financial relations of the modern world. A major depression, starting in any area, leads to trade and financial repercussions elsewhere. Conversely, a strong revival in any important country proves a stimulus to other countries. The principal variations between countries, as already noted, are to be found in minor recessions or recoveries which did not reach proportions large enough to affect economic relations with other countries.

II. THE SEARCH FOR CAUSES

The popular explanation of business depressions has always been *political*—"they are the result of the policies of the party in power." In the United States depressions were for many years commonly attributed to the Democrats; but in 1929 responsibility was shifted to the Republicans. In other countries the political explanation appears to have been somewhat less common.

The parties in power at the beginning of each of the American depressions since the Civil War were as follows:

1866-67	Republican	1907-08	Republican
1873-78	Republican	1913-14	Democratic

1882-85	Democratic	1920-21	Democratic
1890-91	Republican	1929-33	Republican
1893-97	Democratic	1937-38	Democratic

While unwise political policies may undoubtedly affect business adversely, it seems obvious from the foregoing that American depressions cannot be explained primarily in terms of changing political administrations. They appear to fall on the just and the unjust alike. Moreover, their international character affords sufficient evidence that the causes lie deeper than the domain of politics.

The explanation of depressions has long been sought by professional and amateur economists.

The phenomenon of recurring depressions has challenged the thought of widely divergent types of individuals, and the number of diagnoses and prescriptions offered is legion. Causes, remedies, and control devices have been suggested by mathematicians, physicists, engineers, businessmen, and politicians, as well as by professional economists; and it is characteristic that each discoverer is certain that *he* has found the true explanation or solution.

It is impossible here to present a detailed statement of the many types of theories—not to mention the numerous variations and refinements—that have been advanced. A brief outline of the more important explanations suggested by professional students is, however, essential to an understanding of the complex and baffling nature of the phenomenon under consideration. In the summary which follows, we are interested only in revealing the many varieties of explanation and remedy, not in appraising their validity.

A. Solar Changes and Crop Failures

The good years and the lean years, known to man at least as far back as Biblical times, have not unnaturally suggested to many individuals that the cause of business depressions must somehow be rooted in weather conditions and crop yields. Since depressions appear to occur with some degree of regularity, the thought arose—Might not the bad harvests be due to periodic fluctuations in the weather resulting from cosmic conditions?

This type of explanation proceeds from the assumption that solar cycles, of one kind or another, produce corresponding weather cycles on the earth. Recurring sun spots and the movement of Venus in relation to the earth have been the most popular explanations of meteorological changes. Elaborate statistical computations have been made to determine whether sun spot cycles and Venus cycles *time* with weather cycles; and, in turn, whether climatic cycles *time* with business cycles.

While neither of these correlations has been satisfactorily established, the thought persists with some that the most logical explanation of the periodical character of cycles is to be found in periodic solar perturbations. It may be noted, in passing, that if depressions were rooted in natural phenomena, their cure would be beyond the power of man. At most their effects might be alleviated—as Joseph mitigated them in Egypt by providing stock piles of food.

B. Psychological Oscillations

Another type of explanation is rooted in human psychology. The simplest form of the psychological explanation is that businessmen in the mass are subject, like any single individual, to alternating periods of optimism and pessimism. More often the psychological explanation is looked upon not as the initiating cause of sharp changes in business conditions but rather as a factor which intensifies the degree of fluctuations. Favorable trade conditions, for whatever reason, generate a spirit of optimism; optimism leads to recklessness; and recklessness sooner or later ends in disaster. Similarly, a crisis and business recession generate pessimism—which spreads with cumulative effects throughout the economic system. Business recovers only when it begins to appear that conditions are not as bad as feared and that the curtailment of production may have been overdone.

C. Defective Banking Systems

Since American depressions in the nineteenth century were immediately preceded by banking panics, many observers naturally regarded bad banking as the primary cause of business depressions. The sequence appeared to be as follows: unsound banking organization and practice; loss of confidence; runs on banks; inability of banks to meet depositors' demands; and, finally general financial and trade paralysis. These panics, because of their sensational character, were often referred to as volcanic eruptions or sudden earthquakes disrupting otherwise *normal* economic conditions.

It was a natural assumption, therefore, that the remedy for depressions lay in removing defects in banking organization. It was in part with this thought in mind that a national banking system was established during the Civil War to provide a uniform bank note currency in place of the heterogeneous issues of the various types of state banking institutions. When the national system did not succeed in preventing the great banking panics of the seventies, the eighties, the nineties, and 1907, the Federal Reserve System, based upon European central banking models, was conceived.

The Federal Reserve Act contained numerous provisions designed to strengthen individual banking institutions and to safeguard lending operations. More important, it created central reserve reservoirs which might be drawn upon in time of emergency.

The Reserve System was, moreover, designed to control the business cycle—to prevent the development of a panicky situation. The concentration of reserves in the Federal Reserve Banks was supposed to make it possible to restrain any dangerous credit expansion that might be developing.[2] The principal means of checking unhealthy expansion was to raise the rate of interest at which member banks could borrow from the Federal Reserve.

D. Monetary Deflation and Falling Prices

The observation that commodity prices always fall rapidly during periods of business recession has led numerous writers to conclude that the cause of depressions is to be found in the factors responsible for the declining prices. They explain the fall in prices in terms of monetary deflation—ascribed by some to a change in the value of the monetary unit, and by others to a reduction in the supply of currency in circulation.

Those who hold this point of view naturally conclude that the solution lies in some form of monetary management. One school of thought emphasizes modifications or adjustments of the monetary standard in which prices are expressed. Another would simply prevent any decrease in the quantity of money in circulation—either by means of bank credit policies, as outlined in the preceding section, or by Treasury currency issues. If, perchance, a recession had already begun, the remedy would be to inject an additional supply of money into the channels of circulation.

This monetary control philosophy was implicit in the bank credit policies developed by central banking institutions; it underlay the American "greenback" and "free silver" movements of the 1870's and the 1890's; and it was involved in the gold devaluation and price *re*-flation movements of the early 1930's both in the United States and other countries. In recent years, however, attention has been shifted in the main from monetary manipulation to fiscal policies designed to stabilize national purchasing power.

E. Price Rigidity

An alternative price explanation runs in terms not of a general decline in prices but of *uneven* declines. While some prices fall sharply as soon as a depression gets under way, others are highly resistant; and accordingly, the general price structure is described as rigid, or sticky, rather than flexible. The resistance to downward pressures in certain parts of the price structure is ascribed to monopolistic or organizational controls which prevent essential price and cost readjustments. When depression begins, industries seek to maintain prices by curtailing production schedules as demand declines. Similarly, labor organizations resist wage reductions, thereby maintaining costs on a high plane.

Those who hold this theory contend that an incipient industrial depression could readily be checked by prompt downward wage and price adjustments. A quick reduction in the prices of industrial commodities would, it is held, immediately restore effective demand and thereby obviate the necessity of curtailing output. With industrial output and employment maintained, the demand for agricultural products would be sustained; and equilibrium would thus be preserved or quickly restored. It is emphasized that price adjustments must be universal in character; in all sections of the economy the price mechanism must function *freely*—in order to clear the markets of goods, to preserve balance, and to permit continuous production. Accordingly, emphasis is placed upon the elimination of monopolistic restraints on production and trade—whether originating with management or with labor. Genuinely free competition and a flexible price structure would, it is believed, ensure a high degree of business stability.

F. The Shrinkage of Profits

A very different type of explanation of depressions is built upon the fact that capitalistic business enterprise is conducted in response to the profit motive. Since business commitments are undertaken in the hope of profits, if anything happens which seriously reduces or even threatens to reduce profit margins, business commitments are quickly curtailed and depression ensues.

While numerous factors which might affect profits have been suggested, those most commonly stressed are rising costs of production. If wage rates increase more rapidly than prices, the profit margin is impaired; and, similarly, if the prices of raw materials rise faster than the prices of finished products. It is pointed out that during the early stages of a period of business expansion when costs are relatively low, the profit outlook appears exceptionally good. Hence, expansion is stimulated and speculative activities are encouraged. But as the boom develops, the growing scarcity of materials and labor gradually results in rising costs, narrowing margins of profit, and eventually contraction and depression.

A variation of this interpretation emphasizes the growing scarcity of loanable funds during a boom period. In consequence, interest rates rise to prohibitive levels; indeed, funds for further expansion eventually become unobtainable at any cost. Thus retrenchment is in due course inescapable. (It will be observed that this is an *under*savings rather than an *over*savings explanation. See page 52.)

This line of interpretation does not offer much hope of any easy remedy. Depression appears as an inevitable outgrowth of the conditions which developed in the preceding boom period.

G. Overproduction and Underconsumption

The terms "overproduction" and "underconsumption" in a sense express the same thing—for production is *over* in relation to consumption and consumption is *under* in relation to production. Nevertheless, some writers have emphasized overproduction as a primary cause of depressions, while others have stressed the lack of consumptive power as the source of the difficulty. Hence it is necessary to consider the two points of view separately.

Overproduction explanations are of several types. The simplest runs in terms of a general business expansion leading to speculative activities, inflation of values, and serious maladjustments in financial and commercial markets. The volume of production meanwhile runs ahead of current consumption. A refinement stresses the accumulation of business inventories—the increase in current purchases in trade channels having exceeded the increase in sales to ultimate consumers. In either case a period of readjustment becomes necessary in order to restore balance.

A variant of this theme calls attention to the jerky, or fitful, character of economic progress. It is observed that new technological discoveries and business innovations tend to come in waves, which produce occasional periods of intense business activity. When such a creative burst has spent itself, a period of rest and recuperation follows. A refinement emphasizes that it is necessary for consumption to expand sufficiently to absorb the sudden increase in productive capacity before a new expansion can occur. Another suggestion is that the business crisis results from the fact that expansion occurs at very unequal rates in different industries, resulting in serious maladjustments within the industrial structure.

The overproduction explanation is sometimes more concretely related to the construction industry—including housing and commercial and industrial building. It has long been noted that activity in this industry shows very wide fluctuations—years of intense activity being followed by years of subnormal construction. Since no small part of the housing construction is speculative in character—built for *potential* buyers rather than to *order*—it is easy to expand well beyond current or early prospective requirements. A suspension of building activity eventually occurs, either because margins of profit have been reduced or because buyers can no longer be found. Once the building boom flattens out, the resulting unemployment and shrinkage of income quickly affect other types of business, and general depression ensues.

In recent years this general conception has been broadened to cover not only *construction* but all *durable* goods—including household furniture and equipment, automobiles, and other commodities whose consumptive use is spread over a period of more than two years. Since the life of durable goods can be materially stretched if conditions necessitate, the demand for such commodities is less constant than for perishables and other quickly consumed commodities. Consequently, some draw the conclusion that the entire business system revolves around fluctuations in the durable goods markets—expanding and contracting as these industries are prosperous or depressed.

Under-consumption explanations center on the availability of purchasing power in the hands of the public with which to buy the goods offered for sale. Deficient purchasing power theories are of three principal types.

The simplest is that the aggregate money income received by the masses of the people as wages and salaries is less than the aggregate value of the consumer goods offered for sale—the difference representing the profits accruing to capital. In the Karl Marx version this difference represents *surplus value* expropriated by capitalists. According to some modern versions a deficiency of purchasing power *always* exists; but in others it is held to arise only in periods of business expansion.

The second type of purchasing power theory is tied in with the *relative* movements of wages and prices. It is contended that in periods of prosperity prices advance more rapidly than wage rates—as a result of which *real* purchasing power is progressively restricted. As soon as reserves of savings and consumer credits have been exhausted, the volume of goods that can be purchased inevitably declines and depression follows. The advance in prices is explained in various ways—by scarcities, by speculative activities, and by an expansion of bank credit.

The third type of purchasing power explanation is more complex and involves the phenomenon of *oversaving*. This explanation finds the source of the difficulty in the distribution of money income among the various groups in society, and the way in which this income is allocated as between consumptive expenditures and saving for investment. During periods of prosperity when employment is abundant and incomes are increasing, and when large fortunes are being amassed by business enterprisers and speculators, an increasing proportion of the national income is directed to savings channels. Hence new capital construction, and in due course additional production of consumer goods, increases faster than consumer expenditures, the resulting accumulation or glut of commodities in wholesale or retail markets leading to a collapse of prices.

The remedies suggested for overproduction or underconsumption naturally vary with the explanation offered. One type of overproduction remedy stresses financial restraints on further expansion. Another emphasizes industrial stabilization programs designed to keep production in adjustment with consumption. Still another approach is to stabilize the construction industry by withholding government projects in time of boom and expanding them when recession begins.

Underconsumption remedies call for such varied procedures as: credit expansion to make good the deficiency in purchasing power; increasing money wages, especially in the lower-income groups; subsidies to farmers and to tenant operators; restricting the savings of the rich by surtaxes; and reducing business savings by high corporate levies or special taxes on undistributed income.

The striking impression given by the foregoing brief summary of depression theories is one of divergence, of conflict, and of confusion. A more complete and detailed exposition would serve only to enhance this impression. It is scarcely necessary to add that none of these theories can be regarded as generally accepted by professional students. The fact is that there is little if any more agreement today with respect to causes than was the case a generation or so ago. Nor is there any greater unanimity of view with respect to remedies. The prescriptions suggested, as indicated in the foregoing analysis, naturally reflect the varying types of diagnosis.

There has, however, been a tendency in recent years to center attention upon fiscal policy as a means of controlling fluctuations in business. In brief, the thesis is that when business activity begins to overreach itself, the situation may be eased by a curtailment of net government expenditures; and, conversely, when business is slackening off—for whatever reason—an expansion of net government outlays would provide the necessary stimulus for recovery. Indeed, this conception commonly referred to as "compensatory fiscal policy," is regarded by some as a new panacea with which to maintain continuously a state of full employment. Its merits will be considered in Chapter X.

III. IS THERE A SINGLE CAUSE?

As the foregoing analysis suggests, nearly all students

of depressions, or of the business cycle, have been in search of a single cause. The recurring character of depressions and the alternating phases of the business cycle—from depression to recovery, to prosperity, to crisis, and again to depression—have suggested to most students that there must be some fundamental or underlying explanation. Some have searched for this cause in physical or psychological factors, while others have sought to find it within the operations of the capitalistic system. The hope has persisted that by rigorous analysis, or inductive study, *the* cause might be identified, thus making possible the application of an appropriate remedy.

There appears no valid reason for assuming that there must be a single underlying cause.

The modern economic system is a highly complex mechanism. It operates in response to various motivating influences, and it is composed of many interrelated parts. Within a given country the operation of the economic system might be disturbed by a variety of changes affecting the relations between: wages, prices, and profits; consumption and saving; banking and business; agriculture and industry; and, more broadly, government and business. Moreover, the economy of each country is connected through trade and financial operations with the economies of other countries. In so complex and delicately adjusted a mechanism, why should one assume that the source or place of disturbance should always be the same?

While analogies may easily be ovedrawn, it may be helpful to reflect that the human body is also a complex mechanism, the effective functioning of which depends upon the health and proper adjustment of such basic organs as the brain, heart, lungs, liver, and kidneys, and such secondary ones as the pancreas and the adrenals. A physician does not assume that the recurrent illness of a patient is always attributable to the same organic disorder. Rather he is prepared to find one or another of several possible sources of derangement—or to discover complications.

In a similar way an economic diagnostician might possibly find the source of a particular business derangement—either in a breakdown of the banking machinery, in overexpansion, in speculation, in a distortion of prices in relation to wages, in rising costs which impinge upon profits, in restrictive taxation or other government policies, in foreign trade relations, etc. Or there might be complications—several maladjustments at once.

But, it is often urged, the periodical character of depressions and the regularity in the pattern of business cycles strongly suggest a single underlying explanation rather than multiple or varied causes. If an individual became sick at fairly regular intervals, and if the illness always seemed to run a typical course, would not one conclude that there must be a basic cause—a disorder that resulted in a gradual accumulation of poison in the system?

One answer is that business depressions do not, in fact, occur with any high degree of regularity. The dates given on page 40 above indicate that depressions have occurred frequently but at far from regular intervals. All that can be said about the pattern of the business cycle is that once a recession begins—for whatever cause—the effects are cumulative, curtailments at one place inevitably resulting in retrenchment elsewhere; and, similarly, that when recovery once begins—for whatever reason—the forward movement is self-propelling. Even so the rapidity and the extent of the downswing, the length of the depression, the rate of advance, and the duration of the prosperity period show no uniformity.

The view that depressions are always caused by the same factor is disproved by the record.

The historical record reveals many different types of strain or maladjustment at the period of crisis—a fact which largely accounts for the many types of theory that have been advanced. In the nineteenth century, as we have seen, American economic depressions were commonly preceded by banking panics accompanied by a breakdown of the monetary system; but since the establishment of the Federal Reserve System, this has not been the case. Moreover, few European depressions were preceded or accompanied by banking panics.

Prior to the First World War the United States was a country in which the volume of money savings was *deficient* rather than *excessive*. That is, we found it necessary to borrow abroad and to expand bank credit to meet the financial requirements of business in periods of expansion. In the 1920's the reverse was the case; out of superabundant savings we absorbed all the securities floated in the home markets, loaned vast sums abroad, and still had large amounts left over. Depressions occur in undeveloped countries with meagre savings as well as in rich countries with a high saving rate.

The crisis of 1873 came at the end of a period of great activity in railroad building and in construction generally. The collapse of 1920 came at a time when railroad, public utility, and housing construction had been at subnormal levels for many years. The break in 1929 followed a period of abnormal activity in the capital goods industries. The depression of 1937 followed a period of subnormal activity in these industries.

In the months preceding the collapse of 1920, wage rates had about kept pace with rising commodity prices. Preceding 1929, wage rates had been gradually rising, while commodity prices had been slowly declining. Preceding the break in 1937, wage rates had been rising much faster than commodity prices.

In the spring of 1920 there was a sharp curtailment in consumer buying—known as the "buyers' strike"; in 1929 there was little if any decline in retail buying until after the break had occurred; in 1937 retail trade was very active until well after the recession began.

In 1837 the collapse occurred in real estate markets. In 1920 it was in commodity markets. In 1929 it was in the security markets.

Divergences such as these are incompatible with the idea of single causation. They clearly support the view that a highly complex economic mechanism may get out of gear in more than one way—sometimes at one place and sometimes at another.

In this chapter we have been interested solely in reviewing the history of business fluctuations, the explanations that have been advanced with respect to causes, and the various types of remedies that have been proposed. The problems involved in mitigating or eliminating business depressions will be considered in Chapter X.

CHAPTER III

THE GREAT DEPRESSION OF 1929

The complex character of the economic system and the varied types of maladjustment to which it is subject can best be illustrated by an account of the factors and forces responsible for the great depression which began at the end of the 1920's. While of shorter duration than some of the depressions of the nineteenth century, it was more far-reaching geographically and more devastating in its consequences than any which the world had hitherto experienced.

To understand the sources of disorder which rendered the world economic system particularly vulnerable in the late 1920's, it is necessary to review economic developments reaching as far back as the First World War. Some of the disturbing factors were essentially international in character, while others were a reflection of domestic trends in particular countries. The more important of the developments contributing to the ensuing disequilibrium are briefly sketched below.

I. INTERNATIONAL MALADJUSTMENTS

As indicated in Chapter I, there had developed by the end of the nineteenth century an economic and financial organization world-wide in the scope of its operations. This world system, was, in the language of economists, in a state of balanced equilibrium. All important industrial countries were on the gold standard; budgets were everywhere in a comfortable position, if not in all cases actually in balance; and international trade, service, and credit operations were so adjusted that foreign exchange rates fluctuated only within narrow, and automatically self-correcting, limits. The economies of debtor and creditor countries were adjusted to the underlying requirements of such relationships: the former had developed the export surpluses essential to the procurement of the foreign exchange with which to meet interest payments; the latter had import surpluses—interest being in effect received in the form of imported materials which could not advantageously be produced at home.

The First World War thoroughly disrupted the international equilibrium of the world.

Stated in fundamental economic terms the war forced most European countries to sacrifice much of their accumulated wealth and also to mortgage their future. First, there was an extensive movement of gold from the European belligerents to other countries for the purchase of war supplies—which served to undermine currency foundations in some countries and to accumulate excessive reserves in others. Second, there was an extensive liquidation by the belligerents of investment holdings abroad. Third, foreign borrowing, through both public and private channels, was resorted to on an unprecedented scale.

Thus the European nations were transformed, wholly or in large part, from net creditors to net debtors, whereas neutral countries and the United States, were quickly converted from debtors to creditors. To these financial changes were shortly added the complications resulting from the assessment of stupendous reparation obligations against the defeated powers.

These vast financial shifts were not accompanied by corresponding changes in the producing or consuming power of the nations involved. The borrowings of the war period were used for destructive rather than constructive purposes; instead of an expansion of producing and debt-paying power in Europe, the war resulted in a great decrease in such power. On the other hand, the war had stimulated a great expansion of both industrial and agricultural producing power in the United States and other countries lying outside the principal war theatres. In short, the economic structure of the world was in no way adjusted to the requirements of the changed situation.

The international disequilibrium, particularly in Europe, was further complicated by the territorial readjustments resulting from the war. The new states carved out of the old Russian, German, and Austro-Hungarian empires, in seeking to achieve economic independence, inevitably disrupted long-established commercial and financial relationships. Similarly, the dismembered countries found it necessary to reorganize their economic activities in the light of changes in frontiers and dislocations of former trade connections. The resulting shifts, and the accompanying confinement of commerce within more restricted boundaries, seriously affected the economic life of a large portion of continental Europe.

The internal fiscal and monetary stability of most European countries was also undermined.

The financial requirements of the war were so enormous and so exigent that in no country was it deemed possible to meet the costs from current tax levies. The result everywhere was an enormous growth in the public debt, which was not matched by a corresponding increase in tax-paying capacity. The degree of fiscal deterioration of course varied widely in the several countries, being, with the exception of Russia, less among the Allied nations and greater among the central powers.

The combined result of these *external* trade and financial maladjustments and the *internal* fiscal and monetary deterioration was reflected in the depreciation of the foreign exchanges. During the war period actual depreciation was checked by control devices, and the full extent of the disruption which occurred was not fully revealed until exchange restrictions were removed after the end of the conflict.

The consequences of these maladjustments were often obscured by new credit extensions.

In 1919-20 the United States government made substantial loans to European countries for relief and rehabilitation, and at the same time American industrial and banking corporations extended large credits on a commercial basis. Meanwhile, the schedules of reparation payments had not been determined, and the international debt obligations were in suspense. This continuing flow of funds to Europe served to support the international exchange situation during the critical period in 1919-20.

In the immediately ensuing years the volume of supporting credits declined greatly, while reparation installments now had to be met. The result was a rapid disintegration of the financial and economic structure of a large part of continental Europe—necessitating, in the interest of international economic security, the formulation of a series of co-operative stabilization plans.

Each of the stabilization plans granted extensive reductions in the amount of reparation or international debt payments, and also provided for large reconstruction loans by the creditor nations to the afflicted countries. An important objective of the program was the restoration of the gold standard and the stabilization of the foreign exchanges as indispensable foundations for the reestablishment of normal trade and financial relations.

Following this stabilization program of the middle twenties, there ensued a new period of private credit extension from the economically stronger to the economically weaker countries. Such credits were advanced by Great Britain, France, Sweden, and other creditor countries, as well as by the United States, and they were extended to other parts of the world as well as to Europe. However, the outstanding feature of the late twenties was the vast extension of American private loans to Central Europe, especially to Germany.

During this period the defeated countries were nominally meeting reparation obligations, as scheduled; and, in turn, installments on interallied debts were being regularly paid. But this flow of funds in the liquidation of war obligations was being made possible chiefly by the continuing flow of credits from the United States to Central Europe. In fact, the inflow of new credits to Germany was roughly double the outflow on reparation account. Moreover, the reparation receipts were substantially smaller than transfers to the United States on interallied debt account.

Thus what appeared, superficially, to be a gradual liquidation of war indebtedness and the re-establishment of international financial stability was in reality but an augmentation of the international credit disequilibrium. Net indebtedness to the United States was constantly increasing, with no corresponding expansion of European debt-paying capacity. In the earlier years of this period the new credits extended by the United States were chiefly long- or medium-term in character, but in the later years, especially in 1929-30, they were mainly short-term credits, payable within a few months. The same was true of British credit extensions during this period. As we shall presently see, this short-term credit situation was a factor of paramount influence in the financial debacle of 1931.

International trade policies were not adjusted to meet the economic needs of the situation.

The changed debtor-creditor relationships resulting from the war and postwar trends discussed above called for profound alteration in the flow of international commerce. Instead of facilitating the essential shifts, postwar commercial policies, generally speaking, worked in the opposite direction. The desire to achieve economic self-sufficiency, to provide employment, and to prevent Germany from regaining her former position in international trade led many countries quickly to increase their protective tariffs in the early postwar years. In particular the increasing restrictions on imports by creditor countries continued to work at direct cross purposes with the trade necessities involved in servicing the mounting international indebtedness.

In due course the increasing barriers to trade began to cause apprehension. The League of Nations Assembly eventually called an international conference to consider this vital problem. The World Economic Conference of May 1927 unanimously emphasized the need for arresting the protectionist movement and liberalizing commercial policy in general if the laboriously re-established monetary and credit system were to be maintained. The conference concluded that "The time has come to put a stop to the growth of customs tariffs and to reverse the direction of the movement."

In ensuing months some slight progress was made in this direction. Numerous contemplated increases in tariff were postponed and a number of trade arrangements designed to improve commercial relations were concluded. But in late 1928 and 1929 the movement for higher protection again gained momentum in Europe, as a direct result of the increasing depression in agriculture in various countries. It was, moreover, stimulated by the alarm and resentment felt over the increased duties of the Smoot-Hawley Tariff Act of the United States, which after a year of discussion was finally passed in June 1930.

During the 1920's the world agricultural situation also became increasingly unstable.

The restriction of agricultural production in Europe during the war had enormously stimulated agricultural output in other parts of the world, especially in North America. The quick recovery of European agriculture after the war was not accompanied by corresponding readjustments in agricultural output in other countries. As a result, the postwar period was one of persistent decline in the prices of farm products, especially those which were exported in quantity. Wheat, cotton, wool, silk, sugar, and coffee declined rapidly from 1924 on, while in the late twenties, rice, tea, cocoa, jute, hemp, and flax fell sharply.

Meanwhile, there was a progressive accumulation of unsold stocks of farm products in terminal and other warehouses. With such supplies hanging over the markets and with production constantly increasing, the world agricultural situation was highly vulnerable. Both in the United States and elsewhere, solutions were being sought through the medium of government policies of various types designed to support the prices of farm products.

Many countries were still confronted with difficult internal financial problems.

The war left everywhere a heavy legacy of public indebtedness. Notwithstanding increases in taxes, the mounting costs of government in most countries served to prevent the attainment of fiscal stability. The situation was further complicated by the apparent necessity of large internal public loans for relief and reconstruction. In many cases public credit was extensively employed in order to develop home industries and achieve economic self-sufficiency. In many countries, also, banking institutions made extensive loans for industrial development in line with national programs but without adequate attention to economic realities.

Unbalanced budgets rendered difficult the problem of maintaining monetary and foreign exchange stability. Moreover, the growing expansion of credit—both public and private—created a highly vulnerable situation, once a business recession, for whatever reason, got under way.

II. MALADJUSTMENTS IN THE UNITED STATES

In many respects the economic situation in the United States during the 1920's was strikingly different from that in other parts of the world. The fiscal situation was easy, and the public debt built up during the war years was being steadily reduced. There was no possible threat to the dollar in the international exchanges, for the United States had a huge gold reserve and large current net receipts from abroad. Meanwhile, also, a great industrial expansion had occurred. Despite these favorable factors the economic position of the United States in the late twenties was vulnerable in certain important respects.

In considering the developing situation within the United States, it is essential, first, to sketch briefly the general trend of business in the early postwar years. From early 1919 to the spring of 1920 there was a business boom, stimulated by the replacement (both in the United States and Europe) of depleted stocks of commodities required for ordinary consumption. This boom was accompanied by rapidly rising commodity prices, especially in consumer goods lines. The so-called "buyers' strike" of May 1920 was followed by a very sharp depression involving a precipitate decline of prices and a drastic liquidation of commercial credit. Recovery began late in 1921 and continued with slight interruption until the spring of 1924. Then came a sharp curtailment of industrial production which lasted, however, only until the autumn of that year. Another moderate recession occurred in 1927 when Ford automobile production was in suspense. On the whole, however, the period from 1922 to 1929 is not inaccurately described as one of great and well-sustained prosperity.

A number of factors had combined to produce the great business activity of the 1920's.

The first, though not the most important, was the great expansion of foreign trade made possible by the extensive outpouring of credit to which reference has been made above. Of greater influence were the enormous expansion in the field of construction, made necessary by the shortages resulting from the war, and the phenomenal growth of the automobile industry. These particular developments require a word of explanation.

During the war period, building operations were largely suspended except in fields directly related to the war program. Moreover, during the brief prosperity period of 1919-20, there was but a moderate increase in building activity. The suspension of construction for five or six years during a period of steady population growth inevitably served to create a great shortage of housing accommodations. The recovery of 1921 was undoubtedly stimulated by the increase of construction which began early in the year and steadily gained momentum. With the return of prosperity there was a cumulative increase in all forms of construction, including industrial plant and equipment and railroad and public utility replacements and improvements.

The phenomenal growth of the automobile industry was closely related to developments in housing. The higher levels of income made it possible for greatly increased numbers of people to own automobiles; and, in turn, the ownership of automobiles greatly stimulated the housing industry by shifting population from urban to suburban regions. Similarly, also, the growth of the automobile necessitated a vast program of highway construction. Thus widespread business activity was cumulatively accelerated.

Economic expansion was also facilitated by the liberal use of credit. In addition to the extensive international loans to which reference has been made, credit also played a large role in the domestic field. On the consumption side, sales on the installment plan made possible a substantial increase in purchases of automobiles and a wide range of household commodities. Similarly, houses could be bought on time payment plans involving but moderate initial investment. State and local governments employed their credit in floating securities for the purpose of financing highway construction and other public enterprises. In addition, commercial bank credit was extended on a large scale for speculative activities.

By the late 1920's a number of disquieting factors were in evidence.

The first two of these related to the international situation and have in part already been discussed. The world agricultural crisis was bearing heavily upon American markets. Food prices were steadily declining, and world stocks were accumulating. Moreover, banks throughout the farming sections were in distress and failures averaged more than 800 annually. The international credit situation was becoming increasingly precarious. The flow of sustaining credits from the United States to Europe reached its maximum in 1928, declining sharply in 1929. Meanwhile, there were no corresponding improvements in the ability of continental debtors to meet obligations out of their own resources. Increasing tariff restrictions both in the United States and in Europe denoted rather a declining capacity to pay.

During the early twenties the expansion of housing facilities proceeded at a faster rate than the increase in population, with the result that the accumulated shortages were being steadily reduced. The high point in housing construction was reached in 1925, after which such building declined steadily. The automobile expansion, based in part upon the suburban movement and in part upon the creation through low-price policy of new markets among the lower-income groups, appeared to many observers to be approaching the saturation point. In this case, however, cessation of Ford production in 1927 and early 1928, incident to a basic change in model, laid the basis for a new production bulge in 1929. Construction of railroad equipment reached its maximum in 1923 and tapered off rapidly after 1926. Construction outlays by public utilities and industrial enterprises, however, continued to increase moderately through the late twenties.

While there was no apparent threat of collapse in the construction field there was undoubtedly growing caution with respect to further expansion. Moreover, the extensive dependence upon credit support, both in housing and in the related fields of household equipment and automobiles, rendered the situation vulnerable the moment a business recession and accompanying shrinkage of income began—for whatever reason.

Mention must also be made of the fact that during the late twenties the phenomenon of technological unemployment was beginning to manifest itself. Boom periods had ordinarily been accompanied by acute labor shortages, but this was not the case, generally speaking, in the twenties. A survey made by the Brookings Institution[1] during this period revealed that workers displaced by technological improvements in certain industries were finding serious difficulty in obtaining employment elsewhere. Moreover, there appeared to be considerable slack in the general labor market in 1929.[2]

The national income was becoming increasingly concentrated. During the prosperity period of the twenties there was a rapid increase in the total national income. The *per-capita* income from current production activities increased between 1919 and 1929 by as much as 23 per cent. This increase was not, however, participated in equally by all portions of the population. The aggregate dollar income of the farm population showed a slight decline after 1925. Wage income increased in absolute terms but did not quite keep pace with the increase in national income as a whole. The greatest increase occurred in the high-income groups, including salaried officials and receivers of profits from business enterprise. Moreover, there was a rapid growth in the number of income recipients in the higher-income brackets.[3]

The increasing concentration of income in the higher brackets and also the rising level of urban incomes generally were serving more or less automatically to increase the proportion of the aggregate national income set aside as money savings. That is, although the flow of current income into trade and service channels continued to expand, it expanded less rapidly than the flow of funds into investment channels. While an abundance of funds was thus available with which to construct new plant and equipment, it was evidently clear to business enterprisers that prospective consumptive demands were not sufficiently large to warrant as much expansion as the available funds made possible. The evidence shows conclusively that the volume of money savings seeking investment was very much greater than could be absorbed by security flotations for purposes of plant construction.[4]

This changed ratio between the flow of funds into consumptive and investment channels served to explain, in large part, a number of significant developments of the late twenties. On the one side, the restricted purchasing power in consumer goods channels helped explain the great expansion of installment credits and the efforts through high-pressure advertising and salesmanship to overcome what was called "sales resistance." On the other side, the plethora of funds seeking investment outlets provided the basis for such events as the following: the intensive efforts of investment bankers to expand loans abroad; the issuance of vast blocks of investment trust and holding company securities, not for the purpose of financing new capital construction but for acquiring ownership control; and the phenomenal flow of funds into the security exchanges for the purchase of the outstanding stock of existing corporations. The resulting security market inflation was of course enhanced by the extension of commercial bank loans for speculative purposes.

The stock market in 1929 was in a highly vulnerable position. At the first evidence that the boom market was over and that a substantial reaction was in store, there would inevitably be quick and heavy liquidation. Individuals who had bought securities outright would naturally desire to cash in on their profits before it was too late, while those who had purchased on margins would be forced to liquidate. Under these circumstances any substantial decline in the market was in danger of becoming a rout. And a reaction could be produced whenever any considerable number of large investors or speculators decided that the time had come to withdraw from the market.

Inasmuch as the situation the world over was thus vulnerable in a number of very important respects, it was only a question of time until a break might be expected somewhere—the precise moment and place being perhaps more or less accidental. Moreover, as the preceding chapter has indicated, once a serious break occurred at any place in the complex mechanism, the effects would presumably spread rapidly throughout the entire economic system. To understand the relationship of the various sources of maladjustment discussed above, it is essential to trace in some detail the unfolding, development, and ramifications of the world depression of 1929-33.

III. THE COURSE OF THE WORLD DEPRESSION

The diagram on pages 74-75, showing quarterly changes in business conditions in leading countries, indicates that the business recession had begun in various places in the world before the well-known crisis in the New York stock market in October 1929. In Australia and the Dutch East Indies an industrial depression was clearly in evidence as early as the last quarter of 1927. The year 1928 showed business recession setting in early in the year in Germany and in the third quarter in Finland and Brazil. In 1929 Poland showed a decline in the first quarter, Canada and Argentina in the second, and Italy, Belgium, Egypt, and the United States in the third. In most cases, however, the extent of the recession was not pronounced.

The diagram is separated at the middle of 1931 because the depression was marked by two clearly defined stages. The first phase resembled in many respects the business recessions of former times. The second, beginning in the late spring of 1931, was featured by the collapse of the international monetary and credit system.

The first phase, 1929-31, was comparatively moderate in character.

The most striking and significant developments during the first phase of the depression were as follows: a drastic decline in the prices of stocks; a sharp fall in the prices of foodstuffs and raw materials; a marked decrease in world trade; a rapid reduction in the flow of new international loans; a substantial curtailment of industrial production; and a corresponding reduction in employment and purchasing power.

The average of stock prices fell between September 1929 and June 1931 as much as 60 per cent in New York, 46 per cent in Berlin, 43 per cent in London, and 38 per cent in Paris. The prices of a selected group of "world market" foodstuffs fell from 50 to 60 per cent between 1928 and the middle of 1931, and industrial raw materials showed comparable declines, ranging from 42 per cent in the case of copper to 72 per cent in rubber. The prices of manufactured goods fell only about half as much as those of agricultural products. World trade declined about 15 per cent in quantity terms and 40 per cent in terms of value. The flow of international loans and short-term credits declined rapidly in 1929-30, and disappeared in 1931. Industrial production in the United States declined over 30 per cent.

During this first stage of the depression there were recurring waves of optimism as to the prospect for early

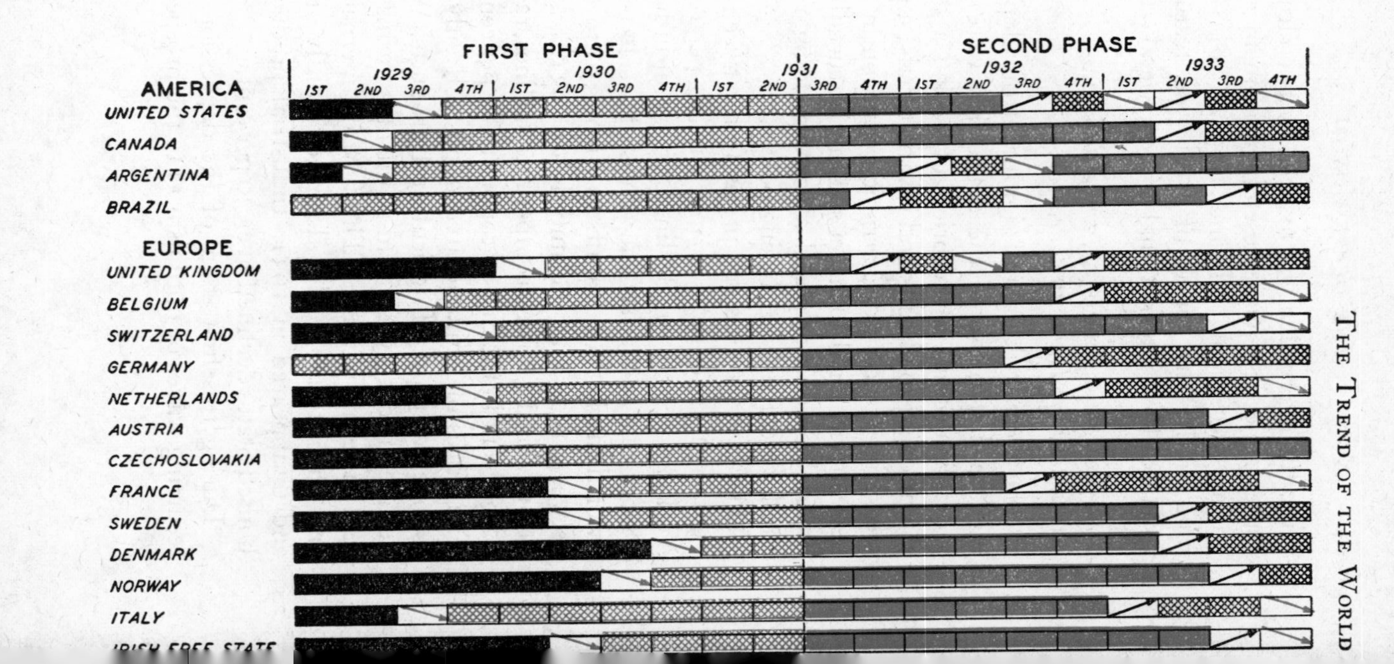
FIRST PHASE
SECOND PHASE
1929
1930
1931
1932
1933
1ST
2ND
3RD
4TH
AMERICA
UNITED STATES
CANADA
ARGENTINA
BRAZIL
EUROPE
UNITED KINGDOM
BELGIUM
SWITZERLAND
GERMANY
NETHERLANDS
AUSTRIA
CZECHOSLOVAKIA
FRANCE
SWEDEN
DENMARK
NORWAY
ITALY

DEPRESSION, 1929-33[5]

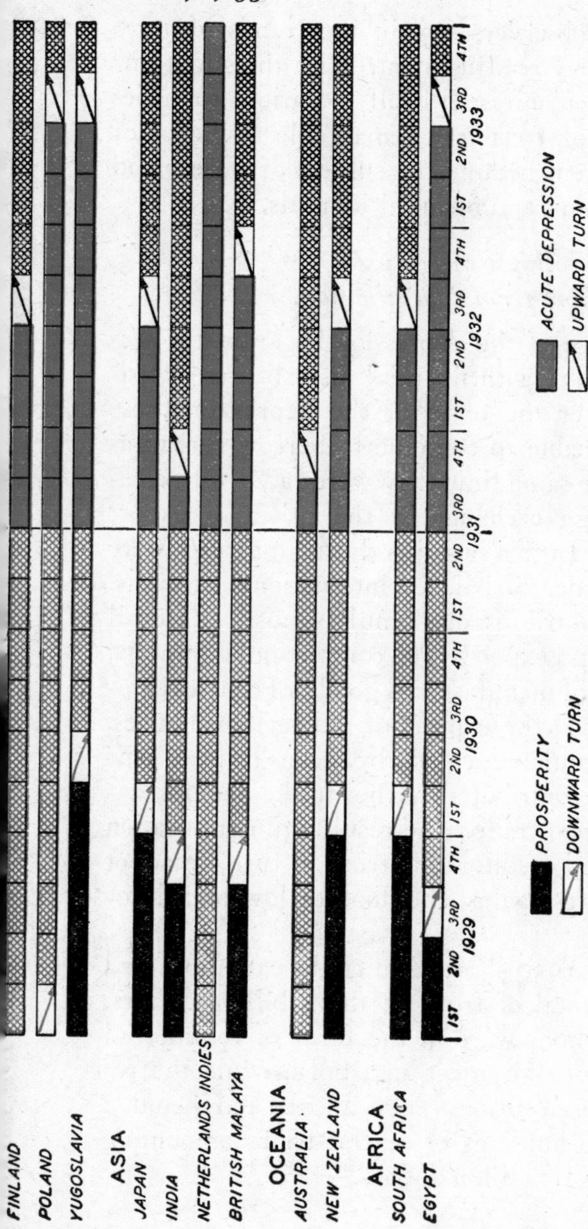

recovery. Many observers saw in the trends of 1930 evidences of orderly readjustment. With the slight improvement which manifested itself in various countries at the beginning of 1931, the remarkable resiliency of the economic system became the subject of widespread comment in economic and financial journals.

The international collapse of 1931 was precipitated by the short-term debt situation.

The acute phase of the depression began in the second quarter of 1931 with financial disturbances in central Europe. After the onset of the depression these countries were unable to continue to borrow abroad as before, and at the same time they were faced with a reduction of foreign exchange as the prices of export commodities fell. In this situation drastic measures were resorted to in order to balance international accounts. Many debtor countries strove simultaneously to curtail imports and expand exports. The contraction of imports, consisting chiefly of manufactured goods, of course correspondingly reduced the exports of industrial countries. Exports were stimulated, chiefly by means of price concessions, and this contributed further to the demoralization of international trade. The resulting intensification of competition led creditor countries, in turn, to adopt protective measures against the flood of low-priced imports.

By the end of 1930 short-term credit extensions had reached a huge total of from 12 to 14 billion dollars. Some 7 or 8 billions were in the form of commercial credits arising out of trade transactions, while the remainder represented *financial* investments, and included foreign exchange holdings of central banks amounting to approximately 2.5 billion dollars.[6]

The credit and financial position of Central European countries grew rapidly weaker in the early months of 1931. French investors withdrew a substantial volume of their short-term funds in Germany; and many Germans, uneasy over the rise of Nazism, began to transfer funds abroad in the hope of greater security. The result was a gradual drain on the gold and foreign exchange holdings of the Reichsbank. In March Germany and Austria announced a customs agreement—which was construed as a violation of the treaties of peace. This action led immediately to large withdrawals of funds from Austria, which was quickly followed by the failure of that country's largest bank. These events produced a panic among the short-term creditors of all Central European countries, and the ensuing flight of capital forced the abandonment of the gold standard in Austria and Hungary and the suspension of the bulk of international debt payments, both public and private.

This collapse produced a profound shock in every financial center of the world, and there was grave apprehension over the ability of the capitalistic system anywhere to withstand the strain. In an effort to stem the tide of financial dissolution in Central Europe, drastic steps were soon taken by the governments and financial institutions of the creditor countries. The Hoover moratorium of June suspended reparation and war debt payments for a period of one year; and the short-term creditors of Germany and Austria agreed to "standstill" agreements with their debtors. Large new short-term loans were extended to Germany, Austria, and Hungary by the principal central banks and by the Bank for International Settlements. In addition, various means of restricting capital outflows were adopted by some of the debtor countries.

While these measures served to retard the process of financial disintegration in Central Europe, new strains soon developed elsewhere. The freezing of a huge volume of short-term funds in Central Europe inevitably led to apprehension over the safety of short-term funds in other quarters, and a mad scramble began for the repatriation of liquid funds while there was yet time. The most immediate and by far the most serious effect was the strain placed upon Great Britain.

Great Britain was on the whole in a strong creditor position. But her short-term obligations abroad exceeded her short-term claims against other countries. Her long-term investments could not quickly be converted into cash, while at the same time a large part of her short-term claims had become unrealizable because of the situation in Central Europe. Meanwhile, however, Britain's own short-term obligations to foreigners were payable on demand.

Within a short time a run on the relatively slender gold reserves of the Bank of England precipitated a foreign exchange and monetary crisis. In an attempt to meet the strain and prevent a collapse of the financial and monetary structure, the Bank and the British Treasury contracted loans in the United States and France during the late summer of 1931 to the amount of 650 million dollars. But even these resources were insufficient to meet the double drain occasioned by the simultaneous withdrawal of foreign funds and the flight of British capital which followed the revelation of a difficult budget situation. On September 21 the British government took the momentous step of abandoning the gold standard.

In October the strain was transferred to the United

States. As in the case of Great Britain, the long-term debts due to the United States were of no immediate use, and the American short-term claims were largely frozen. As a result of large withdrawals from the United States of short-term claims held by foreigners, principally bank deposits, American gold soon began to flow abroad—in the months of October as much as 338 million dollars. Thanks to the enormous accumulation of gold in the United States resulting from war and postwar trade and financial relations, this country managed to withstand the strain. While there was grave concern for a time over the increase of internal hoarding and the flight of capital, the outflow of gold soon ceased.

Great Britain's abandonment of the gold standard in September 1931 precipitated a wholesale breakdown of the international monetary system. As many as 15 countries abandoned the gold standard in the fourth quarter of 1931, and five others followed in early 1932.

The disintegration of the gold standard in turn profoundly affected commercial policies.

The struggle to maintain financial solvency, the collapse of international credit, and the sudden alteration in the terms of commercial competition resulting from the new depreciation of currencies with respect to gold led to utter turmoil and confusion in the field of commercial policy. Within 16 months general tariff increases were authorized in 23 countries and increases on individual items or groups of commodities in 50 countries. At the same time, quantitative restrictions in the form of import quotas, prohibitions, and licensing systems had been imposed in 32 countries.

In due course, many countries, especially those of

South America, defaulted outright on international indebtedness, while others adopted novel devices for relieving the strain of foreign payments. Various countries declared "transfer moratoria" under the terms of which annual payments to foreign creditors would be made in domestic currency to a designated institution within the country, but would not be subject to conversion into foreign currencies except under certain prescribed conditions. In many cases, even current payments on account of commercial transactions were "blocked" or suspended, and a considerable part of international trade thus came to represent merely forced loans by exporters in one country to importers in another.

Finally, out of all these difficulties grew the system of clearing arrangements, under the operation of which a substantial portion of international trade was reduced to barter terms. Since a clearing arrangement could be operated successfully only between two countries, the use of such arrangements naturally tended to bring about a direct trade balance between each pair of countries. The growth of this bilateral balancing process greatly reduced the scope of roundabout trading operations, diverted commerce from its accustomed channels of economic advantage, robbed the trade process of much of its necessary flexibility, and served to intensify the vicious interaction between trade shrinkage and financial and monetary disintegration. Whereas in the spring of 1931 the value of international trade was still 60 per cent that of 1929, by the middle of 1933 it had shrunk to 34 per cent.

The ultimate consequence of this series of national measures—the suspension of gold payments, exchange controls, increased tariffs, import quotas, monopolies, licensing systems—each of which was introduced with a view to maintaining the stability of a particular country—was to disrupt completely the international monetary and credit system. However unavoidable or inescapable some of these policies under existing circumstances may have been, once the breakdown of the international monetary system had begun, the net result was greatly to reduce production, increase unemployment, and impoverish the people of the world.

The collapse of the international monetary system intensified the American depression.

The repercussions were of course first manifested in the field of foreign trade, but they quickly ramified throughout the economic and financial system. The index of industrial production fell from 70 in June 1931 (1929 = 100) to 48.7 in July 1932. The prices of American foodstuffs further declined from an average of 70.6 in March 1931 to 42.8 in March 1933, while raw material prices fell from 69.4 to 49.4.

The shrinkage of industrial output and of corporate earnings, together with increasing pessimism as to the ability of the economic system to withstand the strain to which it was being subjected, led to renewed drastic declines in the prices of securities. Although the index of stock prices in New York had already shown a decline of 50 per cent from the peak in 1929, between March 1931 and July 1932 two thirds of the remaining market values were wiped out.

The prices of bonds also declined heavily during this period. Up to the middle of the year 1931 they had remained practically stationary; indeed, as is common in periods of depression, they rose several points during the first year of the recession. But after June 1931 the collapse in the prices of low-grade bonds was comparable to that of stocks; and even high-grade issues suffered a heavy depreciation. In a twelve months' period following July 1931, bond prices fell on the average more than 25 per cent.

This wholesale shrinkage in values produced a grave debt crisis. Even before the depression began, the persistent decline in agricultural prices had created a difficult farm-debt problem. Mortgage obligations incurred on the basis of wartime prices of farm lands could not readily be met even on the basis of prices obtaining in 1928-29. With the drastic decline in agricultural prices which came during the first stage of the depression, the farm-debt problem was rendered acute; with the further precipitate collapse in 1931-32 the meeting of farm-debt obligations became virtually impossible.

Meanwhile, other debts were becoming increasingly burdensome. In the field of urban mortgages, large numbers of individuals whose incomes were steadily shrinking were unable to continue meeting interest and mortgage installments, and many urban real estate mortgage companies were in default. The railroads seemed threatened with wholesale bankruptcy, while many public utility and industrial corporations were also in serious condition. Grave concern was manifested over the stability of insurance companies and savings banks and of trust and endowment funds which were directly dependent upon the continuance of the flow of interest and mortgage payments. State, city, and local government units, which had for years been borrowing for various and sundry purposes, were finding it increasingly difficult to meet interest obligations. Involved in this network of relationships was the safety of the investments of all classes of people.

The final stage in the process of disintegration was the collapse of the American banking system.

The mortality rate of the country banks—already very high—increased rapidly in 1930, and with the collapse of 1931-32 the whole rural credit structure was undermined. For years city "correspondent banks" had been carrying their country bank clients along in the hope of gradual improvement. But the situation which developed in 1931 made it apparent that it was only a question of time until this support would have to be withdrawn. Many city banks were, moreover, heavily involved in urban real estate financing, and when this situation broke, wholesale bank failures became inevitable.

Meanwhile, also, the decline in the value of securities was adding to banking difficulties; and a "race for liquidity" began. As margins on collateral loans became inadequate, payment was immediately demanded, and often the collateral had to be taken over by the bank and sold at a loss. The shrinkage in the value and income of bonds directly owned by banks also presented a serious problem. Fearful of still further declines, and often in need of cash, the banks attempted to unload their holdings of second-grade bonds. The combined result of the liquidation of the collateral of distressed borrowers and of their own investments was to demoralize still further the security markets. The greater the efforts of the banks to save themselves by the liquidation of securities, the greater became the demoralization of security values.

In due course the fear engendered by the financial situation led to a renewed flight of funds from the United States to other countries, and also to extensive hoarding within the United States. The flow of gold abroad was resumed on a large scale; in the six months January-June 1932 the net outflow was 620 million dollars. The situation was relieved slightly by the moderate recovery which occurred both in business activity and security prices in the second half of 1932. But in the winter of 1933 the continued strains finally culminated in panic and the collapse of the banking structure.

The bottom of the depression, generally speaking, was reached in mid-1932.

The most striking fact pertaining to the great depression was the comparative shortness of the acute stage—the quickness with which recovery followed collapse. The diagram on pages 74-75 indicates that sustained recovery began in India and Australia as early as the fourth quarter of 1931. In the third quarter of 1932 improvement began in the United States, Germany, France, Finland, Japan, South Africa, and New Zealand, while in the fourth quarter there was an upturn in the United Kingdom, British Malaya, Belgium, and the Netherlands. The index of industrial production in the United States rose 9 points—from 58 to 67—between July and October 1932. This improvement, however, proved short-lived and it was followed by a new decline during the banking crisis in early 1933. By March 1933 the index of industrial production had declined to 60.

It should be emphasized that while in many countries a turn was evident in the second half of 1932, the recovery movement remained somewhat sporadic in char-

INDUSTRIAL PRODUCTION IN SELECTED COUNTRIES, 1929-32[7]

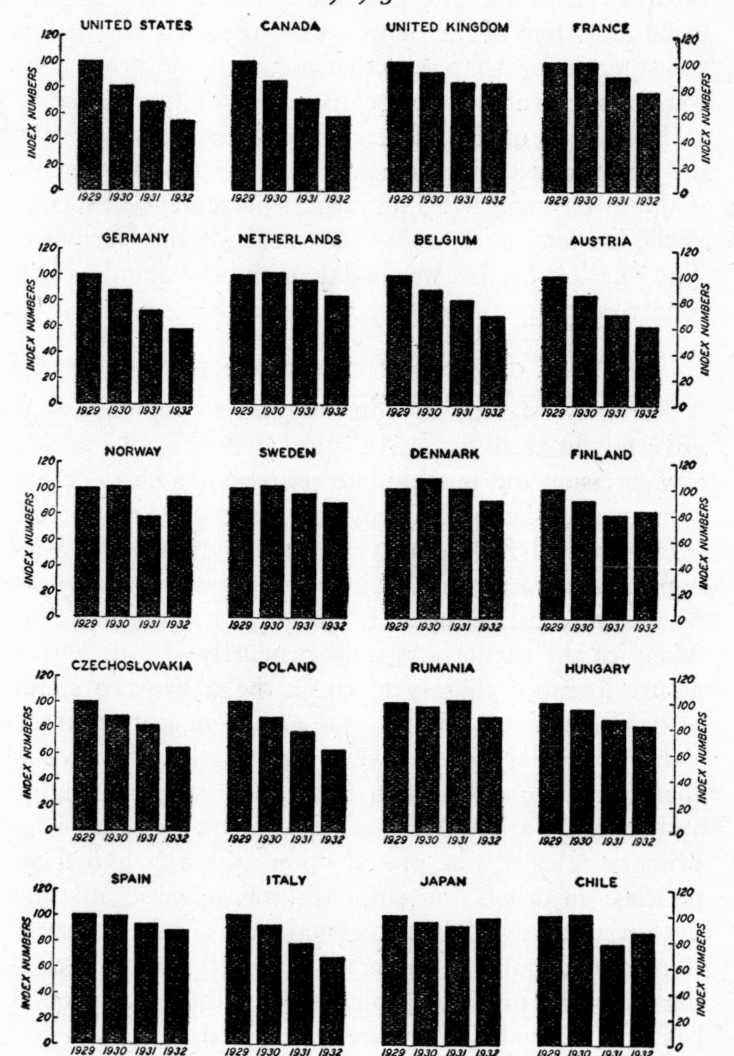

acter and moderate in proportions until the spring of 1933. Perhaps the safest statement would be that in general the bottom of the depression was clearly reached in the summer of 1932, but that a strong and broad forward movement did not begin until nine months later.

The effects of the depression upon the volume of industrial production in selected countries is shown in the diagram on page 85. The largest percentage drop was in the United States, followed by Canada and Germany. The smallest decline was in Japan and the Scandinavian countries.

IV. GOVERNMENT INTERVENTION

For the first time in industrial history the powers of government were extensively invoked to stem the tide of depression and to stimulate recovery. In part because of a growing belief that government could be a sort of balance wheel for the private economy, but more perhaps because of practical exigencies, governments everywhere were called upon to adopt remedial measures. Many of the earlier acts were primarily of a defensive nature intended merely to check the downward spiral of deflation or to bring relief to groups in acute distress. Other measures were, however, essentially offensive in character, designed to start the stalled economic engine and promote a new forward movement. In some cases primary reliance was placed upon monetary and fiscal policies; in others the emphasis was upon stimulating industrial and agricultural revival. Some of the measures were deflationary in character, directed toward reducing costs and prices as a means of establishing a sound basis for revival. Others were designed to raise prices, either by monetary policy or by increasing purchasing power in the hands of the public. A brief summary is necessary in order to reveal the widely divergent character of the policies adopted by leading countries.[8]

Widely varying types of government aid were tried.

In Great Britain, the gold standard was abandoned; fiscal stability was maintained; agriculture and industry were protected and encouraged by new commercial legislation; and employment was stimulated through the granting of subsidies, particularly for the construction of houses.

France maintained (until 1936) the value of the currency; vainly tried to maintain a balanced budget; and sought to reduce costs and prices in industry. But with this deflationary policy was coupled an extensive program of agricultural aid through subsidies and the control of production and prices, and extensive appropriations for public works as a means of relieving unemployment.

Belgium followed in the main a deflationary policy until the spring of 1935; but it then devalued the currency, reorganized its financial system, and embarked upon a systematic policy of stimulating recovery, especially by means of expenditures for public works.

In Germany two distinct stages are in evidence—before and after the emergence of the Nazi party. In the former period major emphasis was placed upon monetary and credit stability, the balancing of the budget, and the reduction of costs and prices with a view to stimulating exports. In the second period the government exercised strict control over production, prices, and trade, and largely eliminated unemployment by removing a large number of workers from the labor market and by increasing the number of jobs through extensive programs of public works and vast outlays for military purposes.

The Swedish government, contrary to prevailing assumptions, did not adopt an extensive recovery program. The currency was linked to the pound sterling; the budget was only moderately unbalanced; aid was extended to agriculture; and provision was made for the relief of unemployment. In Norway, as in Sweden, primary emphasis was placed upon monetary and fiscal measures. The currency was adjusted to the pound, and vigorous efforts were made to maintain a balanced budget.

Finland remained on the gold standard, and attempted to maintain a balanced budget through rigid economies and increased taxation. On the other hand, extensive aid was extended to agriculture, and appropriations were made for public works as a means of relieving unemployment.

The government of Denmark carried through a very extensive program, involving not only the alleviation of distress but the regulation of production, trade, and prices.

Poland maintained the gold standard; endeavored by rigorous methods to maintain a balanced budget; reduced "inflexible prices" by negotiation or decree; and "stabilized" industry by means of syndicates or cartels. A moratorium was proclaimed on agricultural debts, and financially distressed industries were relieved by a compulsory general bankruptcy law.

The Italian program extended to practically every phase of economic activity, great emphasis being placed upon the control of production, prices, and wages. Gold parity was maintained until the autumn of 1936, and systematic but unsuccessful efforts were made to keep the budget in balance.

The Austrian government, during the acute stage of the depression, devoted its energies chiefly to the re-establishment of financial stability, with the co-operation of the League of Nations. The gold standard was definitely abandoned in 1933. Relief aid, particularly to agriculture, was extended throughout the whole period.

The government of New Zealand concentrated attention upon monetary, credit, and fiscal policies. The gold standard was abandoned and fiscal stability maintained. Extensive aid was given to agriculture, and a public works program was instituted.

The Australian recovery program is distinctive for the systematic effort made to lower costs of government and the level of commodity prices by means of reductions in wages and interest rates. At the same time relief was extended to distressed debtors and to the unemployed.

In Japan we find perhaps the most extreme case of inflationary action. Not only was the gold standard abandoned, but public credit was extensively employed for the promotion of industry, the development of foreign trade, and the carrying out of a military program. No effort was made to maintain a balanced budget, and most of the government's loans were placed directly with the central bank.

In the United States government intervention involved two stages. In the first stage, under the Hoover administration, the primary effort was directed toward arresting the depression. In early 1930 the administration obtained agreements from important industries, notably railroads and public utilities, to continue their production programs as usual, especially capital construction. In the same year the Federal Reserve lowered rediscount rates and engaged in extensive open-market operations with a view to easing the money market situation generally. The Railroad Credit Corporation was organized in late 1931, the Reconstruction Finance Corporation in February 1932, and the Home Loan Bank System in June 1932. Meanwhile, also, the Agricultural Marketing Act of June 15, 1929 provided a 500 million dollar revolving fund for the stabilization of agricultural prices.

The second stage is best described as the 1933 program of the Roosevelt administration. The principal planks were: (1) reconstructing the shattered commercial and investment credit system; (2) extending financial aid to and underwriting the credit of distressed industries; (3) restoring agricultural purchasing power by restricting production and by financial aids of various types; (4) stimulating exports and raising the general level of commodity prices by reducing the value of the dollar; (5) promoting and financing public works to provide employment and purchasing power; (6) raising wage rates and adopting industrial codes under the National Recovery Administration; (7) establishing public credit on a sound basis by reducing expenditures and balancing the federal budget. Within a few months, however, this last principle was abandoned in favor of an extensive unbalancing of the budget as the surest means of increasing purchasing power and "priming the industrial pump."

No real correlation is discoverable between government policies and recovery.

In the light of the widely divergent policies in the various countries and of the further fact that the course of the depression followed a similar pattern in leading industrial countries, it seems apparent that government intervention could not have been a primary factor in checking the downward course of the depression and initiating a recovery movement. The two measures most widely acclaimed as having been effective were the abandonment of the gold standard and the expansion of public credit.

The time at which recovery began in the various countries does not, however, correlate closely with the dates at which the gold standard was abandoned. It is true that recovery was less rapid in Belgium, France, the Netherlands, and Italy, which remained on the gold standard, than in Great Britain and Germany, which abandoned it. On the other hand, the United States and Canada, which departed from gold, recovered little more quickly than the gold bloc countries of Europe.

Nor is any close connection observable between fiscal policy and recovery. The departure from gold was in some cases accompanied by deflationary fiscal and credit policies, while in others it was combined with inflationary measures. Among the countries showing most rapid recovery, Japan and Germany made prodigal use of public funds; in contrast, Great Britain, Australia, and Sweden were conservative in public finance, striving to maintain a strong, stable fiscal situation. The recovery was more rapid and extensive in Great Britain and the Scandinavian countries, which followed conservative fiscal policies, than in the United States, which ultimately made extensive use of public credit with a view to "priming the industrial pump." Moreover, the American recovery was as marked during the budget economy period of 1933 as during the pump-priming which followed.

The recovery movement in the various countries began at different times and followed a highly irregular course. The monthly indexes of industrial production, shown on page 93, reveal the trends in 20 countries from January 1932 to the end of 1936. A sustained forward movement in industrial production began in Japan and Chile in February 1932; in Belgium, Sweden, and Hungary in the late summer and early fall of 1932; and in the United Kingdom in the last quarter of 1932. In the United States, Canada, Germany, Poland, and Czechoslovakia, no sustained upward movement occurred until the spring of 1933.

As the chart reveals, the recovery movement showed little uniformity in the various countries. The expansion of industrial production once under way was more or less continuous in Japan, Germany, Sweden, the United Kingdom, Hungary, and Chile, but the rate of expansion varied considerably. In Poland and Czechoslovakia the recovery was gradual and of only moderate proportions. In Belgium production remained practically stationary until 1935. In France, after a year of expansion, production declined throughout 1934 and showed little improvement in 1935.

In the United States the upward movement was sporadic and very irregular. After the sharp rise in production in the spring and early summer of 1933, there was a substantial recession in the autumn. Through 1934

THE COURSE OF INDUSTRIAL PRODUCTION, 1931-36[9]

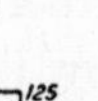
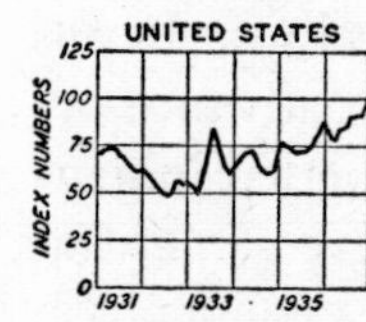
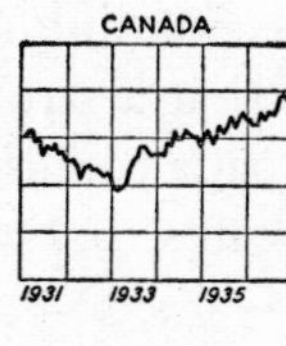
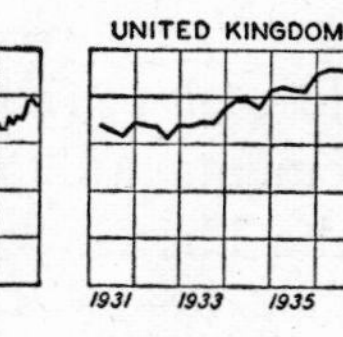
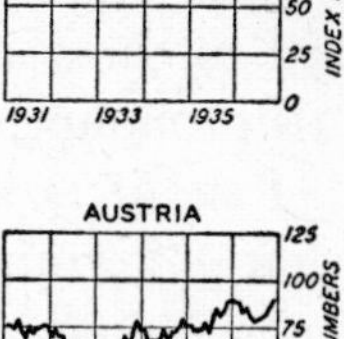
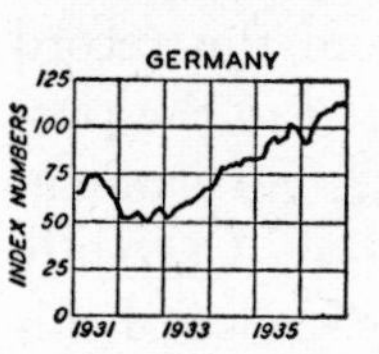
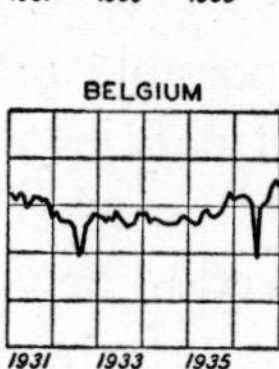
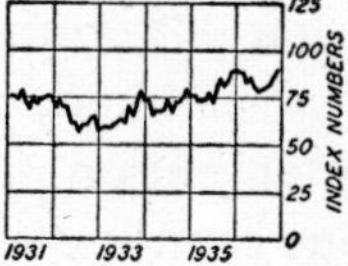
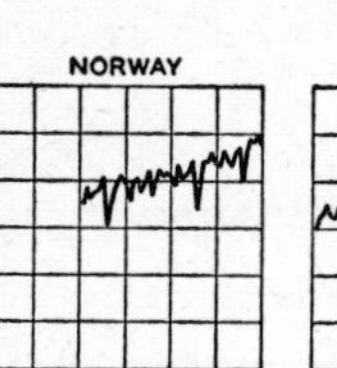
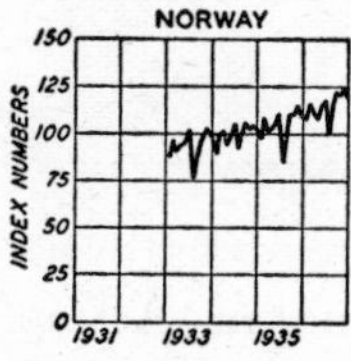
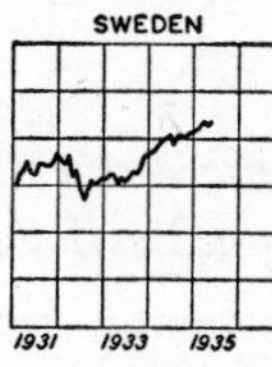
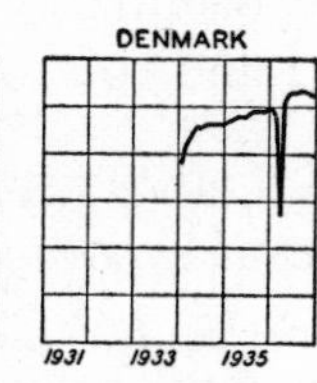
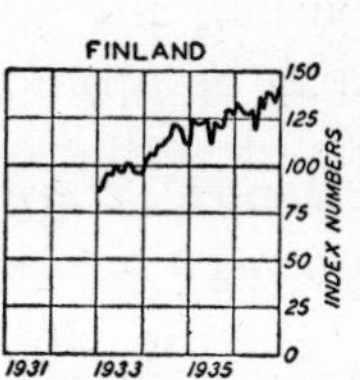
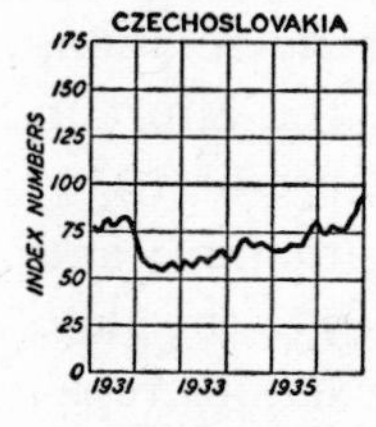
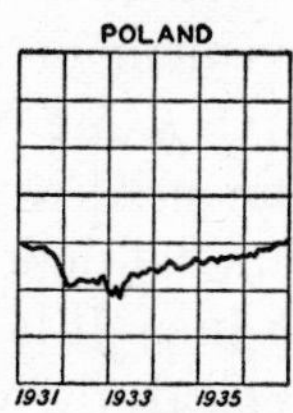
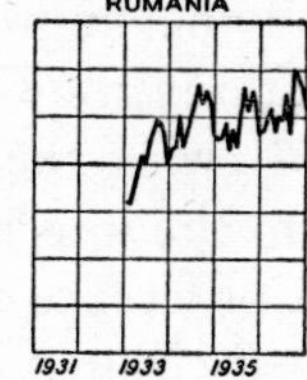

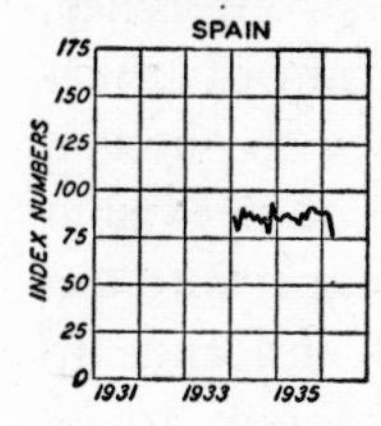
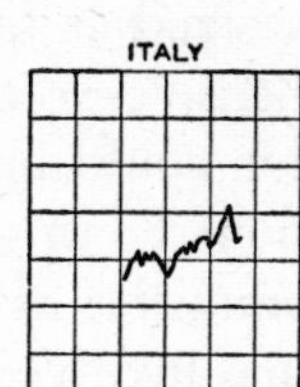
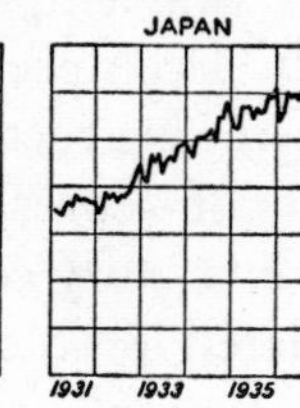
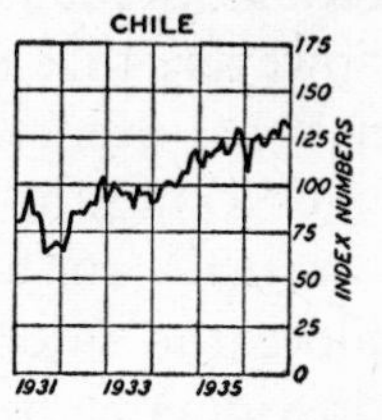

and the first half of 1935 there were periodic advances followed by more or less corresponding declines. It was not until the middle of 1935 that a strong advance occurred. The movements in Canada corresponded in general to those in the United States, but were somewhat less pronounced.

Thus it is impossible to determine from the record what government policies were best adapted to the purpose in hand, or even whether, on balance, government intervention proved to be a constructive force. Certainly one cannot discover, from the available evidence of this period, any sure formula by means of which recovery may be promoted and controlled.

Attempts were also made to control the situation through co-operative international action.

At the Conference for Concerted Economic Action held in 1930, emphasis was placed upon the removal of tariff barriers and the improvement of trade relations with Europe. Nothing, however, came of the effort in this direction. Following the financial collapse of 1931, attention shifted to the international debt situation; and at the Lausanne Conference of June-July 1932 the slate was virtually wiped clean as regards the vexatious reparations problem. It was emphasized at this conference, however, that only a comprehensive program of international economic reconstruction could hope to succeed in checking the tide of depression. To this end provision was made for a preparatory committee of experts to explore the interrelated problems involved and thus to provide the basis for an international program to be implemented at a subsequent international conference.

After a year of intensive study by the preparatory committee of experts, the World Economic Conference convened in London in June 1933. The preparatory committee had emphasized that the crisis could not be solved by piecemeal measures—that a broad solution involving both monetary and economic measures must be sought.

The World Economic Conference foundered as a result of divergent monetary policies. The United States at the last moment refused to accept any commitment with respect to the stabilization of foreign exchanges and chose this moment to announce its faith in independent national action. The conference thus failed to achieve any of its fundamental objectives. Meanwhile, however, the recovery movement, as we have seen, was already under way.

This analysis of the great depression of 1929, and of the varied, divergent, and even conflicting, types of government efforts to ameliorate and stimulate recovery, serves further to emphasize the conclusion reached in the preceding chapter that there is no single cause of economic disorders and no simple formula for checking a decline and bringing about a recovery. A similarly detailed study of other depressions would reveal differing types of initial maladjustment, varying degrees of depression intensity and duration, and eventual recoveries that were unconnected with government policies. Perhaps the most striking fact disclosed by this study of the 1929-33 depression is that recovery eventually began everywhere, regardless of the type of government policy being pursued.

It does not follow from this fact, however, that business depressions must always be allowed to "run their course and that, once bottom has been reached, recovery will automatically ensue." The following questions remain for consideration: (1) Can preventive measures, undertaken prior to the onset of a depression, either by government or business, or by the two jointly, be helpful in stabilizing the situation? (2) Once a recession is under way, can defensive measures minimize the shock and arrest the process of disintegration? (3) Can measures be taken by government and/or business enterprise which will stimulate early recovery? These issues will be considered in Chapter X.

CHAPTER IV

OTHER FACTORS RETARDING ECONOMIC PROGRESS

While it became apparent long ago that recurring business depressions slowed down the rate of material advancement, it was generally believed that otherwise the economic system operated with reasonable satisfaction—promoting the most rapid progress possible. In short, the only major problem appeared to be to discover the cause and cure of depressions. This point of view prevailed, in fact, until very recent years, and it is still widely held.

The present chapter will be devoted to an analysis of factors other than *cyclical,* which have affected economic progress over the past century. It will be focused on the motivating forces underlying long-term economic growth in a highly developed capitalistic society. It will review briefly the traditional conception of economic progress; outline the emergence of divergent views; set forth the conclusions reached in a comprehensive inductive study by the Brookings Institution; and discuss other theories pertaining to economic retardation which found expression in the decade of the 1930's.

I. THE TRADITIONAL CONCEPTION OF PROGRESS

The classical economists took full use of our productive resources for granted. That is, they started with the assumption that the existing supply of labor and capital is *normally* fully employed. Such a phenomenon as persistently *idle* plant capacity or *chronic* unemployment had virtually no place in either nineteenth or early twentieth century economic thinking. Except for occasional periods of depression, we produced all that could be produced "in the given state of the arts."

Moreover, it appeared that general overproduction was impossible. It was observed that the market value of the goods and services produced is *necessarily* equal to the sum of the wages, interest, profits, etc., accruing to those who participate in the processes of production; hence available purchasing power is always adequate to buy the entire annual production. The kinds of goods produced were seen to be dependent upon the desires of the public as manifested in the market place: If the public's desire for commodity A increases, while that for commodity B decreases, it would obviously pay to shift production from line B to line A. There might be a failure to gauge market demands correctly, and a consequent misdirection of productive effort, with attendant losses. But there could be no chronic state of maladjustment or persistent failure to utilize existing productive capacity.

Similarly, such a conception as "excessive savings" seemed meaningless. If the people save more, they simply increase the demand for and production of capital goods as compared with consumer goods. As one writer put it:

> That which one spends for consumers' goods virtually hires men to produce that class of goods, while that which one spends for producers' goods virtually hires men to produce that class of goods. The more money there is spent for producers' goods, the more rapidly they will accumulate. This means that the more thrifty the people are, and the more inclined they are to live on less than their incomes and to spend the remainder for tools, the better equipped with tools they will be.[1]

That capital expansion could continue for an indefinite period without any concurrent increase in consumption was a not uncommon view. This position is illustrated in the following explicit statement:

> Is there no economic limit to the deferment of consumption? The answer is that there is none save . . . the continuance of such consumption as is essential to the proper sustenance of life. In economic theory the indefinite extension of the roundabout process is a logical aim. A society is conceivable in which men may for several generations (which means indefinitely) be content to get along with salt, bread, milk, and a loin cloth the while they are industriously and profitably engaged in the production of machines and equipment of every sort.[2]

Unlike Mill and the early classicists who attached relatively little importance to capital,[3] later writers, as already noted, came to regard capital as the great creative force. Accordingly, it appeared that the greater the curtailment of consumption and the greater the volume of saving, the more rapid the increase in man's power over nature. While the ultimate purpose of increased capital was to make possible greater consumption, it was held that consumption must constantly be restrained in the interest of rapid economic advancement. Capital formation leads the way; rising standards of living follow in due time in consequence of increasing efficiency and declining cost and prices. The only likely drag on the wheels of progress seemed to be a lack of thrift—*under*-saving rather than *over*saving.

II. DIVERGENT VIEWS

From time to time conceptions at variance with the foregoing found expression. In the early nineteenth century a few European writers—notably Lauderdale of Scotland, Malthus of England, and Sismondi of France

—emphasized the importance of steadily expanding consumption and noted the possibility of excessive saving. These writers were in the main, however, concerned with the causes of recurring crises rather than with the possibility of chronic retardation of capital growth.

In the middle 1880's certain American writers argued strongly that the world was suffering from an over-expansion of capital goods—such as manufacturing plant and equipment; warehouses; railways, canals, and tramways; water and gas works; and telegraph lines. In a comprehensive survey of the world situation, Carroll D. Wright, United States Commissioner of Labor, concluded that "On all sides one sees the accomplished results of the labor of half a century. This full supply of economic tools is the most important factor in the present industrial depression."[4] David A. Wells, noted business analyst, concluded that "The supply of the great articles and instrumentalities of the world's use and commerce has increased . . . in a far greater ratio than the contemporaneous increase in the world's population or its immediate consuming capacity."[5] Though these writers were concerned chiefly with explaining the depressions of the late seventies and the middle eighties, the implication of their analyses reached beyond the phenomenon of the business cycle and suggested a slowing down if not the end of progress.

In 1918 the present writer challenged the whole traditional conception with respect to the motivating force in capital expansion.[6] It was pointed out that when individuals save money they do not as a rule exercise a direct demand for capital goods; they merely provide funds which business managers *may* use in constructing new capital. At the same time, it was observed, the restriction of consumption incident to saving "tends to restrict the profitable use of new capital and hence to retard the rate at which such capital will be created." The result is "a permanent, though variable, lag in the rate of expansion, and a prevention of the continuous use of the full productive capacity of society." The reason why restricted consumption tends to check capital formation is that "the entrepreneur who assumes the risks and directs the creation of new capital is in quest of profits"; and the outlook for profits is favorable only when the flow of funds into consumptive channels is large and increasing. "Expanding consumption is the controlling factor."

In verification of this analysis it was pointed out that the only periods in which capital expansion in the United States had been rapid were the so-called "eras of extravagant consumption." It was explained that this phenomenon—involving a *simultaneous* increase in the flow of funds into consumption channels and into investment channels—was made possible by a rapidly evolving commercial banking system which provided a continuously expanding volume of available liquid capital.

Up to the time the foregoing was written, the United States was a country in which the volume of money savings set aside for investment purposes was commonly much less than the needs for new capital construction. In short, we had *under*saving. The writer, however, called attention to the fact that in a pecuniary society there might develop a situation in which savings would be *excessive,* that is, greater than the demand for funds for capital expansion. In such a situation, it was pointed out, the continuance of large savings would "serve to check the demand for the products of expanding industry and thus retard the creation of new capital."

Finally, it was contended that the allegedly automatic mechanism of fluctuations in the interest rate could not be depended upon to prevent either undersaving or oversaving and thus to maintain the desired balance between saving and spending. "Neither the rationalistic reactions of a multitude of individuals in the matter of saving, nor the behavioristic psychology of the masses as conditioned by social and economic environment (whatever theory of individual motivation one may prefer) will serve to furnish automatically the precise amount of saving required in a pecuniarily organized society."

In the decade of the 1920's the importance of expanding consumption was emphasized increasingly. In business circles it was repeatedly stated that it was easy to expand production—that market outlets presented the real problem. Business executives were seeking to expand sales in domestic markets through high-pressure advertising and extensive consumer credits, and they were enlisting the aid of the government to obtain larger outlets abroad. Labor leaders, and also numerous writers, were beginning to stress expanding purchasing power as the basis of sustained prosperity. Slackness in the labor market in a period of great prosperity suggested to some professional economists the possibility of persistent technological unemployment.

With the advent of the great depression, some of these tentative ideas and conceptions quickly became deeply rooted convictions.

III. THE INDUCTIVE STUDY BY THE BROOKINGS INSTITUTION

The conclusions of the classical writers referred to above were not derived from inductive study of the operation of the economic system. They were based in the main on assumptions and deductive reasoning therefrom. Moreover, most of those who challenged the traditional assumptions based their conclusions on more or less casual observation of economic conditions and forces. What was evidently needed was a comprehensive inductive investigation; and, fortunately, accumulating factual information was beginning to make such an inquiry feasible.

In the early 1930's the Brookings Institution undertook a pioneering study of the operation of the economic system with special reference to the possible bearing of the distribution of income upon economic progress. Did the way in which current national income was divided among the various groups in society serve to retard capital development and improvements in living standards? Was there any validity in the conception of *under*consumption or *over*saving? Concretely, was there any evidence supporting the view that productive capacity had outrun consuming capacity? Were the assumptions underlying the traditional approach valid? Since the investigation was not directly concerned with the causes of depression, it was confined to the period prior to the economic collapse of 1929.

The results of this investigation were published in 1934-35 in four volumes—*America's Capacity to Produce*, *America's Capacity to Consume*, *The Formation of Capital*, and *Income and Economic Progress*. The analysis is here recapitulated in the simplest possible terms, with some slight refinement and amplification in the interests of clarity. Since the entire analysis was closely integrated, it is essential to review the successive steps in the inquiry.

Step 1: Determination of Excess Capacity

The preliminary inquiry was to determine whether our productive resources were in fact fully utilized. It is obvious that in periods of depression both capital and labor resources are only partially employed. But was there any substantial slack at other times? Were we producing at reasonably full capacity in periods of so-called prosperity?

The survey of American productive capacity and output covered the entire period from 1900 to 1929; but since the data were less adequate for the earlier years, the primary focus was on the prosperity period of the twenties. The purpose of this section of the study was simply to determine how much slack, if any, existed in the economic system as it actually operated.

The conclusion reached was that, with full allowance for frictional elements and for the flexibility essential to a dynamic economic system, American productive capacity was not being fully utilized, the slack, even in good times, being in the magnitude of 20 per cent. That is to say, with available plant and equipment, raw materials, transport facilities, labor supply, and financial resources, the economic system as an integrated whole could readily have turned out at least 20 per cent more goods and services than were in fact produced.

It is noteworthy that the extent of the unused capacity was not appreciably reduced in the peak years of the boom. This finding ran directly counter to the general belief that during a period of business expansion we inevitably soon reach a point where productive resources become fully employed and scarcities begin to prevail, with a resulting rise in prices. But in the late twenties there did not develop any shortage of labor and materials, nor did industrial prices rise. The explanation is that during this particular boom period capital outlays went not so much for additions as for replacement of obsolescent equipment by new units of greater efficiency. The result was an economizing in the use of labor which served, in effect, to increase the labor supply.

It was also apparent from the survey running back to 1900, even earlier in some industries, that idle productive capacity was no new phenomenon. Except in occasional boom years, industrial slack appears to have been characteristic of the American economic system. A striking illustration of the possibility of increasing production was found in the expansion which occurred after the United States entered World War I in 1917.

Step 2: The Division of National Income

The next question to be considered was whether the way in which the national income was distributed might be responsible for the failure to make full use of our productive resources. The first requirement was to ascertain the facts as to how the national money income was actually divided among the public as a whole. Since statistical information relating to the distribution of individual income by classes was reasonably satisfactory only for the year 1929, the detailed analysis was concentrated on that year.

This analysis showed an extraordinary concentration of income in the higher levels in 1929. The *aggregate* income of the 6 million families (21 per cent of the total) with incomes of less than $1,000 amounted to only 3.5 billion dollars, or 4.5 per cent of the total. The 11,653,000 families under the $1,500 level received a total of only 10 billion dollars. At the opposite extreme, 36,000 families having incomes in excess of $75,000 received as much as 9.8 billion dollars. Thus one tenth of one per cent of the families at the top received practically as much as 42 per cent of the families at the bottom of the scale.

Moreover, the evidence showed that income was growing faster at the top than at the bottom. During the prosperity period from 1922 to 1929, the percentage of the aggregate national income accruing to wage earners declined slightly and to farmers materially; while that accruing to salaried employees and investors increased. Income tax returns showed a steady increase in the percentage of families in the upper income ranges, especially in the highest brackets.

It also appeared that over the entire period from 1900 to 1929 there was a gradually increasing concentration of income in the higher levels. The growth of great fortunes was attracting the attention of economists as early as 1905[7] and became a political issue under President Theodore Roosevelt. Because of fluctuations in business conditions the tendency toward increasing concentration was by no means uniform; but the evidence is unmistakable that it was greater in each succeeding boom period and that over the three decades as a whole there was a more rapid growth in income at the top than at the bottom of the income scale.

Step 3: Income Distribution and the Volume of Savings

The disclosure of a great and apparently growing disparity in incomes did not of itself warrant the conclusion that the existing distribution of income accounted for the failure to make full use of productive resources. The question had still to be faced whether the way in which money income is distributed has any bearing on total demand for the products of industry. If the income distribution is highly concentrated in the upper levels, will not a larger proportion simply be spent for luxuries and a smaller proportion for necessities—without affecting the total outlay? Or perhaps less would be spent for consumption goods as a class and more for capital goods. In other words, does not the way in which income is divided merely affect the character of the demand, and hence the character of the resulting productive operations without having any effect upon total output? This, it will be recalled, was the basic assumption of the traditional theory.

The third step, then, was to determine how those at various income levels do, in fact, dispose of their incomes. (1) How are consumptive expenditures at different levels of income apportioned among the various types of consumer goods? (2) How is the income allocated as between consumer expenditures as a whole and savings for investment?

First, the available data revealed that, as family incomes increase: *aggregate* expenditures for each of the major classes of consumer goods rise steadily; the *proportions* spent for such basic necessities as food, shelter, and clothing decline, while the percentages going for health and education, "conventional" necessities, and luxuries rise rapidly. The study thus revealed an enormous potential demand among the lower-income groups for the primary necessities of life, and an even greater potential demand for conveniences and luxuries. In short, *potential* consuming power was enormously in excess of the nation's existing capacity to produce.

It might almost seem that it was unnecessary to establish this rather obvious conclusion. But at the time the study was made many leaders of public thought, confused by the phenomenon of congested markets, were alarmed at the prospect of chronic overproduction of consumer goods, both industrial and agricultural. This view lay at the basis of the curtailment of output and share-the-work programs of the early thirties. Moreover, as we shall see in Section VI below, some professional economists still hold the view that consumptive habits are relatively fixed, and hence aggregate consumptive demand will increase but slowly as national income rises.

Second, the evidence shows conclusively: that those in the lower-income groups save a negligible percentage of their incomes; that the percentage saved rises steadily through the middle brackets; and that the proportion set aside for investment in the upper levels of income rises rapidly and often runs as high as 40 or 50 per cent. Savings are negligible at the bottom of the income scale because earnings barely, often hardly, suffice to cover minimum consumption requirements. As incomes rise, savings become possible; and as the margin above basic necessities increases, the figures show that savings progressively expand. In the high-income brackets a substantial percentage of the income is *automatically* saved.

In 1929 the great bulk of the money savings was

made by a very small percentage of the population. Less than 1 per cent of the nation's families—those having incomes in excess of $20,000—contributed as much as 54 per cent of the aggregate family money savings. The upper 8 per cent—with incomes above $5,000—contributed approximately 84 per cent of the aggregate family savings. At the opposite extreme, 59 per cent—with incomes less than $2,000—accounted for only about 1.6 per cent of the net family savings.

It follows from this analysis that an expansion of income among the poorer classes would sharply increase aggregate consumer expenditures relatively to aggregate savings. Practically all of the increased income accruing to those in the lower-income levels would go for additional consumption.

The investigation also indicated that the percentage of the total money income directed toward savings channels was increasing over the thirty-year period as a whole. While the trend was naturally affected by periodic fluctuations in business activity, the general upward tendency was clearly in evidence. It was particularly marked during World War I and throughout the prosperity period of the twenties.

From this analysis two conclusions were derived which could be stated in the form of laws, or generalizations, as follows:

The higher the general level of income of the population as a whole, the greater will tend to be the proportion of the aggregate that is saved.

The greater the concentration of the national income in the hands of a small percentage of the population, the greater will be the proportion of the aggregate national income that is saved.

In the three decades under review both of these factors were operating to increase the ratio of savings to consumption. The per-capita income increased nearly 40 per cent, an increase which was shared by all classes. But at the same time an increasing proportion of the total was going to those in the higher-income levels. This second factor was primarily responsible for the rapid increase in the proportions saved during the period under investigation. It was this, rather than any apparent change in the saving habits of the average individual, which accounted for the increasing percentage of the national income that was directed into savings channels.

Step 4: Restricted Consumption and Capital Formation

Granted that the existing distribution of income tended to increase the flow of funds into savings relatively to consumption channels, the next question was—What bearing did this have on the operation of the economic system? Did the increase in the rate of savings promote or retard economic progress?

As a preliminary, it is necessary to reveal the several stages involved in the process of capital formation. In traditional theory money savings and capital formation were usually looked upon as identical concepts; indeed, the term "savings" was commonly used simply to connote the amount of new capital actually constructed. This conception, that capital formation and money savings are identical, was based on the explicit assumption that when an individual saves money, he is demanding capital goods instead of consumption goods.

Observation reveals, however, that in a complex

pecuniary society the process of creating new capital *usually* involves three distinct stages: (1) the decision by the receivers of money income to save rather than spend such income—this we call *money saving;* (2) the purchase of securities with the money saved—this we call *market investment;* and (3) the use of these savings funds by business enterprisers who employ labor and materials in the actual construction of new, procreative capital—this we call *capital formation.* Each of these stages is influenced by particular forces or considerations, and it may be said they are *independent variables.*

In the first stage—the refraining from consumption or the decision to save money—the main considerations involved are the desire to provide security, to enlarge future income, to build an estate, etc.; and, as we have seen, much saving in the higher-income levels results from the simple fact that beyond a certain point it is difficult to spend at all. The individuals who save money income are not themselves as a rule interested in demanding or constructing new plant and equipment; they merely make funds available.

In the second stage—the investing in securities—the primary consideration is the safety of the funds that have been saved. This depends upon the prospective stability of business conditions. When the situation appears favorable, virtually all money savings are promptly invested marketwise—either directly by the individual savers or indirectly through savings institutions. But in periods of instability the *hoarding* of cash by individuals and savings institutions is practiced on an extensive scale. Thus, in any given time period the amount of money savings and the amount of market investment in new securities may diverge sharply.

In the third stage—the employment of investment funds in constructing capital goods—the decisions are in most cases made by different people from those who save money and invest in securities. In a highly developed capitalistic society, such decisions are commonly made by business enterprisers who employ savings funds in their profit-making activities. In gauging the situation, they are not motivated by the same considerations which govern the decisions of individuals to save money. They are influenced by a combination of factors which may best be described as the *general business outlook and the prospect for profitable expansion.*

Since the motivating factors in the three stages in the roundabout process of capital formation are thus largely independent, there never was any reason for assuming that the volume of money savings, of market investment, and of capital formation would ordinarily be identical. Moreover, the assumption has never been in accordance with the facts.

Until recent historical times the great bulk of the money savings was not invested at all, but was hoarded—chiefly in the form of precious metals—a practice which has continued in such countries as China and India even to the present day. The problem of finding investment outlets for accumulating savings during the early stages of capitalistic evolution has often been noted by economic historians.

In the United States prior to World War I the volume of money savings made by the American people was ordinarily quite inadequate for the needs of American businessmen bent on expanding plant and equipment—the deficiency of funds being met in part from foreign borrowings and in part from commercial bank credit expansion. Issues of securities frequently remained "undigested" for long periods of time, being carried meanwhile by underwriters and speculators largely by means of bank accommodations. Commercial banks also made direct extensions of credit for investment purposes both to industry and agriculture. Investigation shows that in 1914 something like two thirds of all the credit extended by commercial banks had gone for investment purposes.[8] After World War I the balance between savings and capital formation in the United States was reversed. That is, the volume of current money savings thereafter greatly exceeded the volume of new capital construction. In England and other advanced countries, current savings have long been greatly in excess of the amounts demanded for domestic capital expansion. There have even been cases in which in a given year a nation had a large supply of money savings and *no* domestic flotations of securities for purposes of new capital formation.

The crucial question in this fourth step of the analysis was whether restriction of consumption promotes or retards capital growth. In analyzing the influence of *restricted* consumption, it was necessary to consider two situations: one in which the flow of funds into consumptive channels is *positively* declining; and another in which it is increasing, but less rapidly than the flow into savings channels. In either case, it will be observed, consumption is *relatively* restricted.

The evidence assembled showed: (1) that declining consumption is usually accompanied by declining rather than expanding capital formation; (2) that the growth of physical capital is in general adjusted to the growth of consumption; and (3) that only a part of the money savings available in the twenties was used to expand plant and equipment.

The first point had been tentatively established by the writer's earlier studies referred to on page 102, where it was shown that the only periods of rapid capital expansion in our history had been periods of so-called extravagant consumption. The more comprehensive production data available in later years indicated conclusively that aggregate consumption and capital formation expand and contract together; they do not move in opposite directions.[9]

With reference to the second point, the traditional assumption had been that rapid capital growth might continue for an indefinite period irrespective of the rate of consumption growth. Even writers who emphasized the importance of consumption assumed that all money savings would automatically be used in building new plant and equipment. No maladjustment was foreseen until long-continued expansion resulted in a congestion of unsold goods in consumer markets. The piling up of inventories, it was held, would eventually break consumer goods prices and bring on depression.[10]

The facts showed that during the prosperity period of the twenties production of consumer goods was largely on a hand-to-mouth basis, with output closely adjusted to sales prospects. There was no accumulation of inventories in consumer goods markets. Instead of producing all the goods possible and pressing them into consumptive channels, businessmen were in the main holding production in leash, adjusting output to the volume of current orders. This is the explanation of the unused productive capacity, which remained practically constant in percentage terms throughout the period 1922 to 1929.

Moreover, the expansion of new plant and equipment was apparently being held in check by the existence of unused productive capacity. With the materials and labor supply available, it was readily possible in these years to build much more plant and equipment than was actually constructed. The facts showed that the building material industries were operating at much less than capacity and that there was substantial unemployment in the construction field.

The demand for capital goods is a *derived* demand—derived, that is, from the demand for consumption goods. While the expansion of capital goods may, here and there, run ahead of current demands for the products which the new capital could turn out, aggregate capital formation is on the whole closely adjusted to the demand for consumption goods. In fact, the construction of machinery and equipment is, under modern conditions, usually undertaken largely on the basis of orders from the consumer goods industries. The base of the economic pyramid is consumption.

The third point—the failure to use all available money savings in creating new capital—was established by comparing the volume of security flotations for purposes of new capital formation with the volume of money savings available for the purchase of such securities. The data showed that the supply of investment money greatly exceeded the demand for funds with which to finance new capital construction. In 1929 the volume of money savings available for market investment in securities was roughly three times the volume of new capital construction financed through corporate issues and mortgages. The discrepancy existed throughout the twenties and was steadily increasing.

When the supply of investment funds exceeds the

market demand therefor, what becomes of the excess? Depending upon circumstances, it may be (1) held as idle cash, (2) invested in existing corporate securities, and (3) invested in new corporate issues the proceeds of which are devoted to the purchase of existing corporate securities. In the late 1920's little, if any, was held as idle cash; much was invested through the securities markets in already outstanding issues; and very large amounts were invested in new issues, the proceeds of which were used to buy control of existing enterprises rather than to construct new capital.[11]

The employment of savings funds in purchasing already outstanding securities inevitably led to a progressive rise in the prices of such securities. Instead of producing new plant and equipment, the excess savings served in effect to raise the market prices of existing plant and equipment, that is, the value of the ownership shares outstanding in the market. Quite apart from security purchases made on bank credit, the demand flowing from redundant savings was a powerful contributing influence in the bull market of the late twenties.

It should be understood that the money profits, or capital gains, realized by those who sell securities at advancing prices, are not withdrawn from the economy. The profits derived from stock market inflation—as is of course also the case with profits derived from inflation in commodity markets—serve to augment the onward flow of *money* income. The proceeds of such capital gains may be spent for consumer goods or again be directed to investment channels, as the owner thereof may decide.

The conclusions reached in this section of the analysis may be succinctly summarized as follows:

(1) Money savings, market investment, and actual capital formation are independent variables.

(2) Capital formation expands rapidly when consumption is also expanding, not when it is contracting.

(3) The growth of productive capital is adjusted not to the volume of money savings available for investment but to the growth of consumptive demand.

(4) The rapid growth of money savings as compared with consumer expenditures in the twenties retarded rather than accelerated the growth of productive capital. The "excess" savings which entered the investment market served to inflate prices of existing capital goods and to produce financial instability. A larger relative flow of funds through consumptive channels would have led to a larger utilization of existing productive capacity and also to a more rapid growth of plant and equipment.

Step 5: Methods of Redistributing Income

The foregoing sections of the analysis comprised the diagnosis of factors restraining the rate of economic progress. The remaining problem was to consider means whereby the primary source of difficulty might be mitigated.

In the final volume—*Income and Economic Progress*—consideration was given to a number of methods which might be employed to improve the distribution of income and thereby establish a more effective ratio between consumptive expenditure and saving. The complex character of the problem was expressed as follows:

> All the world loves a panacea. But anyone broadly experienced . . . knows that there is no single formula by which desired results can be brought about. . . . Sound proposals for a better system for the distribution of income cannot be oversimplified nor can the prospect of general amelioration come

through attention to a single phase of the process. The ultimate distribution of the national income is brought about through an elaborate process of pricing goods; determining wage and salary payments; disbursing premiums and bonuses; accumulating surplus and determining other aspects of corporate fiscal policy; operating profit-sharing, insurance, and pension schemes, both public and private; and carrying out an elaborate system of taxation and government expenditure.

Methods of bringing about a different division of income are of two broad types—the one direct and the other indirect. The direct method involves a modification of the income stream at its source—that is, in the disbursing offices of the business corporation. The indirect method involves an unmodified initial distribution and then a subsequent redistribution through the medium of taxation machinery.

The indirect method, through tax reform, it was pointed out, does not reach to the heart of the problem. The *re*distribution necessary to redress the situation by the tax method involves a costly process of gathering in the money from those with high incomes and transferring it through the public treasury to the low-income groups. This can be accomplished on an extensive scale only through the medium of doles, subsidies, pensions, and free services, or by extensive participation of the government in business enterprise—all of which have repercussions upon production. Thus, while according a significant place to modifications of the tax structure, we could not regard tax reform as an all-sufficing, or even a major, remedy.

The most effective means of modifying the distribution of income was held to be to alter the stream at its source—that is, within the business enterprises where the income is generated. Consideration was given to three alternative methods of increasing mass buying power: raising wage rates; sharing profits; and reducing commodity prices.

Increasing wage rates was recognized as having a part to play in this process of modifying the division of currently produced income. Because people are preoccupied with *money* income, it is essential that at least a portion of the gains from technological progress be received in the form of more dollars in the pocket. But we held that the wage rate increase method was relatively ineffective because the benefits of wage increases are not quickly and broadly distributed to the population as a whole. As a rule, wage increases occur in given plants or, at best, in particular industries, and the direct increase in purchasing power is thus very limited. Even a universal increase in wages would confer no benefits upon roughly 50 per cent of the consuming public, notably the farm population. In this connection, attention was called to the fact that the wage increase method of distributing the benefits of industrial progress had been a major factor in producing the disparity between industrial and agricultural prices—which in turn led the government to seek other means of raising the purchasing power of the farmers.

Profit sharing was regarded as a better method than wage increases because it might furnish a direct stimulus to efficiency. However, profit sharing could be successfully operated only in the more profitable corporations and could be applied only to workers who have comparatively permanent tenure, which means that its benefits would often not accrue to the lower-paid workers.

Price reductions in line with increased productivity was considered the most effective means of improving the distribution of income.

> The price reduction method has an outstanding advantage over other methods in that the benefits are extended automatically to the entire population. A general increase in money wages . . . will increase the buying power of the wage earning group; but it will not directly improve the position of the equally important portions of the population which do not work for wages. . . . A reduction of prices gives to *every* purchaser a larger return for his money.

This method, it will be seen, places emphasis upon an ever-broadening distribution of the new income generated by technological progress. The dynamic requirement is to increase income among the masses of the population sufficiently to provide the essential consumption outlets.

Such a process also automatically improves the ratio of spending to saving. That is to say, with the ever-increasing concentration of income which characterized the past replaced by an ever-broadening diffusion of income, outlays for consumption would expand relatively to savings for investment.

The price reduction method, it was pointed out, is in keeping with sound business policy. In most cases the expansion of buying power resulting from reductions in price brings a direct increase in demand for the products of the company making the price reduction, and thus makes possible further expansion of the business. Experience has proved that companies which have reduced prices as productivity has increased have been successful in improving their competitive position and have obtained larger rather than smaller aggregate profits. In fact, this large volume, low-unit cost principle is the basis of the mass production system of some of America's most successful modern industries.

IV. THE EVIDENCE OF LATER YEARS

As was to be expected, an investigation which arrived at conclusions fundamentally at variance with the traditional body of economic theory gave rise to no little controversy. The major criticisms which were advanced in connection with the several sections of the analysis are discussed in the Appendix. Meanwhile, in the years which have elapsed since the completion of the study, much additional evidence bearing on some of the basic questions involved has become available. Does this evidence lend support to the conclusions reached in our study of the relation of the distribution of income to economic progress? Or does it tend to confirm traditional conceptions?

A. The Discrepancy between Money Savings and Capital Formation

In our studies we submitted evidence showing that the traditional assumption that all money savings are automatically used in creating new capital was not borne out by the facts. The volume of individual savings available for investment was greatly in excess of the total volume of security flotations for capital expansion purposes (refundings eliminated). Moreover, a substantial part of the proceeds of these issues was used for purposes other than capital construction. The portion of the funds raised in the security markets by corporations and municipalities that was used for actual capital expansion for the entire period 1921 through 1945, according to compilations by Moody's Investors Service, is shown in the accompanying chart.

Since 1934 the Securities and Exchange Commission has also made compilations from prospectuses, which

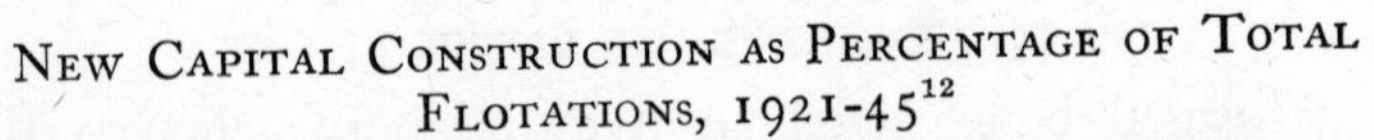

New Capital Construction as Percentage of Total Flotations, 1921-45[12]

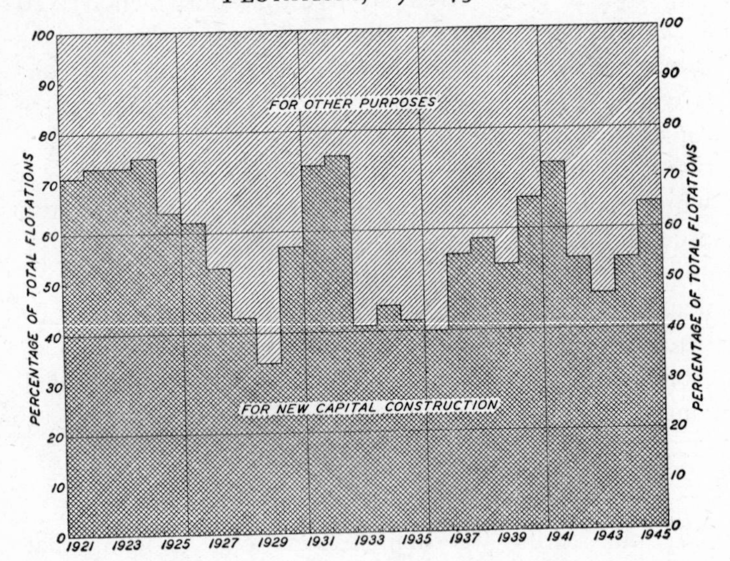

show the proportion of the net proceeds from corporate flotations which are devoted to capital expansion. These figures correspond closely with those made by Moody's Investors Service.

The funds not devoted to actual capital formation are used for a variety of corporate purposes which differ widely at different times. In the late twenties the greater part was used to purchase the securities of other corporations, chiefly shares of stock. In the thirties, the excess money savings were used mainly to buy government issues and seasoned private securities.[13] Since World War II the expanding volume of business, coupled with a rapidly rising level of costs, has made necessary a great increase in the volume of working capital—needed for the larger pay rolls, etc., a substantial part of which has been derived from the investment market.

B. The Expansibility of Consumption

Later evidence drawn from extensive income and family budget studies made under governmental auspices strongly confirms our tentative conclusions as to the indefinite expansibility of consumption.[14] All of these studies indicate marked increases in consumption per family in each successive higher level of income—although the *percentage* spent declines. Because the bulk of the families are in the lower-income levels, a widely diffused increase in national income is thus accompanied by a very great expansion in aggregate expenditures for consumer goods. The studies also reveal an allocation of expenditures for major types of goods, very similar to those shown in earlier, less extensive, family budget surveys.

The very great expansion in aggregate consumption that occurs in periods of rapidly rising national income is strikingly revealed by the developments since 1939. The increase in national production and income, stimulated by war preparedness, led to a rapid increase in consumer expenditures through 1940 and 1941. Moreover, despite wartime restrictions civilian consumption actually increased throughout the war years—in terms of real goods and services. In 1947 per-capita consumption was over 40 per cent higher than in 1939.[15]

C. The Pattern of Savings

Later budgetary surveys also confirm our analysis with respect to the varying amounts saved at different levels of income. They show that negligible savings are made in the low-income groups, that the proportion saved rises steadily through the middle-income classes, and increases rapidly in the higher-income levels.[16] Thus the proportion of the aggregate national income that is saved reflects both the general level of income and the degree of income concentration. Estimates subsequently made by the United States Department of Commerce of the aggregate volume of money savings in 1929 are in line with our estimates for that year.[17]

D. Reversal of the Savings Trend

The Brookings Institution studies showed that a gradually increasing percentage of the national income was being directed to savings channels, especially during the twenties. While available data with respect to money savings are far from satisfactory, it appears that in recent years the trend has been reversed. For example, individual money savings in the highly prosperous year 1941 equaled 11.7 per cent of the national income; in 1946 the figure was 8 per cent; and in 1947 it was 6 per cent. It might appear, superficially, that this reversal refutes our general analysis of the factors governing savings. In fact, however, it illustrates the overwhelming importance of income concentration on savings. On the one hand, rising incomes in the lower levels gave the masses large savings margins; but on the other hand the *disposable* income—after taxes—and hence the savings capacity of the well-to-do and wealthy classes was greatly reduced. The net result was a decline in the over-all savings ratio.[18]

E. The Controlling Importance of Consumption

The significance of expanding mass purchasing power is strikingly illustrated by the developments since 1945. At the end of the war much unspent purchasing power had accumulated, and at the same time current incomes continued at a very high level. As soon as concern over transition difficulties and the continuance of government controls disappeared, industry hastened to adjust its plans to the enlarged market possibilities. The first step was to expand the output of civilian consumer goods to the limits of existing productive capacity; and the second step, following hard upon the first, was to increase plant capacity in order to realize the new potentialities. The expansion of plant and equipment is best shown by the figures covering output of producers' durable goods and industrial construction. In 1929 such capital expansion amounted to 7.4 billion dollars. In the good year, 1941, it was 8.5 billions. In 1945 it amounted to 7.7 billions. In 1946 it rose to 14.1 billions; and in 1947 to 19.3 billions.[19] Again, the expansion of capital followed the lead of expanding consumption.

V. CONTEMPORARY VIEWS ON ECONOMIC RETARDATION

In recent years many professional economists have become concerned with the problem of long-term economic progress. The persistent, apparently chronic, unemployment in leading industrial countries during the middle thirties led many to question the dependability of automatic economic forces to restore prosperity and also to ensure continued economic expansion. Moreover, the new conceptions which emerged exerted a profound influence on government policy in many countries.

A. The Keynes Theory of Underemployment

The most influential study of the forces responsible for protracted unemployment is that published in 1936 by the British economist, John Maynard Keynes.[20] The problem, as he saw it, was to explain why the economic system was continuing to function at a subnormal level —in a sort of equilibrium, but with persistent unemployment. While Keynes' analysis reflected his preoccupation with the causes of the protracted depression during which he wrote, it extended, in its implications, to the fundamental factors upon which the perpetuity of the private enterprise system depends.

The "essence of the theory" is set forth by Keynes himself in the following language:[21]

When employment increases, aggregate real income is increased. The psychology of the community is such that when aggregate real income is increased aggregate consumption is increased, but not by so much as income. Hence employers would make a loss if the whole of the increased employment were to be devoted to satisfying the increased demand for immediate consumption. Thus, to justify any given amount of employment there must be an amount of current investment sufficient to absorb the excess of total output over what the community chooses to consume when employment is at the given level. For unless there is this amount of investment the receipts of the entrepreneurs will be less than is required to induce them to offer the given amount of employment. It follows, therefore, that, given what we shall call the community's propensity to consume, the equilibrium level of employment, *i.e.* the level at which there is no inducement to employers as a whole either to expand or to contract employment, will depend on the amount of current investment. The amount of current investment will depend, in turn, on what we shall call the inducement to invest; and the inducement to invest will be found to depend on the relation between the schedule of the marginal efficiency of capital and the complex of rates of interest on loans of various maturities and risks.

. . . The effective demand associated with full employment is a special case, only realised when the propensity to consume and the inducement to invest stand in a particular relationship to one another. . . . This optimum relationship . . . can only exist when, by accident or design, current investment provides an amount of demand just equal to the excess of the aggregate supply price of the output resulting from full employment over what the community will choose to spend on consumption when it is fully employed....

Our interpretation of the meaning of this statement may be summarized as follows:

1. When national income is expanding, consumptive expenditures do not increase proportionally; hence the percentage directed to savings channels increases.
2. It would not pay businessmen to increase the output of consumption goods proportionally to the increase in total income —because consumers would not buy that amount of additional commodities.
3. There will be less than full employment except when new capital construction happens (occasionally) to be just equal to the volume of savings funds.
4. The amount of new capital construction depends on the *inducement* to business managers to invest in new plant and equipment.
5. The inducement to invest exists only when money market rates of interest are lower than the marginal productive efficiency of capital equipment.

There are some points of seeming resemblance between Keynes' theory and the conclusions reached in the studies outlined in preceding pages. First, Keynes notes a tendency for consumption to increase less rapidly than savings as national income expands. Second, he implies that restriction of consumption may retard capital expansion rather than stimulate it; indeed, at one place he characterizes as an "absurd fallacy" the idea that "current investment is promoted by individual saving to the same extent that present consumption is diminished."[22] Third, he points out that money savings are not always fully used in expanding plant and equipment; in fact, this is the phenomenon with which his analysis is primarily concerned.

Nevertheless, Keynes' analysis has little kinship with that of the Brookings Institution. It diverges sharply at crucial points, and the ultimate implications with respect to the future of the private enterprise system are fundamentally at variance from ours. It seems desirable, therefore, to indicate the principal differences and to appraise the validity of Keynes' argument. Phases of his discussion which are not germane to our analysis are omitted from consideration.

Keynes attributes the relative increase in money savings to weak consumptive desires.

He contends that the rise in the proportion saved when national income is expanding is primarily due to psychological factors governing the propensity of the *average* man to consume. "The fundamental psychological law . . . is that men are disposed, as a rule and on the average, to increase their consumption as their income increases, but not by as much as the increase in their income."[23] These psychological characteristics of human nature—together with social practices and institutions which also affect the volume of consumption—"though not unalterable, are unlikely to undergo a material change over a short period of time except in abnormal or revolutionary circumstances."[24]

This analysis is in line with the traditional assumption that the amount of savings is primarily a reflection of the thrift habits of the average individual—of the masses of the people. It would appear that aggregate national savings increase only as the *ordinary* individual becomes inherently more thrifty. This approach overlooks the great importance of the savings of *extraordinary* individuals—those with very large incomes. As we have shown in a preceding section, without any change in individual propensities to be thrifty, the proportion of the national income saved may rise sharply because of an increasing concentration of income in the hands of the wealthy. Keynes made only casual mention of the concentration of income as a factor in the expansion of savings; it finds little place in his basic analysis.

The first assumption, that consumptive desires are weak, is belied by the facts. Family budget studies, as we have indicated, show conclusively that consumption expands not slowly but rapidly as income increases. It is true that the *proportion* spent declines and the *proportion* saved increases as income rises. But the explanation of the phenomenon is found not in a low *propensity* to consume but in a strong *disposition* to provide for the future as and when rising incomes afford a margin above the primary necessities of life. Keynes' failure to ascertain from factual studies the true nature of the phenomenon led him, as we shall presently show, to wholly unwarranted conclusions.

The interpretation of the lag in capital formation is lacking in consistency.

Although he suggested at places that consumptive demand is of controlling importance—that it would not pay business enterprisers in quest of profits to construct new capital when consumption is declining, or increasing but slowly—Keynes forgot this completely when analyzing what he calls the inducement to invest. In accounting for the failure of money savings to be fully used in constructing new capital, he concentrated on the spread between the market rate of interest and the productivity of additional capital. He assumed that money savings available for investment are typically taken off the market through the medium of bond issues or other interest-bearing obligations and that the corporate manager gauges the outlook for profit by comparing the rate of interest he will have to pay in the money market with the prospective yield from the new capital equipment.

However he did not consistently adhere to the view that new capital construction depends upon the decisions of business enterprisers. At times he shifted from the calculations of business borrowers to those of individual savers and explained why the latter do not always devote their money savings to new capital construction. He attributed this to what he calls "liquidity preference"—meaning that under certain conditions it seems wiser for individuals to hold current savings in cash or equivalent rather than to venture them in new plant and equipment.

It should be apparent that if the demand for consumer goods increases but slowly because of a weak propensity to consume, the outlook for sales of additional consumer goods produced by additional capital would be *bad*—irrespective of the rate of interest. The spread might be ever so favorable, and yet it would not pay to produce goods which by hypothesis could not be sold.[25] Similarly, if consumer demand is inadequate, it would be immaterial whether individual savers were interested in holding their savings in liquid form or disposed to lend them freely. The dark outlook for profitable investment would leave the entrepreneur with no incentive to borrow, or for that matter to use his own savings directly in building new plant and equipment.

Keynes' analysis of the capital formation process is

thus essentially different from ours. He makes no clear differentiation among the three distinct stages in the money-saving, market-investment, capital-formation process. In his thinking there are at the most two stages —money saving and "investment"—by which he means actual capital formation. Thus he failed to appreciate the fact that expenditures for consumption plus new capital formation may be less than total national disbursements and to understand the effects of "excess" savings upon the prices of already existing capital instruments. In fact, it is the operation of the *market-investment* process which determines in general the market rate of interest; when the supply of money savings is large relative to the volume of new security flotations, the use of money savings in buying already outstanding securities serves to bid up their prices, with a resulting decrease in yields.

The analysis of controlling factors in capital expansion has two vital defects.

(1) Keynes' thesis that the inducement to invest is found in the spread between interest rates and the productivity of added units of capital implies that the margin of profit is primarily, if not exclusively, measured by the difference between the cost of borrowed money and the output of the new unit of capital. This traditional theory is open to criticism on two grounds: first, many industrial corporations under modern conditions raise no funds for capital expansion through the medium of interest-bearing obligations—the reason being that shares of stock involving no interest cost provide much greater flexibility to management. Second, interest is in general a negligible element among the factors of cost.

It should be noted here that Keynes had finally become doubtful about the adequacy of the investment inducement. While the strong disposition to save would reduce money market interest rates, he believed that the productivity of new capital would diminish even more rapidly—thus leaving scant inducement to invest. Nor could government monetary policy with safety be depended upon to bring about sufficient reductions in market interest rates. "I am now somewhat skeptical of the success of a merely monetary policy directed toward influencing the rate of interest."[26]

(2) Keynes adhered to the classical conception of the declining productivity of additional units of capital. He assumed that the added physical units of capital have merely the same effectiveness as those they replace and that since they are applied to natural resources under conditions of diminishing returns, the productivity of additional units necessarily declines. Nowhere in his book does one find any reference to technological progress and the ever-increasing productivity which results from constantly improving capital instruments. When one recognizes the fact that new capital units are usually much better than old, as indicated in Chapter I, the outlook is completely altered.

Notwithstanding the extraordinary and continuous increase in productivity in modern times, made possible by science and technology, Keynes' position in 1936 was almost identical with that of John Stuart Mill in 1848. He went so far as to say:

> A properly run community equipped with modern technical resources . . . ought to be able to bring down the marginal efficiency of capital . . . to zero within a single generation; so that we should attain the conditions of a quasi-stationary community.[27]

Like the classicists, Keynes saw little chance for continued economic progress.

Since he adhered to the classical conception that additional capital inevitably means declining productivity, he was preoccupied with *equilibrium* in a virtually stationary industrial society. Starting with a condition of under-employment in time of depression, his analysis led him to conclude that as employment and income expand, the lag in consumer demands tends to prevent private enterprisers from providing full employment. If, by chance, in some period of business buoyancy, we should attain full employment, the situation would quickly be undermined by the growing disparity between consumption and savings.

Keynes' reasoning thus led him to a dead-end street so far as private enterprise is concerned. Despairing of the latter, he looked to the government and to public enterprise as the primary source of new investment and employment.

This static conception is diametrically the opposite of that set forth in our *Income and Economic Progress.* Building on two established facts—the vast expansibility of consumer demand and the *in*creasing productivity of improving units of capital—we contemplated a dynamic rather than a static society. Since the new units of capital mean constantly expanding output per man-hour, there is an increasing social dividend to be distributed. The only question then is whether it is possible by means of an ever-broader dissemination of the gains resulting from technological progress to alter the ratio of consumption to savings.

Keynes' pessimism rested on a misconception of the primary source of expanding savings.

Since in his view the over-all ratio of savings to spending is determined by the low propensity of the *average* man to consume, with a consequent tendency for savings to increase, it appeared impossible to correct the maladjustment, that is, to reduce the percentage of the national income saved. On the contrary, as the wealth of a nation increased, the evil, in his view, could only be progressively aggravated.

But when one discovers from budget studies showing the savings made at different levels of income that the *primary* factor affecting the savings ratio is the increasing concentration of income in the hands of the wealthier classes, it is easy to see how the spending-saving ratio may be improved. It might obviously be brought about by a reduction in the number and magnitude of high incomes—by means of taxation or otherwise. More important, as a continuing process, a reduction in the savings ratio may result from a constantly broadening distribution of *newly generated* income, made possible by technical advances.

A concrete illustration will reveal the possibilities in this latter method. Let us assume that in a given year the disposable national income is 100 billions, and that 80 billions of this is directed to consuming channels and 20 billions to savings. Assume, further, that in consequence of a high concentration of income 18 billions of the savings were made by individuals having incomes in excess of $5,000 annually and 2 billions by those with incomes of less than that amount. Assume now that technological progress in the ensuing twenty years serves to increase national income from 100 billions to 150 billions, and that all the benefits of this technological advance accrue to those having incomes less than $5,000. In this situation, those with incomes in excess of $5,000 may still be presumed to save 18 billion dollars. Those with incomes less than $5,000 would now be able and disposed to save somewhat more than before. If we assume that *their* savings tripled, now reaching 6 billions, aggregate savings would become 18 billions plus 6 billions, or 24 billions. But the proportion of the total national income saved would, nevertheless, have been reduced from 20 per cent to 16 per cent. As shown on page 124, a much greater reduction in the savings ratio than this actually resulted from a combination of factors operating in the United States between 1929 and 1947.

A resort to government spending would not solve the basic problem posed by Keynes.

A growing disparity between consumption and saving would not be corrected by a government spending program. An expansion of income resulting from government activity would have precisely the same effect as an increase of income flowing from private activity. Keynes did not attempt to show that, when the masses derive income from government sources, the "fundamental psychological law"—that is, the allegedly weak propensity to consume—is altered. Indeed, he recognized at one place that the fundamental difficulty remains even with government spending.[28]

Moreover, there is no reason to assume that a substitution of government capital expansion for private capital expansion would overcome the inevitable tendency (as Keynes saw it) toward declining productivity.

The additional units of public capital might well be even less productive than new units of private capital. So long as one adheres to the classical assumption with respect to the declining productivity of additional capital, economic progress is obviously impossible—whatever the form of economic organization. A static society is the most that can be anticipated.

It should be added that Keynes did not face the long-run fiscal implications of the resort to government spending. Unlike many of his followers, he did not specifically contend that an ever-increasing public debt is of no consequence. This fundamental long-run issue was simply ignored.

B. The Mature Economy Conception

In the United States in the late thirties there developed a variation and extension of the Keynes philosophy which came to be known as the mature economy conception. This point of view reached its culmination in the discussions of the Temporary National Economic Committee.

This school of thought built on the Keynes thesis that the relatively fixed consumption habits of the *average* man inevitably result in chronic over-saving. To this was added the view that the economic stagnation of the 1930's was largely due to the disappearance of the frontier and the declining rate of population growth. The two conceptions were united as indicated in the following quotation:

> It is just because we have developed, in our highly dynamic society, firmly fixed institutions and habits affecting the income elasticity of saving that we cannot rely upon autonomous increases in consumption to provide full employment *once the*

extensive expansionist stimulus to investment has largely disappeared. . . . We shall be compelled to seek full employment of our resources by deliberately injecting a new stimulus to investment.[29]

Consumption habits were assumed to be virtually fixed. "We have to recognize that we are dealing here with a [consumption] function that is highly stable and is not easily changed."[30] So long as we had abundance of room for expansion and population was rapidly increasing, total consumption requirements, and hence capital requirements, might increase rapidly; but, once the frontier disappeared and the rate of population growth was restricted, the demand for *additional* food, clothing, shelter, and other consumer goods would be negligible. Thus the only means of finding outlets for money savings and providing for full employment seemed to be to substitute public investment for private investment.

The conception that the disappearance of the frontier and the declining rate of population growth necessarily produced stagnation is readily disproved. The American frontier disappeared around the turn of the century. Moreover, the *rate* of population growth began to decline in the United States as early as 1850. Yet this entire period, especially from 1900 to 1930, was one of extraordinary economic expansion. This expansion found its stimulus and its sustenance in the steadily expanding mass purchasing power and consumption which characterized the era.

Nor, if we look at the world as a whole, does the argument that economic growth is necessarily checked by the passing of frontiers find support. After 1900 no extensive new areas involving large capital investment were opened up; yet the wealth and income of the world continued to expand with great rapidity.[31] Sweden affords an excellent illustration of economic expansion during a period of slow population growth. During the first thirty years of the present century, the increase in population in Sweden was only 20 per cent, but the increase in production was over 300 per cent. The story is not essentially different in France and the United Kingdom.

Since it was assumed that consumer desires were comparatively static, these writers, like Keynes, naturally gave no thought to the stimulus to further capital expansion that might come from an ever-broadening distribution of national income. Nor did they indicate how a mere shifting from private enterprise to government enterprise would stimulate consumption relatively to savings.

This American school did, however, attempt to face the fiscal problem involved in a permanent public investment program. In varying degrees confidence was expressed with respect to the fiscal implications of such a policy. The problem of fiscal stability will be discussed in Chapter VIII.

PART II

LOOKING FORWARD

Part I of this analysis looked backward. It was noted that a century ago economists emphasized a law of diminishing returns from natural resources and a law of increasing population which, operating together, appeared greatly to restrict the possibility of advances in the plane of living. As late as 1848 John Stuart Mill foresaw a virtually static society in the not distant future.

In the ensuing century the law of diminishing returns was engulfed by a law of increasing returns. In agriculture and mining, as well as in transportation and manufacturing, productive output per unit of labor and capital employed, constantly increased—not only during the territorial expansion period of the nineteenth century but even more so in the early decades of the twentieth century. Simultaneously, there occurred an unprecedented rate of population growth and an unprecedented improvement in living conditions. This astonishing outcome, as we have seen, was the result of a scientific and technological revolution accompanied by extraordinary improvements in economic organization.

In Part II we shall seek to gauge the economic potentialities of the future and to indicate the essential requirements for making the economic system function effectively. With a view to clarifying objectives and providing criteria by which to appraise national policies, the first two chapters are devoted respectively to a discussion of economic goals and alternative methods of organizing and conducting economic activity.

CHAPTER V

NATIONAL ECONOMIC GOALS

A clear and precise perception of our national economic objectives or goals is the essential first step in the formulation of a national economic program. The goals provide standards or criteria by which to measure the soundness of national economic policy and also the methods employed in carrying them into effect. What then are the major economic goals of the American people? Do we know what we want? Is there any agreement as to the economic objectives toward which our national policies should be directed, or are the various economic and political groups which make up the nation in basic disagreement?

Public discussions of economic issues inevitably tend to emphasize differences rather than agreements—for that is a primary purpose of *discussion.* When such discussions are conducted by political leaders or by spokesmen for special economic groups, they appear as controversies and commonly generate so much heat and bitterness as to convey an impression of deep-seated, irreconcilable differences in philosophy. Such contrasting terms as conservative and radical; progressive and reactionary; forward looking and backward looking; the new order and the old order—all serve to emphasize disagreements and conflicts, and to obscure whatever measure of accord there may be with respect to basic national objectives. These apparent differences in underlying economic philosophy have been greatly magnified by the economic, social, and political developments of recent decades. The profound maladjustments which have taken place and the attendant suffering have naturally stirred emotions deeply and provoked such a welter of controversy that we have seemed to be in profound disagreement with respect to the very highways that we wish to travel.

In the light of this prevailing confusion, it seems desirable at this place to center attention upon the basic objectives of American economic life. In the author's view current controversies relate not so much to goals as to the methods and policies designed to achieve the desired results. It is believed that a vast majority of the American people would agree that the goals stated below constitute the primary objectives of national economic policy.

GOAL I. A PROGRESSIVELY LARGER TOTAL NATIONAL INCOME

That our aggregate national production is far from adequate to satisfy the needs and desires of the American people is apparent from common observation as well as from statistical evidence. Almost every individual feels keenly that he should have more income in order that he may have a higher standard of living for himself or family. Every organized economic group in society is constantly striving to increase its income and improve its economic position. Political parties are always committed to a program of greater national income—evidenced by such slogans as "a full dinner pail," "a chicken in every pot and two cars in every garage," "one third of our population ill-clothed, ill-housed, and ill-fed," and by perpetual promises of perpetual prosperity. The only doubting voice one hears is that of the occasional philosopher or religious leader who expresses the thought that we would perhaps be more truly happy if we were less materialistic and more devoted to the simple life.

The case for a progressively larger total national wealth and income is buttressed by other considerations than individual needs and desires. A nation is potentially stronger from the military point of view. Moreover, increasing wealth is regarded as essential to prestige in the family of nations.

GOAL II. A PROGRESSIVELY WIDER DIVISION OF NATIONAL INCOME

The American view appears to be that the gains resulting from technical improvements and increasing efficiency in production should accrue in large measure to the masses of the population. That is, we wish to see a progressively broader distribution of income among the many rather than increasing concentration in the hands of the few. Such a goal meets the approval of the masses for the obvious reason that it benefits them directly. But there are also reasons why it commands the support of all classes.

First, higher incomes among the masses make—within broad limits—for individual efficiency. The evidence indicates that a substantial proportion of the American people are still on a plane of living too low for health and efficiency and adequate educational training.

Second, a broad distribution of national income is essential to the economic growth of the nation as a whole. The continuous expansion of industry, agriculture, and mining depends upon *markets*, and our only permanently expansible markets are those which are found in the unfulfilled desires of the great masses of the people. Whether the stimulus to economic growth springs from expanding mass consumption or from preceding capital development, there can be no doubt that the wants of the masses constitute the primary ultimate markets. What we are interested in is a dynamic, growing society; and maximum growth is dependent upon a progressive expansion of the buying power of the great body of consumers.

A narrow distribution of national income, it is worth noting, is inconsistent with the democratic ideal. It is of the essence of democracy to share in the fruits as well as to participate in the operation of the economic and political system. A society in which the gains from increasing productive efficiency were increasingly restricted to the comparatively few could not be regarded as democratic, in the deeper meaning of the term.

This goal does not imply that we wish to have complete equality of income; for this would not be consistent with the realization of the third goal, now to be considered.

GOAL III. A SOCIETY IN WHICH INDIVIDUAL REWARDS ARE BASED PRIMARILY ON WORK PERFORMED

It has always been a principle of the system of individual enterprise that the individual should be paid for what he does, and not according to his needs. A national goal of rewarding each individual without reference to the work performed appears so repugnant to the basic thinking of the American people as scarcely to require comment. It should be observed, however, that the proposition that rewards should be directly related to productive contributions is not a capitalist doctrine merely. The Socialist party does not advocate the communal idea of equal pay regardless of productive output. Nor does the present-day Communist party. In the constitution of the U.S.S.R., Article XII, appears the following principle: "From each according to his ability; to each according to his *work*."

This principle of basing income on work performed is, however, not quite universally applied. First, some members of society, because of mental or physical incapacity, are unable to work; and for reasons of humanity we provide for such unfortunates through private or public charity. Second, those who have reached the age of retirement and are under the social security system are provided with old-age benefits. Third, we recognize, to a limited degree, the system of inheritance under which individuals may receive income resulting from the work of their forbears. These exceptions do not, however, undermine the basic philosophy that everyone is expected to earn his bread by the sweat of his brow, and that the harder and more intelligently he works the more bread he should get.

GOAL IV. INCREASING ECONOMIC SECURITY

Economic *in*security is a product of the modern highly developed industrial era. The agricultural pioneer, the medieval feudal serf, and the slave all possessed economic security—at some level. But the free and independent worker of the modern age has long been faced with periodic loss of income in consequence of fluctuations in the labor market.

A greatly increased measure of individual economic security is regarded as a goal of primary importance. Without reasonable stability of income, no one can make adequate provision for the hazards of sickness and the requirements of old age, or plan personal and family development programs with any assurance that they may be carried out.

The recent establishment of the *social* security system was a recognition of the importance of providing, through the agency of government, a minimum of economic security for many classes of people. Similarly, present-day emphasis upon the restoration and maintenance of a state of full employment evidences a conviction that the provision of the *individual* security which flows from steady employment is a paramount requirement.

GOAL V. THE GREATEST POSSIBLE DEVELOPMENT OF THE CAPACITIES OF EVERY INDIVIDUAL

An economic system which stultified the individual and resulted in human deterioration would obviously not be acceptable to the American people. The system must rather provide a stimulus to individual initiative and promote the development of latent capacities. Such a system aids directly in achieving that expanding national production upon which the realization of progressively higher standards of living depends.

This goal is of the very essence of democracy, the strength of which is directly dependent upon the power of the individual units of which it is composed. It is, moreover, essential to the achievement of that self-realization, the desire for which is so deeply ingrained in human beings.

Human intelligence applied to the processes of production under favorable conditions constitutes the ultimate basis of economic advancement. With this in mind, we have provided a vast free elementary and public school system, supplemented by extensive vocational education programs, and also by subsidized institutions of higher learning. In short, we have endeavored to give everyone the best possible training, mental and physical, with which to realize his personal potentialities.

Closely related to—indeed an essential part of—the principle of individual development is the conception of free choice in economic affairs. Except in time of war, the individual is under no compulsion with respect to the type of economic activities in which he may engage. Everyone has the right to determine for himself what kind of occupation or career he wishes to follow and to acquire such training as may be necessary; he has the right to quit his job if he does not like it or thinks he can better himself elsewhere; he has the right to shift from one occupation to another; he has the right to move from place to place if he thinks he can improve his position by so doing; he has the right to decide for himself for what purposes he should use his income. This lack of compulsion by external authority applies equally to laborers, professional groups, and businessmen both large and small. The opportunity to realize one's ambitions may, of course, be handicapped by various factors; but the opportunity for individual development through the exercise of free choices is virtually unrestricted.

GOAL VI. OPPORTUNITY FOR EVERY CAPABLE INDIVIDUAL TO EARN HIS OWN INCOME

Self-help has been regarded as a cardinal principle of the American system. Instead of a situation in which large numbers of people are dependent upon the state or charitable institutions for economic support, we have coveted a society in which every individual who is not physically or mentally defective shall have the opportunity to *earn* his own living. The poorhouse and the dole, necessary though they may be, have never been regarded as satisfactory substitutes for remunerative work.

A remunerative occupation appears indispensable to the maintenance of individual self-reliance and to the development of latent capacities and talents. It is likewise indispensable to the self-respect and personal independence of the individual citizen—so essential to a virile democracy. Without adequate work opportunities our society will deteriorate physically, mentally, spiritually, and politically, as well as in terms of material wealth.

[The author must express some doubt whether this conception is as deeply ingrained in the American philosophy now as formerly. The desire for security has become so compelling that increasing numbers of people appear to treasure security above freedom and self-reliance.]

These goals, it is believed, represent the basic economic *objectives* in which the American people are interested. In any case, it seems clear that if we could move steadily in the directions indicated, we would be enjoying well-rounded economic progress and moving toward the larger goal of economic democracy.

CHAPTER VI

ALTERNATIVE TYPES OF ECONOMIC ORGANIZATION

The long history of civilization has witnessed numerous forms of economic organization. The widely divergent types reflect: the varying degrees of social complexity existing at different stages of economic evolution; the need for security or protection from external aggression; and also conceptual differences with respect to the inherent merits of various kinds of organization. The family, the tribe, the feudal manor, and the nation illustrate the widening scope of the organizational unit within which economic activities have been conducted.

The central issue with respect to economic organization relates to the location or division of power and responsibility. In the family, tribe, manor, and absolute monarchy power rested with the acknowledged head or ruler. Decisions with respect to economic activities were made at the top, and the responsibility for execution was delegated down the line to the individual members of the group. Historically, security considerations were commonly of such paramount importance that centralized authority appeared indispensable. Except in a few isolated cases, it was not until recent centuries that conditions became such as to permit consideration of other than dictatorial methods of economic or political organization.

In modern times four major conceptions of economic organization have taken form. At opposite extremes are the so-called free enterprise system and communism. The former holds, in brief, that the surest means of promoting economic progress is by developing the individuals who comprise society, by according to each the fullest possible measure of freedom of decision in economic matters. Communism, on the other hand, emphasizes, at least in practice, the top group or state as the source of wisdom and initiative.[1] The individual members of society, who take orders instead of make decisions, are regarded as of secondary importance.

In between free enterprise and communism we find a compromise system commonly called state socialism, which calls for public ownership and management of certain selected industries, with freedom of initiative permitted to continue elsewhere. Between, also, are certain hybrid systems in which private enterprise operates under the general overhead control of the government. While these major types of organization are seldom found in pure form, they do represent fundamentally divergent philosophies.

I. FREE ENTERPRISE

In the feudal system of the Middle Ages, economic society was organized from above, the masses of the people being servants of the lord and king and exchanging labor and fealty for subsistence and protection. Following the disintegration of feudalism in western Europe in the fifteenth and sixteenth centuries, the centralized control of economic activities continued in modified form under the city-states and national governments. The essence of the so-called mercantilist system was that the growth of national wealth and power could best be fostered by means of extensive government regulations of trade and industry.

The free enterprise conception emerged out of eighteenth century philosophical discussions.

During this period attention was gradually shifted from man-made law to natural law. This fundamental change in viewpoint may be explained in part as a natural reaction against the excessive restrictions imposed upon the individual by the mercantilist system. However, it also strongly reflected the influence of developments in the field of natural science. It was in the sixteenth and seventeenth centuries that such men as Galileo, Kepler, and Newton discovered and formulated basic laws governing the physical world. In due course these scientific discoveries came to exert a profound influence upon men's ideas in other realms of thought. The question was inevitably raised, Is not man as much a part of and subject to an ordered universe as the physical earth on which he has his setting? It was conceived that there existed a system of natural law which, if it were not interfered with by governments and other human institutions, would always lead to progress.

Blackstone, the great English jurist of the common law, contended that there had been established by the Creator a simple system of natural law or ethics and that the constitution and frame of humanity had been so contrived that if we but pursued our own "true and substantial happiness" we could not fail to be in tune with the universe of nature. William Godwin held that it was the function of society not to make law but merely to interpret "that which the *nature of things* has already decreed." Rousseau declared all social institutions vicious in their effects upon free-born man.

In accordance with this philosophy the individual

members of society, not the state, constitute the true source of power. The idea came to prevail that if each individual is left free to follow his own inclinations and develop his own potentialities, the nation, as an aggregate of individuals, will in like measure become affluent and powerful. Adam Smith, the Scottish philosopher, wrote in 1776 that each individual in pursuing his own welfare and happiness is led as by a divine hand to promote the welfare of his fellow men.

This new philosophy of natural law in due course had a profound effect upon practical affairs. Innumerable laws restricting the freedom and the initiative of the individual were repealed. The mercantilist system was gradually overthrown, and industry and trade were relieved from a multitude of hampering regulations. National boundaries came largely to be ignored through removal of barriers to the free international movement of trade and currency and the migration of people from country to country. Ultimately, the conception of a world society—economically speaking—was born, in which men would be free to live wherever they might desire and to conduct their business operations without reference to national boundaries.

These conceptions found their fullest opportunity for development in the young United States of North America. The founders of the American system of government, notably Jefferson and Madison, were steeped in the European literature which set forth the natural law philosophy and its conception of individual freedom. The Declaration of Independence gave eloquent expression to the inalienable rights of men to life, liberty, and the pursuit of happiness. So from the very beginning our American system emphasized the vital significance of the unfettered human being in the scheme of things.

In the nineteenth century, nearly everywhere the role of government in relation to economic activity was regarded in the main as passive. The functions of government were confined to safeguarding the rights of individuals and to handling a few general problems where centralized authority was essential, as in provision for national defense and the maintenance of a unified currency system. It was not regarded as properly the function of government to engage directly in economic enterprise or to regulate private business, *except* when such business tended to become monopolistic in character.

The economic and political system of the nineteenth century is sometimes referred to as an *unorganized* society, one lacking in social purpose. It is contrasted with a "planned economy," which has as its goal the welfare of the people. Nothing could be more misleading than this comparison. The so-called system of *laissez faire*, or noninterference, was itself a plan or method by which, according to the belief of its advocates —who were the great constructive liberals of their day —economic progress and human advancement could best be promoted. It was the belief that this system would promote the most rapid economic development and that the benefits would be disseminated among all classes of people. So deeply convinced were they of the merits of individual freedom in economic affairs, that they insisted that the burden of proof rests on those who propose government restrictions that would limit individual initiative.

Certain incentives and mechanisms were relied upon to achieve desired social ends.

The essential stimuli to productive effort were seen to exist in the selfish propensities of mankind. Since almost every individual is primarily interested in furthering his own welfare, the only incentive necessary to induce exertion is the opportunity to engage freely in whatever line of enterprise appears most promising and to reap the rewards personally. Thus, enterprising men would constantly be seeking new means of enlarging their incomes. This necessitates the right to own or borrow private property and to derive profits from its use. Those who do not possess property should in any case be free to shift from one employment to another in quest of higher wages or more congenial employment.

Competition and the price system were depended upon to maintain balance and ensure equity. The test of what would pay best was found in the market places where the desires of the public find expression in relative market demands for goods and services. If the demand for commodity A, for whatever reason, is relatively weak and the available supply is large, the resulting decrease in price will, if the situation persists, discourage production. Conversely, if the demand for commodity B is strong, the accompanying rise in price will encourage added production. Thus it appeared that the relative changes in the outlook for profit, resulting from changing market prices, automatically adjust production in accordance with the desires of the people as expressed in the markets. Prices and profit margins would guide the allocation of productive resources in response to the desires of the consuming public.

Competition among producers was also depended upon to ensure fair prices to the public. In order to increase the profit margin, producers would strive to reduce costs by increasing operating efficiency. Having reduced costs, a producer is in a position to increase sales by quoting prices below those of his competitors. Thus prices tend downward in line with the costs of the most efficient producers. This competitive process naturally involves the continuous elimination of obsolescent or otherwise inefficient, high cost, *marginal* establishments. The fit, as gauged by ability to sell at a minimum price, alone survive—the survival being due to the exceptional service rendered the consuming public.

This competitive process also appeared to prevent excessive rates of profit for any considerable period of time. If for the moment industry A offered exceptional opportunities for profit, the flow of additional capital in that direction would soon expand output and reduce prices to the normal level. If any particular company obtained unusual profits through superior technological developments, necessity and opportunity would quickly drive other companies to match these advances in the arts of production. Indeed, the producer of superior efficiency today may well become the relatively inefficient of tomorrow. The race is to the swift, and there is no resting place.

The price which people pay for the free choices and the productive incentive of a private enterprise system is found in the profits permitted to those who venture their private capital in business undertakings. Profits would not always be forthcoming, for many companies and individual enterprises would fail every year.

Moreover, exceptionally high profits gained by the far-seeing and efficient would under free competition be transient. Taken as a whole, it was believed that the rate of profit would tend toward the minimum essential to induce enterprises to assume the inevitable risks involved.

The private enterprise system thus described, commonly referred to as *laissez faire*, was never characteristic of the entire economy of nations. In most countries it was gradually and incompletely substituted for former systems involving a large measure of centralized control. Moreover, in due course the expanding size, scope, and complexity of business organization led to new forms of regulation designed to overcome certain weaknesses of competition and to prevent the growth of monopoly. Nevertheless, it may fairly be said that, in varying degrees, the private enterprise system was the dominant form of organization in nearly every important country through the nineteenth century and the early decades of the twentieth.

II. COMMUNISM

The terms communism and socialism are commonly used more or less indiscriminately in popular discussions of economic systems. A clear distinction is seldom made even in the literature of social reform or in the official statements of communist and socialist leaders. For example, Marxian communism was long referred to as "scientific" socialism to differentiate it from the state or group socialism advocated by others. Many of the so-called socialistic societies of the early nineteenth century were referred to as communal experiments.

Even today the American Communist party platform describes its goal as that of a socialist society. However, in practice there are basic differences, even antagonisms, between communism and socialism.

Russian communism must be regarded as the true model, for it is based squarely on Marx's philosophy and has been the fountain source of communistic doctrine everywhere. It has embodied the following major conceptions:

(1) The laboring classes are the only producers—the source of all wealth.

(2) Profits are derived by expropriating a part of the wealth created by labor—the surplus over and above wages.

(3) The private ownership of the means of production is opposed to the interests of society, and should not be permitted.

(4) Each individual should contribute to production in accordance with his capacity, but individual rewards should be related to needs.

(5) The wants, or needs, of the people should govern the allocation of productive activity.

(6) A central authority should determine the needs of the people and organize the entire productive mechanism to that end. The state rather than the individual is the source of wisdom and power.

It was a part of the philosophy also that the overthrow of capitalism and capitalistic governments and the establishment of communism could be accomplished only by violent revolutionary methods, and that the perpetuation and full development of the system required its extension to the entire world. The ends sought were held to justify every means of attainment —propaganda, deception, assassination, intimidation, and the ruthless employment of armed force.

The evolution of the communist system in the U.S.S.R. since the revolution of 1917 has involved numerous stages and many modifications. The first stage has been described as a hasty nationalization of the economic system and the establishment of a war economy to meet the immediate requirements of the revolution. After internal order was established and control secured, it was still necessary to go through a long period of experimentation before a genuinely planned economy could be worked out. Indeed it was nearly a decade before a comprehensive plan for the development of the Russian economy was inaugurated. The goals set were altered in subsequent plans and were of course profoundly affected by the coming of World War II.

Under communism the motivation for economic activity comes from the central authority.

In brief, this method of organization involves the development of a master plan which sets forth the national economic requirements and schedules productive activity. The plan first decides what proportion of the nation's energies shall be devoted to the production of capital goods, and what proportion to consumer goods. Because of the importance of rapid industrialization in Russia, it was decided that consumption should be held at minimum levels in order to achieve the most rapid capital expansion possible. The government also determines the quantities of each type of consumer goods and each type of capital goods that should be produced.

In a country where the plane of living is extremely low, little difficulty is encountered in determining what types of consumer goods should be produced. Under prevailing conditions in Russia, food, clothing, and shelter had to have virtually complete priority. It is only in an economy where basic wants have been reasonably well supplied that the allocation problem becomes difficult.

Production is carried out by agencies of the state. Industries are organized chiefly on the individual plant basis. Agricultural production is organized and supervised by co-operative associations. Trade is conducted by store units or larger merchandising groups. The managers of these various agencies are of course employees of the state and subject to the government rules laid down.

Russian communism employs most of the financial machinery characteristic of capitalism. The industrial units hire labor on a money wage basis, purchase raw materials and supplies, and sell finished goods in the market for a price. Wholesale and retail distributors operate similarly. Prices are fixed on an industry-wide basis and are adjusted to cover out-of-pocket costs of production and depreciation on plant and equipment, as well as to provide funds for planned expansion. Since the producing units are owned by the government and operated by government employees, there is of course no *profit* in the private capitalistic sense. Any earnings that may be left after meeting costs and providing for capital expansion belong to the government. The agricultural co-operatives pay farm workers in cash—called "labor-day dividends." It was eventually found necessary, however, to assign to each individual farm family a small plot for personal use, the produce of which may be consumed at home or be sold or bartered in a free market.

The government derives its revenues almost wholly by collecting funds from the socialized enterprises. The process is called taxation—though in effect it merely involves a transfer of the earnings of enterprises owned by the state to the state treasury. Principal sources of revenue for the state budget are: (1) the turnover tax levied on all sales, which accounts for over 50 per cent of the total; (2) collections of the residual earnings of socialized business enterprises; (3) an income tax on the agricultural co-operatives, which agencies are apparently permitted to keep some profits; and (4) income and "cultural" taxes on individuals. The government uses the funds collected to meet ordinary operating requirements and also to finance economic expansion and provide free services to the people in the form of health, housing, and recreation and welfare facilities. While these social services are financed from the state budgets, they are carried out by local governments to which the funds are allotted. At least 50 per cent of the national income flows through the public treasury. Prior to the war the national budget was ordinarily in balance, that is, the treasury collected from the socialist enterprises and their employees the full amount required to carry out the over-all national program.

The original theory that rewards should be based on needs has been abandoned.

Experience revealed that essential output could not be attained unless pay was related to productive effort or contribution. Numerous considerations combined to produce variations in wage rates. Inducements were necessary to attract labor to certain unfavored areas, unattractive occupations, and jobs involving unusual risks or exceptional arduousness. Variations were also made according to the degree of independence and responsibility assumed by the worker and the skill or education required. Finally, wage incentive payments or bonuses were given in order to stimulate output.

General increases in wages over a period of time are related to increases in productivity—resulting either from technological advances or improvements in labor performance. Wages are not, however, permitted to absorb all the gains resulting from increase in efficiency; some part is also expected to be reflected in price reductions.[2]

The vital differences between communism and private enterprise relate to motivation and opportunity.

Under private enterprise individual initiative and self-interest are relied upon to provide the driving force in productive activity and economic development. The right to earn profits on private property constitutes the stimulus for the individual to devise improved methods of reducing costs and to develop new types of industries which in turn create and satisfy new and expanding consumer desires. The variety of products and services made available to the public is constantly increased as a result of scientific discovery, experimentation, and risk taking by individual enterprisers hoping to profit thereby. The distinguishing feature of the private enterprise system is that everyone has opportunity and stimulus to exploit new ideas. And the virtue of competition is that it exerts ceaseless pressure on management to improve productive processes.

Under communism, the ordinary individual is debarred from promoting or developing new products, new industries, or new methods of organizing existing industries. Such innovations must come from the small group who constitute the central authority, or from individuals specifically selected by the state to be the innovators. In their quest, such individuals must conform to government directives, and they are constrained by existing political dogmas and the scientific conceptions of the controlling authorities. The central planning group is not likely to be talented in the realm of technology or industrial organization, and the technical and managing experts—however proficient—have little personal incentive to promote technological advancement. The spur to efficiency provided by potential profits and the fear of losses and bankruptcy which operate in free enterprise are absent under communism, which must depend chiefly upon the *negative* compulsions of loss of position and prestige—supplemented as needed by punitive measures.

Under communism, moreover, the individual is afforded slight opportunity to develop independence, originality, and judgment, or to cultivate his individual tastes and talents. The managers produce what they are authorized to produce, and the individual worker takes the job assigned him by the hierarchical authorities. In short, he serves as ordered and consumes as permitted.

The individual has little voice in the selection of his calling or profession. The needs of the state, as determined by government at the time the individual is making his choice, are decisive. Only the especially gifted youth whose talents are at a premium can exercise some degree of preference with respect to the profession he would like to follow. Once in a profession or calling, the individual has little opportunity to shift.

Nor is he free to exercise personal judgment in the practice of his profession; he must keep in step with established policy. Only in purely technical lines is much leeway allowed. The educational system, which is compulsory to the age of fifteen, is designed to inculcate conformity rather than to encourage independence and originality of thought. What can be taught and how it can be taught are specified by the state authorities.

As a consumer the individual has little freedom of choice; he must conform to the rationing system. While theoretically permitted to own his own home and garden, in practice he lives in a rented abode in the selection of which he has little voice.

Communism is sometimes said to be a true exemplification of democracy because the people through their government own and control all wealth and "devote it to the people's needs." The Russian people do not, however, have any voice in deciding how the national wealth may be used. They are not consulted with respect to the allocation of productive effort. Since there is (almost) no free market in which the people can give expression to the character of their consumptive desires, they cannot influence the character of production. A system which provides no means for the masses to express preferences is a negation of democracy.

A distinguishing feature of communism is said to be that "production is for use rather than profit." This appealing phrase overlooks the fact that profits can be made only by producing commodities that the public wants to use and is hence willing to buy; if they are not useful, or in any case desired, they will not be purchased. Under communism the consuming public, as we have seen, cannot through market demands call forth the production of the things they may most wish to possess.

III. STATE SOCIALISM

Socialism has assumed various forms in the course of its history. Many of the early socialistic societies were mere associations of individuals united to achieve certain satisfactions for the particular group; they were not established by government, nor were they interested in using the power of government to impose their system upon the nation. They were largely Utopian and idealistic, often with a religious purpose, and were usually dominated by the middle classes rather than the wage earners. Such, for example, were most of the ill-fated socialist communities established in the United States in the first half of the nineteenth century. In contrast, state socialism, which is the dominant conception today, stands for a comprehensive scheme of social reform to be carried out by the government. The conception is nationalistic, and is opposed both to associational or group plans and the international socialism of Marx. It is this type of socialism which we shall here discuss.

State socialism resembles communism in contending that labor produces all economic goods—either directly, or indirectly through tools and machinery previously made by labor—and in attacking the perennial exploitation of labor by capital. But instead of violent methods to achieve the goal and ruthless stamping out of opposition it looks to an evolutionary, gradual transformation of society by orderly processes. Its central objective is public ownership and operation of selected industries rather than a comprehensively planned and co-ordinated economic system. It would substitute social ownership and democratic control of industry for the principle of private profit.

Socialism is opposed, in theory, to regimentation of the individual.

Socialism, unlike communism, emphasizes the freedom and the development of the individual member of society. It is opposed to dictatorship and the concept of a party state, either communist or fascist. Both the British and American socialist party programs stress the maintenance of civil liberties and democratic ideals. The American platform would preserve "workers' free choice of occupation, consumers' free choice of goods, and freedom of association for all functional groups." The socialist (Labor) party which came to power in Great Britain in 1945 continued price and wage controls and rationing for the transition era.

The principles governing the selection of industries to be taken over by government are stated in the American party program of 1940 as follows:

> Wherever private exploitation of a limited natural resource is highly wasteful, as in the oil, coal and timber industries, there socialization is required, in the interest of this as well as future generations.
>
> Wherever concentration of financial power leads to the restriction of the expansive forces of our economy, as in insurance and investment banking, we propose socialization.
>
> Wherever private monopoly, in the drive for monopoly profit, restricts production to less than is justified by the social usefulness of the product, as in the steel and cement industries, the principle of socialization should be applied.

Wherever concentration of economic power creates a political interest which is too powerful for a democracy to tolerate in private hands, we would put this power in public hands.

Wherever natural monopoly has consumers at its mercy, as in the aluminum industry, socialization is both practical and necessary.

Wherever, as in the railroads, private operation cannot or will not undertake socially needed investment, socialization becomes the order of the day.

Wherever, as in many large-scale corporations, ownership has lost its management function and the business is managed by hired men, these managers should be working for the public instead of for private owners.

Wherever one or more of these conditions exists, it seems that the private profit principle is destroying the very basis of living; that business must be taken over by the public.

The British Labor party program called for nationalization only of the central bank, inland transport, fuel, power, and iron and steel industries, and government supervision of monopolies and cartels.

Socialism would not provide a coherent national program.

Under an economic system in which certain key industries are owned and operated by government, while at the same time private enterprise and free competitive markets prevail elsewhere, it is impossible to achieve co-ordination in the system as a whole. This is because the forces responsible for productive activities lie in part in consumer choices and in part in government decisions which are affected by various factors, including military needs, social goals, and the exigencies of party politics.

Socialism thus possesses neither the advantages of centralized control over production inherent in communism nor the automatic regulatory features of the price and profit mechanism.

Under socialism national production would not be directly responsive to the people's needs.

While most of the major industries might ultimately be owned and operated by the government, agriculture, much small-scale industry, virtually all trade, some types of financial enterprise, and the professions would apparently remain private. A very substantial part of the economy would thus still be operated in accordance with principles of competition. Moreover, instead of state allocation of productive energies socialism would, as already noted, rely upon consumers' free choices in the market.

Consumer choices in the market could not, however, really be depended upon as under private enterprise to govern the allocation of production for the whole economy. This is because consumer choices would not be permitted to determine the relative prices of commodities generally, since prices in the public industries would be fixed by the government. Thus the price and profit mechanism would be crippled, and the responsiveness of competitive markets to the changing demands of the public would be lost.

Motivating forces under socialism, as under communism, would be weak. The operators of state-owned enterprises would have no personal incentive to improve productive processes or exploit new ideas, since they would not be permitted to profit thereby, and by virtue of the government monopoly there would be no competitive pressures or fear of insolvency to spur technological advancement. Patriotism or zeal for the public welfare would provide the only incentive. In practice, officials would doubtless be chosen more for political reasons than for proved technical competency; they would often be retained long after their managerial mediocrity was recognized; and sometimes they would be discharged because of undue enterprise, independence, or disregard of policy considerations.

The outright transfer of private enterprises to the government would obviously lessen the economic power of private individuals. But at the same time it would lodge in the hands of political agencies vastly greater power than was ever possessed by any particular private individual or corporation. It is a fair question whether such power might not be equally subject to abuse. In any case, socialism is not the only means whereby abuses of private power may be curbed. Government regulation, as distinguished from ownership and operation, offers an alternative. (See pages 188-202.)

This discussion has been focused on full-fledged socialism in which most of the major industries would be directly owned and operated by the government. There is apparently no nation today in which this system is fully in operation. In numerous countries, public ownership and operation has been materially extended in recent times, but with the greater part of the economy still under private ownership. Most so-called socialistic countries have mixed systems in which regulation plays a larger role than ownership and operation. Such hybrid economies, as we shall see, differ in essential respects from either communism or socialism.

Attention should here be called to a form of government control which is in no way related to the ideologies outlined above, but has arisen out of practical exigencies resulting from international economic disorganization, or special difficulties with which individual countries are confronted. The loss of foreign investments and the disruption of international trading relations occasioned by world wars have profoundly affected the ability of many countries to maintain a balance in international transactions—to procure imports indispensable to the continuance of economic life. This has led to a variety of control measures designed to protect the nation's currency and to improve the balance of trade. Inevitably this has involved direct intervention by governments in purchasing essential supplies in foreign countries and the making of intergovernmental commodity agreements. This in turn has often necessitated control over important segments of the domestic economy—to keep imports at a minimum and to ensure that domestic production will be adequate to supply domestic requirements and furnish essential exports. Such controls have frequently been employed in recent decades and are found today in most countries; and in the light of present conditions, they may be expected to continue for some time.

This type of government control program is not a conception of radical groups alone. It has, for example, been advocated by leaders of the British conservative party, who look upon drastic, far-reaching measures along these lines as the only certain way of stabilizing the British economy.

This type of control appears almost inevitable where considerations of national security or actual war are involved, and they have had their fullest exemplification in such connections. It is also true, however, that they have been advocated in some quarters as constituting a system of regulation of international economic relations far preferable to what its proponents call the "anarchy" of private international transactions.

IV. HYBRID SYSTEMS

Throughout the world the decade of the 1930's was one of expanding government control over the economic system. The extent of the controls that were developed varied widely in different countries, and the methods employed were often dissimilar. But everywhere the private enterprise system was being modified by hybrid forms of economic organization—partly free, partly controlled by government. This development—at least in its early stages—was not the result of conscious planning by economic theorists or social reformers. It represented rather a drift which began somewhat earlier and was greatly accelerated by the practical difficulties with which nations everywhere were confronted as a result of the world depression.

A new philosophy of economic organization gradually developed in the United States.

Instead of a completely centralized domination of economic life by government—as under communism, fascism, and nazism—and instead of government ownership and operation of selected industries, as under state socialism, the new American philosophy conceived that the function of government should be to *control* the operation of the economic system. Individuals would still be free to own and operate whatever type of business enterprise might seem to offer the best hope of profit, and private enterprise and competition would be depended upon to furnish the spark and driving force for technological advancement.

American development along these lines involved two stages: The first was that of the Roosevelt administration from 1933 to 1940; and the second was that of the year 1946 under the Truman administration. The latter, as we shall presently see, was much more far-reaching in its potential impact upon the operation of the private enterprise system.

The Roosevelt program invoked the powers of government for both recovery and control purposes.

The principal steps involved in the initial recovery program of 1933 have been presented in Chapter III and need not be repeated here. They centered on relief of distressed individuals and enterprises, the raising of wages and prices, and the expansion of purchasing power.

More or less concurrently, the developing government program emphasized reforms and controls designed to promote long-run economic progress and to achieve economic stability. The principal measures and devices were: (1) the removal of barriers to international trade; (2) the support of farm prices and the subsidization of submarginal farm groups; (3) the establishment of minimum wages and the systematic promotion of labor organization and higher rates of pay; (4) the redistribution of income by steeply progressive taxation; (5) permanent relief for the unemployed, the incapacitated, and the aged, and a social security program; (6) control of the issuance of securities and of security exchanges; (7) the use of public credit and the fiscal machinery to offset the stagnation of private enterprise and to stabilize the economy and maintain employment at a permanently high level; and (8) the curbing of monopoly power and the enforcement of competition to ensure reasonable prices.

These recovery and reform measures did not bring about real business prosperity nor achieve stable economic conditions. As noted in Chapter III, the recovery in the spring and early summer of 1933 was followed by a reaction in the autumn, while the year 1934 and the first half of 1935 showed periodic advances and declines. The substantial recovery of 1936-37—proclaimed as an exemplification of what can be done under a government-planned and controlled economy—lasted little more than a year. In 1938 production receded to the level of 1935. The unemployment problem continued with little abatement until the advent of World War II.

These reform measures did not strike directly at the basic principle of private enterprise.

The virtues of individual freedom were extolled, and the advantages of competition were emphasized. Consumer choices in free markets and the price and profit mechanism were in the main relied upon to guide the allocation of productive energies. The goals were the curbing of monopolistic and other alleged abuses of large-scale business, the supplementation of private by public enterprise in neglected fields, the promotion of permanent prosperity by raising the incomes of the masses and lowering the incomes of the classes, and the control of the business cycle by means of fiscal and monetary policies.

In numerous ways, however, this government program did come into conflict with the private enterprise system. In the field of electric power, for example, the government constructed hydroelectric plants and operated them in such a way as virtually to necessitate the sale of competing private companies to the government. The Reconstruction Finance Corporation, with the vast credit resources at its disposal, exerted a powerful influence on interest rates and even on the character and direction of private financing. The resources of the agricultural credit agencies were employed not only to support agricultural income, but also to bring about shifts in farm production in accordance with goals set by the Department of Agriculture.

In many fields the power of government was exercised through regulatory machinery. The detailed requirements were sometimes clearly stated in the legislative acts, but in other cases large discretion was left with the administrators. This often resulted in arbitrary and contradictory decisions which resulted in confusion and uncertainty as to what was legal and what was not. It also placed coercive power in the hands of government officials. (See pages 196 and 198 below.)

The mechanism hitherto relied upon for allocating productive activity was profoundly affected in some sectors of the economy by government price regulation. In transportation and electric utilities, maximum prices had long been subject to control with a view to protecting *consumers*. But in the thirties *minimum* price floors were established for the protection of producers in agriculture and the bituminous coal industries. Prices for most important farm products were not allowed to fall below certain levels; and hence oversupply could no longer be corrected by declining prices. Instead, the government sought to induce essential shifts by means of "benefit payments," which were cash inducements to grow more of certain products and less of others. This support program was financed largely by the consumers of the cities, who paid higher prices for foodstuffs and higher taxes besides. Since farmers as a class got more income than they would otherwise have received, there was less pressure to shift from agriculture to other fields. The sick bituminous coal industry—subject to increasing competition from other fuels—was propped up by minimum prices, adjusted upward as wages advanced. The competitive position of coal in relation to other forms of fuel was further weakened by this process.

More far-reaching in its effects upon the economy as a whole was the policy pursued by the government with respect to labor. The right to organize and bargain collectively through representatives of their own choosing was properly guaranteed to labor by the National Recovery Act. In its desire to raise wage rates, the government sought to strengthen the bargaining position of labor, in what had too often been a one-sided contest, by encouraging the organization of labor on an industry-wide basis. The outcome in numerous industries was the creation of virtual labor monopolies. With labor in a position to shut down whole industries producing essential commodities or services, the quick settlement of wage controversies was imperative in the public interest; hence the government was obliged to play a positive role in effecting agreements. In view of the administration's commitment to the policy of progressive increases in wages and the need for political support, its power was naturally exerted in favor of substantial wage advances, irrespective of the merits of the controversy.

Wage negotiations were thus transferred from individual companies—first to the industry as a whole and thence to the realm of national politics. Henceforth wage negotiations were largely unrelated to economic realities—which reside in individual companies. Indeed, the argument often advanced for general wage increases was that such expansion of purchasing power was essential to national welfare. Once a new level of wage rates was established in one or more key industries, the power of labor was such as to compel similar advances in other industries, regardless of the condition of such industries.

Under these circumstances, true collective bargaining between individual employers and their employees virtually ceased to exist. Moreover, wage settlements ceased to be related to conditions of demand and supply in the labor market. Nor were they related to changes in productivity.

In the year 1946 an effort was made to control the vitals of private enterprise.

The Truman administration, as it faced the problems of postwar readjustment and reconstruction, possessed a vast control mechanism that had been developed to meet the requirements of war. It elected to retain a substantial part of this machinery, notably that pertaining to the allocation of materials and the regulation of commodity prices. Ostensibly these controls were to be retained only to guide and stabilize the economy during the period of transition, but there were many within the administration who were interested in their permanent use. Moreover, after these controls had been abolished and the transition from war to peace production had been accomplished, the President periodically requested their restoration as the only means of checking inflation, preventing business depression, and maintaining full employment.

The basic policy of the government was to maintain national purchasing power at virtually the wartime level, in order to ensure the maintenance of abundant employment. It was the official view that if demobilization and readjustment were left to natural forces, from eight to ten millions of workers would soon be idle. Accordingly, it was deemed necessary to raise wage rates sufficiently to offset the loss of income resulting from the elimination of overtime work and pay and withdrawals of workers from the labor force at the end of the war. To assure the success of this program, it was deemed necessary to prevent a dissipation of purchasing power through rising prices.

But with the same amount of money wages being disbursed for fewer hours of work and less production, a sharp advance in costs was inevitable. In consequence, industrial demands for compensating price increases soon became insistent. The government's test of the need for price adjustments was the profit situation of the industry, actual and potential. Inasmuch as profits, in a period of industrial readjustment with changing wage and raw material costs, were problematical, prices were set on the basis of hypothetical calculations by government statisticians.

Unless the prices to be permitted could be wisely and quickly determined, the process of industrial recovery would be seriously impeded. Since it was recognized that requests for price advances could not be considered on their individual merits, the effort was directed toward establishing price ceilings on an industry-wide basis. In the face of rapidly advancing wages, which both increased costs and sustained "excess buying power," the Office of Price Administration could not possibly keep pace with requirements, and the whole regulatory system soon broke down. After some months of conflict and confusion, during which price control ceased to be effective over a large portion of the economy, the enabling act was repealed by Congress.

The situation had been seriously complicated by White House intervention in the settlement of major wage controversies. The question at issue was always whether the wage increases requested could be granted without compensating price advances, or without so curtailing profits as to prejudice business expansion. The method of reaching a settlement—to last for a year or more during a period of readjustment and uncertainty—was to call in a group of respected citizens to report to the President what the industry was in a position to do. These individuals, ill-equipped and inexperienced so far as the problems of the particular industry were concerned, were expected to render a decision, after a week or so of study, which would be the basis of a definitive settlement.

A hybrid system, involving price and profit control, cannot endure.

Wartime experience in this and other countries demonstrated the impossibility of controlling industrial prices without controlling wage rates and agricultural prices—basic elements of cost. The problem is no different in time of peace. But, since in time of peace the control of wage rates is a practical impossibility in a democratic country, prices cannot be stabilized if conditions are conducive to sharply advancing wage rates.

Assuming that the system could be effectively administered, prices and profits would not be allowed to rise in industries whose products are in high demand by consumers, and thus an expansion of production in such fields would not be induced. Similarly, the maintenance of existing prices in industries whose products are in low demand would serve to check the shift out of such industries. Not only would consumer choices cease to be effective in guiding production, but the government itself could not adjust prices in line with consumer desires because of the powerful opposition of vested interests who want the government to prevent readjustments adverse to themselves.

In the absence of a functioning price and profit mechanism, the allocation of productive effort would thus have to be made directly by the government. With the vital decisions thus taken out of the hands of business enterprisers, the incentive to assume business risks would be destroyed.

The difficulties inherent in maintaining a hybrid system of controlling economic society may be illustrated by British postwar experience. The British Labor party program involved not only state ownership and operation of certain key industries, but also the retention of much of the wartime regulatory machinery, including the control of wages and prices, the allocation of materials, and the rationing of consumption. In the discussion which follows, we are not interested in appraising whether an early resumption of the prewar British system would have enabled Britain to meet the grave difficulties with which it was confronted. We are here interested only in the question whether the British hybrid system can remain hybrid. The following quotation from the editor of the London *Economist*, who had been one of the strongest advocates of "purposive direction" of the national economy sheds light on the issue.[3]

> Here was a situation that should have been easy to diagnose, and a set of controls already in existence more far-reaching than any socialist planner had ever dreamed of. . . . Yet if "planning" is defined not merely as the efforts of the small group of self-confessed planners, but as the net cumulative effect upon the economic system of all the actions and policies of the state, there can hardly be any room for doubt that it has been bad. If ever a community has been more planned against than planning, it has been Britain in the last two years. There has been quite a singular unwillingess to face facts, to adjust ambitions to resources, or to reduce the policies of the various Government departments to a coherent pattern.

In this situation he sees only two alternatives: first, an abandonment of all controls, leaving the painful processes of readjustment and the restoration of reality to be worked out through the operation of free competitive markets; or, second, a truly comprehensive and co-ordinated control program. Such a comprehensive plan, as he sees it, would involve the following steps: (1) making a realistic estimate of the nation's producing capacity; (2) deducting from this the resources (man power and materials) needed for all governmental activities and programs that have been decided upon; (3) deducting the resources needed for all authorized capital construction, including building and repair work; and (4) making adjustment for net imports or exports. The balance would be what is available for the consumption of the people; and "steps must be taken—by taxation, by wage policy or otherwise—to see that they do not have for spending . . . more than is enough to buy this remainder." The remainder would prove to be so small that it would be necessary to "go back to the beginning and drastically reduce government expenditures and capital programs in order to make the consumable residuum large enough to prevent riots in the streets. This of course would be a very painful process. For the politicians, it would be even more painful than 'natural' deflation, since the sacrifice of pleasant dreams that it involves would be more conscious and deliberate. But it is the way in which the planning philosophy would meet the present situation and those who have not the stomach to face it had better seek refuge in *laissez faire*."

The significance of this analysis is to be found in the conclusion that the only remedy for the weaknesses of partial planning is complete planning. The only way out appears to lie in a wholly centralized program involving state determination of what commodities may be produced and in what quantities, and *complete control* over the entire economy. Such a program as it progressed would lead, inevitably, to the regimentation of the masses and would be difficult to differentiate from communism.

A democracy such as ours is inherently incapable of achieving a unified program of government control.

A number of considerations combine to make it impossible for a government like that of the United States to develop and maintain a coherent, comprehensive program of control over economic life. These pertain on the one hand to the nature of democratic government, and on the other to the intricate and baffling character of the control problem itself. It should be emphasized that we are not at this place concerned with devices for preventing business depressions, but with general government *control* over the economic system.

In the first place, the United States government itself is not a unified, law-making organization. With a view to safeguarding the public against extreme or ill-advised government measures, the Constitution provided for a threefold separation of power—a system of checks and balances. Congress can refuse to pass legislation recommended by the president; the president can veto legislation passed by Congress; and the courts, in turn, may nullify acts passed by Congress and approved by the president, by declaring them unconstitutional. Even when the party in power also has a majority in Congress, the president often cannot gain the support of Congress for specific measures which he deems important; and, similarly, Congress sometimes cannot win the president to its point of view.

Second, the government's economic policy is inescapably a mere composite of the policies of past and present administrations. A new administration is inevitably committed to the continuance of many programs and policies already embodied in law or administrative commitments. This is substantially the case even when there is a change in the party in power. An incoming administration cannot simply scrap outright all existing laws and policies and evolve an entirely new government program. At best, the program of any government is a combination of old and new, good and bad. It should be added that if it were possible for a new administration to launch a control program without reference to existing laws and procedures, the greater coherence that might be achieved would in some measure be offset by the loss in long-term consistency.

Third, there is not merely a lack of unity among the three major divisions of government, but even within the executive branch there is divided responsibility. There are numerous so-called independent agencies, whose responsibilities and powers have been defined in legislative acts, and whose officials have a term of office exceeding that of the president. Such agencies are given this special status in order that they may pursue longer term policies free from immediate political considerations and gradually acquire the experience required for wise administration. Again, the precise jurisdiction of government departments or agencies is sometimes ambiguous, providing an opportunity for interagency conflicts. Moreover, virtually all departments, as by inner compulsion, seek constantly to extend their power, influence, and size. This is in part attributable to a natural desire to exert influence believed to be constructive; it is sometimes due to the political ambitions of a cabinet officer or department head; and it is usually affected by the fact that budget authorizations depend upon making a good showing—by pointing to some striking achievement, or by citing the increasing scope of the department's work.

The constant struggle for influence and status is one of the most striking characteristics of government. The game is to get the ear of the chief executive first—or sometimes last. The only place where conflicts can be resolved is the White House; and the president must often compromise in order to maintain peace in the family and an appearance of harmony before the public. Examples of such conflicts are legion. Reference need be made only to such notorious cases as the encroachments of the Department of Commerce in the twenties, the struggle during the thirties between the Public Works and the Works Progress administrations, and the competition for influence at the White House between the departments of War, State, and Treasury with reference to postwar policy with respect to Germany. Of a more permanent character are the differences and the divided responsibility between the Board of Governors of the Federal Reserve System and the Treasury Department over financial policies.

Fourth, under the American governmental system, the *uniting* states did not confer unlimited powers upon the federal government. To protect and preserve the rights of states and keep government close to the people, state and local governments reserved much power over economic affairs to themselves. While the constitutional powers of the federal government have been greatly broadened by court decisions, and while devices of various kinds have been employed to bring about team play and co-ordinated action, there remains a fundamental division of power and responsibility between federal government and state and local units which, whatever the merits from some points of view, serves to impede the development of a truly comprehensive national program.

Fifth, government economic policies inevitably reflect the power and influence of the many special interest groups that strive perpetually for government favor or protection. In the nature of the case, a program resulting in large measure from the pressures of economic blocs cannot be internally consistent. Since such policies are formulated and executed by political parties desiring re-election, vote-getting is necessarily a primary consideration. It is a maxim of politics that it is sometimes necessary to accept or promote unsound policies because of the exigencies of the political situation. Moreover, once one important group has been given protection, others insistently demand similar support—as a matter of right.

The lack of co-ordination or unity of policy likely to exist may be concretely illustrated by reference to the present situation in a single sector of the economy. The national transportation system, consisting of railways, waterways, highways, and airways, has long been subject to government control; and since 1930 numerous commissions and agencies have been charged with responsibility for promoting and developing a co-ordinated national transportation policy. The situation at the present time may be summarized as follows:

The *railways* are controlled by the Interstate Commerce Commission with respect to such operating factors as rates, service, safety, abandonments and acquistions of properties, and the raising of capital funds. Wage rates and working conditions, however, are governed by procedures laid down in the Railway Labor Act. The railways are subject to taxation on rights of way and terminal properties, rolling stock, and corporate earnings. In short, the rates charged are expected to cover all costs and furnish substantial revenues for the support of government—federal, state, and local.

Waterways, in most cases, are constructed and maintained at public expense, these overhead costs being met from annual taxes.[4] The Corps of Army Engineers surveys and recommends projects (military considerations are seldom involved), and Congress appropriates the money. Since waterway projects offer one of the best opportunities for obtaining funds from the federal treasury for the benefit of local constituents, appropriations are popularly called "pork barrel." Actual transportation on coastal waterways, the Great Lakes, and some inland routes is conducted by private companies which are subject to regulation by the Interstate Commerce Commission with respect to rates, safety, and scheduled routes. However, a substantial part of the river traffic is conducted directly by the Inland Waterways Corporation, which is supported by government appropriations. Wage rates and working conditions are subject to the regulations found in the general labor laws. Since the major costs of water transportation are met by the public treasury, and since the waterway pays no taxes, the rates charged shippers are heavily subsidized.

The *highways* have been developed largely by state and local governments. However, national considerations led to the establishment of a federal Public Roads Administration charged with responsibility for the co-ordination of federal and state highway development—the co-ordination being made effective by *contingent* federal appropriations. The costs of highways, including roadbed, and structures, are eventually met out of taxes imposed upon users of the highways. Fixed capital embedded in the highway properties pays no direct taxes to government. Wage rates and working conditions are subject to the regulations in the general labor laws.

Airways are supervised by the Civil Aeronautics Administration, in the Department of Commerce, with respect to fixed properties, such as airports, beacons, etc., which are provided at public expense—federal, state, and local. The Civil Aeronautics Board, an independent agency, controls fares, route patterns, capital issues, and matters pertaining to safety. This board is also authorized to protect the revenues of operating companies by adjustments in rates for carrying mail. Wage rates and working conditions, as in the case of railroads, are subject to the provisions of the Railway Labor Act.

This wide dispersion of regulatory responsibility in the field of transportation, coupled with the lack of uniformity with respect to financial support and taxation status, has resulted in a complete lack of co-ordination. Although the declared purpose of federal regulation (except in the case of air transport) is to "maintain competition and preserve the inherent advantages of each type of transportation agency," the competition is wholly artificial, since the rates charged do not reflect inherent advantages—that is, true costs. The over-all cost of national transportation service has been greatly increased by diverting traffic from cheaper to more costly routes and by diluting the aggregate supply of traffic available for each type of transport. A practical result has been that a substantial proportion of the railway mileage of the country operates at a deficit, except during periods of high business prosperity. The nation is now faced with these choices: suffering deterioration of railway service, subsidizing distressed roads, public ownership and operation, or giving management freedom commensurate with responsibility. (See pages 192-95.)

Finally, the complexity of the economic system is such that its control is beyond the understanding and competency of government officials. There is usually little in the training or previous experience of presidents, cabinet officers, and congressmen to equip them especially for the task of analyzing intricate economic processes and weighing the balance of forces. Technicians within the government may be called upon to make recommendations, but decisions rest with the responsible officials. Moreover, these technical experts are often in disagreement with respect to the significance or potentialities of suggested measures; and since experts are specialists, they do not commonly possess the breadth of knowledge or the vision required for the co-ordination of the control system as a whole.

In the light of the situation outlined in the foregoing discussion, it is not surprising that government programs should contain many conflicting elements, and often be basically inconsistent. For example, the Hoover administration was committed simultaneously to the maintenance of high tariffs, the expansion of exports, and the collection of international debts. Again, various phases of the Roosevelt program were wholly incompatible: (1) The early efforts to re-establish business confidence by the reconstruction of the credit system and the reduction of expenditures to balance the budget were in large measure nullified by the uncertainty arising out of the program of dollar devaluation and currency management. (2) The currency policy necessitated independent national action and thus disrupted the World Economic Conference, called for the purpose of promoting recovery through co-operative international action. (3) The sharp increase in industrial prices fostered by the National Recovery Administration's program of shortening hours and increasing wages worked directly at cross purposes with the Agricultural Adjustment Administration's policy of restoring price parity between agriculture and industry. In the Truman administration, the continuing inflation of prices—officially attributed to the carryover of accumulated wartime purchasing power—was proclaimed as the greatest menace to prosperity; but at the same time it was conceived to be necessary to shorten hours and increase wage rates in order to prevent deflation and unemployment. In 1948 the administration's program called for a vast increase in expenditures for public works, public housing, universal health insurance, national defense, etc. and at the same time demanded a reduction in the amount of money entering the channels of circulation, in order to check inflationary influences.

Such illustrations serve to indicate not only the complex nature of the problems involved in controlling the economy and the breadth of comprehension required, but also the play of political forces and the influence of special economic groups. Under a democratic system such as that in the United States, it is necessary for the chief executive to take account of political forces. Since congressmen are chosen to represent the interests of their constituencies, in the case of most problems which come before them, they are, practically speaking, compelled to view the matter from the standpoint of special economic groups or sections of the country. They are effectively debarred from taking a truly national point of view.

In short, a controlled economy is incompatible with the American system of government, and cannot be effectively administered. A comprehensive master plan is essential to success, and such a unified plan can be developed and carried out only by a strongly centralized national authority.

V. REGULATION COMPATIBLE WITH PRIVATE ENTERPRISE

In the foregoing discussion attention was focused on hybrid types of economic organization in which private enterprise would be depended upon to carry on productive activities and provide the imagination and drive for technological advancement, but with the government exercising, in greater or lesser degree, overhead controls designed to co-ordinate, stabilize, and fructify the economy as a whole. Our conclusion that such a system cannot succeed and cannot endure does not compel us either to turn to communism or to return to completely unrestricted private enterprise—*laissez faire*. It remains possible to maintain a system of government regulation which establishes certain "rules of the game" and sets certain acceptable standards of performance, without assuming the vital functions of business management or destroying the essentials of the competitive free enterprise system.

It should be noted at this place that in certain fields it is universally recognized that competition is impracticable and economically undesirable. In the case of local transportation service, for example, competing lines would simply clutter up the streets and interfere with traffic movement. The situation is somewhat similar with respect to gas, water, and electric facilities. Since the maintenance of competing establishments would involve a wasteful duplication of resources and resulting higher costs, such local utilities are regarded as "natural" monopolies. The postal, telephone, and telegraph services are also naturally monopolistic in character. The railways are mixed; they are frequently monopolies in restricted regions, but seldom so over broad continental areas.

Since natural monopolies are not subject to the *natural* regulation afforded by competition, other means of protecting the public are required. This may be accomplished either by subjecting the rates charged to government regulation, or through government ownership and operation. In practice, sometimes one method and sometimes the other is employed.

Certain types of regulation have been designed to preserve and strengthen the competitive system.

The evolution of business enterprise was accompanied by developments which often tended to restrict or eliminate competition. So-called "conspiracies in restraint of trade" had long been held illegal under the common law. With the development of huge business organizations and "trusts" in the late nineteenth century, it was deemed necessary (Sherman Antitrust Act of 1890) to make combinations in restraint of trade explicitly illegal and subject to appropriate penalties. The underlying conception of the common law and of this antitrust legislation was that the competitive system and its automatic power to ensure reasonable prices should be maintained.

A second factor leading to government regulation was the emergence of certain "evils" or weaknesses of competition. Unscrupulous, short-sighted, or hard-pressed enterprisers often followed practices which were regarded as disruptive to legitimate business. This "cut-throat" competition involved such practices as selling goods without regard to costs and substituting inferior materials and workmanship. The conception developed that the plane of competition should be raised and that business should be conducted in accordance with generally accepted practices and policies. To some extent business groups or associations might be self-regulating in these regards, but they could not go far without being suspected of efforts to restrain trade, and at the same time there would always be an irreconcilable minority, who could not be brought in line. Hence government aid was sought in working out a set of business rules, which were eventually incorporated in state and federal legislation.

The shortcomings of competition were of course of particular interest to government where broad public considerations were indirectly involved. For example, the intensive exploitation of natural resources often appeared incompatible with the national welfare. Where conservation measures appeared essential, it was deemed necessary to establish regulations governing the extraction and use of natural resources. In a somewhat similar way, private enterprise was often disregardful of health considerations. While the wise business manager might pay proper attention to the health and safety of workers and the purity or quality of the product, the shortsighted, negligent, or hard-pressed competitor might not. Accordingly, it seemed necessary to establish certain regulations pertaining to working conditions and to the quality of products—the latter involving standardization procedures and tests to determine the germinating quality of seeds, the purity of food and drug preparations, the tensile strength of materials, etc.

Experience also proved that it was necessary in certain types of business to establish minimum requirements in accordance with the lessons of experience. Commercial banking affords perhaps the best illustration. Experience under private banking had demonstrated that certain practices and policies yielded highly satisfactory results, while others commonly ended in disaster. Since the failure of badly organized and managed banks tended to cast doubt on the stability of all banks, it was of interest to the soundly managed institutions that all should conform to certain general principles of operation. The provisions which were eventually incorporated into legislation pertained chiefly to minimum capital requirements, security for note issues, cash reserves, and the character and duration of loans. While private commercial banking was not abolished, the prestige acquired by the regulated institutions was so great that nearly all banks in due course voluntarily joined the regulated system.

These types of regulation, it will be observed, were not designed to take over vital functions of management or displace the system of private enterprise. They were intended rather to strengthen the competitive system by correcting shortcomings and establishing standards which experience had shown to be necessary. The governing principle is the same as that employed in the regulation of competitive sports; experience shows that rules have to be laid down by some kind of a governing body, that an umpire is necessary, and that penalties must be provided for violations. Such rules of the game do not destroy competition. They raise the plane of competition without interfering with the essential principle. The governing bodies do not undertake to coach the teams or assume other functions of management.

Government regulation is possible without usurpation of vital managerial functions.

In railway transportation the federal government has increasingly assumed control of management functions. The original purpose of federal railway regulation was to make sure that the rates charged in a potentially monopolistic industry should be "fair, just, and reasonable" and not unduly discriminatory. But with the passage of time the power of the Interstate Commerce Commission over the railway system has been extended to include control of: (1) all rates—minimum and intermediate as well as maximum; (2) the division of the proceeds from rates on traffic passing over more than one line; (3) the allocation of rolling stock; (4) extensions, abandonments, acquisitions, and consolidations of railway properties; (5) the extent to which, and the conditions under which, roads can own, control, or operate other transportation agencies; (6) the issuance of securities; (7) plans for reorganization in the event of bankruptcy; and (8) provisions for public safety.

The development of this comprehensive system of control is explained by several considerations. The control of maximum rates was for the purpose of preventing exorbitant charges and unreasonable profits on invested capital; the establishment of minimum rates was to check the evils of competition as manifested in rate wars between competing roads; and the fixing of individual rates was to ensure that the charges were fair and just and that everybody was treated alike. The veto of proposed abandonments of lines was dictated by considerations of public interest or convenience. Control over the flotation of securities and of extensions, acquisitions, and consolidations was designed to prevent changes in the railway setup which the Commission deemed incompatible with national interests. Requiring the Commission's permission to own, control, or operate other transportation agencies was deemed necessary to maintain competition in the transportation field and make possible a proper co-ordination of the national transportation system as a whole. Control over reorganizations was justified as insurance to investors against the repetition of disaster, and as a guarantee that the capital basis for rate-making is reasonable.

The striking feature in this situation is the mixed and varied objectives of this government regulation. The government is concerned with preventing monopoly profits, with preserving competition both within the railway industry and with other forms of transportation, and with guiding the development of the future transportation system of the country. As a result, the railway managers are deprived of the right to use their own judgment with respect to such important functions as: lowering rates in order to attract traffic from other roads and other agencies; developing feeder, rail, truck, bus, or water lines; abandonment of unprofitable spur or branch lines; and borrowing money for any purpose, including refunding operations to save interest and the sale of equipment trust certificates for purposes of improving operating efficiency. The necessity of obtaining approval from a Commission overburdened with a multitude of cases requiring time-consuming hearings, and often reluctant to render a decision until all doubts have been resolved, commonly renders prompt action on the part of railroad managers impossible. About the only functions left completely to private management are the scheduling and operation of trains, personnel policy, and purchasing.

Meanwhile changing conditions have rendered obsolete those basic regulations which were designed to ensure that the railroads should not make unreasonable profits. The monopolistic position occupied by the railroads at the time the Interstate Commerce Act was passed in 1887 largely ceased to exist before 1930.[5] The problem now is *not* to prevent the making of exorbitant profits, but to maintain a level of rates high enough to cover costs and provide for essential improvements in railroad service. Progressive advances in wage rates and other costs in recent years have necessitated such extensive rate increases that loss of traffic is seriously threatened. In this situation the establishment of rates on the basis of original cost, "prudent" investment, or even the reproduction cost of the fixed capital would be wholly impracticable; the only question is whether the level of rates can be fixed high enough to cover advancing costs without losses of traffic that would more than offset the gains.

The question remains: What types of regulation in this field are compatible with the *efficient* operation of the railroads by private enterprise? Since the fundamental requirement for a solvent and healthy industry is reduction in costs of operation, any regulations which deprive management of initiative and power to act quickly on matters affecting operating efficiency are incompatible with the requirements for responsible private enterprise. It is essential either to give private enterprise freedom and authority commensurate with its responsibility, or make the government directly responsible for developing and maintaining efficient railway transportation.

It should be noted that acceptance of the principle of private initiative and responsibility in the railroad industry would not involve the abandonment of government regulations pertaining to working conditions and safety, the establishment of minimum rates, the prevention of undue discrimination, or control over acquisitions or consolidations.

Another illustration of the extension of government control is found in the administration of the Federal Securities Act of 1933. The purpose of this act was to eliminate dishonesty and fraud in connection with the flotation of securities and to ensure that the investing public is furnished adequate information. It was no part of the plan to ensure that the securities issued would be good investments; indeed, it was explicitly stated that "the Federal Government cannot and should not take any action which might be construed as approving or guaranteeing that newly issued securities are sound in the sense that their value will be maintained or that the properties which they represent will earn profit."[6] Moreover, the prospectus in each case must carry the statement that "it is a criminal offense to represent that the Commission has approved these securities or has made any findings that the statements in this prospectus or in the registration statement are correct."

In practice, however, zealous administrators have often gone beyond this basic principle, and held up for long periods of time the flotation of securities which, in the Commission's judgment, seemed to involve substantial risks. The administrators have not infrequently exerted a direct influence upon corporate policies, even where no question of fraudulent statements or inadequate information was involved. In the words of a prominent member of the staff: "In return for the favor of the administrator, the registrant may amend its practices in accordance with the administrator's conception of equity and justice."[7]

The Public Utility Act of 1935, which authorized the breaking up of financial companies holding control of widely scattered operating subsidiaries, specifically authorized the Securities and Exchange Commission to pass upon the soundness of such securities. Here the Commission examines the capital structure of borrowing corporations and in effect decides what percentage of the capital structure shall be represented by bonds, preferred stock, and common stock respectively. The Commission also decides whether new financing is necessary and appropriate to the economical and efficient operation of the company, the purposes to which the proceeds of any issue are to be applied, and prescribes what dividends the corporation may disburse and what reserves it may set aside. The Commission thus exerts a decisive influence upon the financial and managerial policies of such corporations.

The only tenable principle is for the government to confine itself to preventing dishonesty and fraud, and to requiring the furnishing of adequate information. If the Commission undertakes to pass upon the soundness of securities, three results inevitably follow: (1) the time consumed in reaching decisions and raising the funds required by the issuing corporations is greatly increased; (2) extensive control by the government over financial and managerial decisions becomes necessary; and (3) since the government in effect guarantees the soundness of issues, flotations have to be restricted to issues involving a minimum of risk, thereby hampering the development of new enterprises through the use of venture capital.

In the broad field of industry and trade the government has steadily encroached upon the functions of management. The original purpose of government regulation in these areas was to eliminate monopoly and preserve competition. Under the governing legislative acts, any party claiming injury from conspiracies in restraint of trade may bring suit for damages; and actions may also be initiated by the Department of Justice. The Federal Trade Commission was established to conduct general investigations of current practices in given corporations or industries, and to conduct hearings whenever it shall have reason to believe that any firm is "using any unfair method of competition or unfair or deceptive act or practice in commerce." Upon the finding of a violation, the Commission issues a "cease and desist order," which may be appealed by the defendant to the Circuit Court of Appeals. The Commission may call upon the Attorney General to institute proceedings for the enforcement of its orders.

Under this system of regulation, suits brought by the Department of Justice are frequently settled out of court. While not admitting any guilt, the defendant company under a "consent decree" agrees henceforth to conduct certain of its operations in ways specified by the Department of Justice.[8] The large costs involved in litigation, together with the undesirable publicity, naturally give the Department of Justice powerful weapons of compulsion; and innocent companies may feel that compliance is the lesser of evils. Under this procedure a prosecuting agency of government has, in fact, come to play a decisive role in determining how companies shall conduct specific business operations.[9]

The Federal Trade Commission has interpreted its function as not only to prevent practices that are actually in restraint of trade but also to check developments which, in the Commission's judgment, might ultimately become dangerous. This interpretation has moreover been supported by the Supreme Court in the following language:

> Individual conduct, or concerted action, which falls short of being a Sherman Act violation may as a matter of law constitute an "unfair method of competition" prohibited by the Trade

Commission Act. A major purpose of that Act, as we have frequently said, was to enable the Commission to restrain practices as "unfair" which, although not yet having grown into Sherman Act dimensions, would most likely do so if left unrestrained. The Commission and the courts were to determine what conduct, even though it might then be short of a Sherman Act violation, was an "unfair method of competition." This general language was deliberately left to the Commission and the courts for definition because it was thought that "There is no limit to human inventiveness in this field"; that consequently, a definition that fitted practices known to lead towards an unlawful restraint of trade today would not fit tomorrow's new inventions in the field; and that for Congress to try to keep its precise definitions abreast of this course of conduct would be an "endless task."[10]

The Court goes on to say that the Commission may properly regard a given practice as an unfair method of competition if it is merely an "incipient menace."

In another case it has held that it is unnecessary to show either that there has been or may be restraint of trade: "It is not necessary that the power [to control the prices of a commodity moving in interstate commerce] should be exercised. Its existence is sufficient."[11]

According to these decisions actual restraint of trade need not be proved; a majority of the Federal Trade Commission may declare any business practice unfair if, in their judgment, such practice might eventually place a company in a position where it could, if it wished, restrain trade. Moreover, the Department of Justice may order the breaking up of a company into smaller units, even though no restraints on trade or monopolistic practices have been proved or even charged. In this situation it is impossible for business organizations to know what practices are permissible, or even how large they may become. The rules of the game are unknown.

In the first case quoted above, the Supreme Court stated that the general language of the Trade Commission act was deliberately left to the Commission and the courts for *definition*. Thus it is the responsibility of the Commission and/or the courts to formulate definitions for the guidance of business. But neither the Commission nor the courts have made any definitions or laid down any standards or rules. Each case is considered as a special situation.

The heart of the present administrative difficulty is found in the attempt to go beyond the elimination of actual monopolistic practices, and to anticipate developments which might possibly lead to restraint of trade at some future time. In the nature of the case the Commission cannot define in meaningful terms what incipient tendencies might utimately lead to a restraint of trade, or what size of business enterprise is safe and thus permissible. It is as though some commission were empowered to punish individuals not merely for crimes actually committed, but for actions, looks, habits, or practices which in the Commission's judgment "most likely" foreshadowed a commission of crime or an abuse of power at some future date. It would obviously be impossible to cover such a policy adequately by definitions. Similarly, it would be impossible for any individual to know where he stood.

There are two basic issues in this situation. The first is the legal question whether an individual businessman or corporation can properly be *punished* for practices or developments which are not defined and which no one can know will be held objectionable. The second is whether a system of regulation which places in the hands of government agencies undefined powers over the conduct of business operations, the size of business units, and the very structure of industry and trade is compatible with a private enterprise system.

Such agencies can have no sure judgment as to the ultimate outcome of current tendencies or their true significance from the point of view of national welfare. They might well place so many restraints on industry as effectively to check the technological and organizational developments that are essential to a dynamic economic system. It may also be observed that such agencies may be influenced by political considerations, they may be possessed of well-meaning bias, and they may lack adequate understanding of the reasons for and the effects of business practices and tendencies. They may fail, for example, to distinguish between monopoly and mere bigness, they may not differentiate between administered prices (essential in many industries) and monopoly control; and they may identify uniformity of prices in a truly competitive market with collusion in restraint of trade.[12]

Government regulation of trade and industry should be confined to the checking of collusive efforts to eliminate competition. Any attempt to prevent one company from growing at the expense of others is a negation of the very object of competition. Any policy designed to limit size, curb incipient tendencies, or to check the evolution of industry, can only result in seriously retarding economic progress. Moreover, such policies, as we have seen, render it impossible to establish definite or meaningful rules of the game or to set standards which business can follow.

The Commission should be obliged by Congress to draw up a general statement as to the types of practice that are regarded as monopolistic or collusive as of a given time. To keep abreast of industrial developments, such rules should of course be subject to periodic revision. This suggestion implies that no government agency should be empowered to punish business enterprises for practices or methods of organization which are not covered by the existing definitions or rules. Only thus can the uncertainties produced by present policies be removed. Under such a procedure, monopolistic practices can be prevented without the usurpation by government of essential managerial functions.

If the function of government is confined to the elimination of monopoly and the punishment of actual collusive efforts to restrict or destroy competition, the creative power of private enterprise which has been responsible for the extraordinary industrial achievements of modern times can be preserved. Such a method of *regulation*, in contrast to communism, socialism, and hybrid systems of *control*, would ensure the preservation of individual liberties.

The foregoing discussion has related solely to the control and regulation of the production and distribution of goods and services. Government activities of course affect economic life in numerous other ways. Reference may be made to the work of such bureaus as Agricultural Economics, Reclamation, and Standards, and to a wide range of insurance and welfare activities relating to bank deposits, agricultural crops, social security, etc. Such governmental functions are not, however, germane to the theme of this chapter.

CHAPTER VII

THE POTENTIALS OF THE NEXT CENTURY

In the light of present knowledge what may one say with respect to the economic potentials of the next hundred years? Concretely, have the limitations of nature been permanently overcome—with the law of diminishing returns abolished, so to speak? Stating the matter another way, are the resources of nature as a whole adequate to permit a growth of population and rising standards of living in the century ahead comparable to what occurred in the century which is past? Or must we in the not distant future expect a declining rate of economic growth?

It should be noted here that, notwithstanding the achievements of the past century, many observers still view the future with no little concern—quite apart from organizational complications arising out of social and political developments. It is suggested that the technological revolution of the last 50 years will inevitably soon reach its limits. Has not the intensive exploitation of natural resources during the industrial age, accentuated by the devouring requirements of world conflicts, already served to undermine our economic foundations? In short, will not the law of diminishing returns—temporarily obscured—soon reassert its controlling influence?

In order to give concreteness to the analysis of this chapter, we shall pose the problem in the following terms: So far as natural resources and productive capacity are concerned, might the United States a century hence support a population double that of the present day on a plane of living eight times as high as that now prevailing? The reader will bear in mind that we are here concerned only with economic *potentials*, as governed by resources and productive power.[1] The world situation will be reviewed briefly in Chapter XI.

I. THE PRIMARY COMPONENTS OF LIVING STANDARDS

The production requirements for a rising plane of living may best be gauged by analysis of the principal classes of commodities and services for which the public spends its money. The expenditures of the American people in 1946 for the principal groups of consumer goods and services are shown in the following table:[2]

	Billions	*Per Cent*
Food and nutrition	$55	37
Shelter and home maintenance	31	20
Attire and personal care	24	16
Education and health	12½	8
Recreation and travel	21½	14
Miscellaneous	7	5
Total	$151	100

The allocation of expenditures changes materially as income rises.

Budgetary studies reveal that the great bulk of expenditures in the lower-income ranges goes for food, housing, and clothing. Through the middle- and higher-income brackets, the percentage spent for the basic necessities of life falls, while the proportion going for so-called conventional necessities and luxuries rises. Aggregate expenditures for food and nutrition increase at the successive higher levels, but the *proportion* spent for foodstuffs decreases progressively. Outlays for shelter and home maintenance increase more or less in proportion with incomes, while other types of expenditures rise much more than proportionally.[3]

Thus on the basis of actual experience, it is possible to indicate, roughly, what the volume of expenditures for major classes of goods and services would be if the population were doubled and the plane of living were eight times as high. We shall assume a distribution of income similar to the present.[4] Under these conditions expenditures in the various categories would be multiplied as follows:

Food and nutrition—about eight times
Shelter and home maintenance—about sixteen times
Attire and personal care—about twenty times
Health and education—about thirty times
Recreation and travel—about thirty-three times
Miscellaneous[5]

The problem with which we are first concerned is the extent to which such an increase in population and rise in the plane of living would entail drafts upon productive resources. Would the natural endowment of the United States permit so vast an increase in production as would be involved? We shall begin with a consideration of food potentials.

II. FOOD AND NUTRITION

A population of 300 million people in the United States, with living standards eight times as high as at present, would, as indicated above, multiply expenditures for food and nutrition something like eight times. But this would not mean a proportional increase in the *quantity* of food required. As incomes rise, the *dollar* expenditures on foodstuffs increase rapidly, but there is no corresponding increase in the physical quantity of food consumed. Even with allowance for the undernourishment found among certain groups at present, it appears doubtful that the actual *pounds* of food consumed per capita would be greatly increased.

The larger dollar outlays reflect chiefly the influence of two factors—a selection of better quality and more diversified food products, and higher processing and servicing costs. While the higher costs between farmer and consumer would of course have no bearing upon the quantity of food required, the changes in the character of consumption would have important repercussions upon agricultural production.

A great rise in the level of incomes would doubtless mean not only emphasis upon quality products but also a better selection of foods from the standpoint of nutrition requirements. Involved in this process would be a smaller consumption of starches and a greater consumption of proteins and foods containing essential minerals and vitamins, with corresponding shifts from grain and potatoes to animal products, fruits, and vegetables. The net effect of these shifts on the acreage required to furnish the essential food values cannot be determined with precision. The result would vary widely with different products. A complication is found in the fact that a substantially greater acreage is required to produce a given volume of meat or milk for human consumption than to produce a corresponding volume of grain—because the animals must have the usual roughage and also be fed grain.

Our analysis, based on family budget experience at different income levels, indicates that to support a population a century hence double that of the present, on a plane of living eight times as high, would, in over-all terms, impose a draft upon our food producing resources less than three times that of the present. The situation would vary widely, however, with respect to particular kinds of food.[6]

What are the possibilities of tripling the national food supply? An expansion of food production may be obtained: (1) from the opening of additional productive areas; and (2) from increased yields per acre under cultivation. Great possibilities, as we shall see, are to be found in both directions.

Large, highly productive areas remain to be brought under cultivation.

Because of the disappearance of the unsettled frontier in the United States, the expansion of productive land area can henceforth be obtained in the main only by bringing under cultivation fertile land which has hitherto been unavailable. The principal methods are the reclamation of swamp and other low-lying land and the irrigation of dry regions. Since 1900 large areas have been made available for cultivation by such enterprises. Irrigation alone has added 13 million acres, which is roughly equal to the tillable area of the state of Wisconsin. We have made little more than a beginning in the control of floods and preservation of river bottom lands, or in the drainage of swamp areas. In the future modern technology can doubtless bring under cultivation, at costs that are not prohibitive, vast desert areas of high fertility. Preliminary experiments conducted by French engineers in the Sahara have yielded astonishing results. The possibilities may, however, be restricted by an available water supply.

The ocean contains limitless food possibilities. As the respository of the sediment washed from continental areas by innumerable rivers, the ocean of course has a soil of incomparable fertility as well as an abundance of vegetable and animal life. In the light of recent developments in undersea operations, it would seem that the abundant food-producing resources of the ocean might well be tapped in the future. This might involve not merely the extraction of animal, vegetable, and mineral matter, but also the use of the ocean's bed for the production of certain kinds of agricultural crops.

Soil erosion, an age-old problem, is now subject to control.

On the other side of the land-resource picture is the fact that the rich virgin soils of the United States, as well as those of most other countries, have been severely depleted by washing and leaching. Our streams and rivers, once clear and blue, are now dark and murky with the soil from barren hillsides, and productive plains as well.

Fortunately, the ultimate menace was foreseen and remedial measures inaugurated before it was too late. The comprehensive soil conservation program of the federal government is based chiefly on three simple principles: (1) expansion of grass and tree culture; (2) longer rotation periods for cultivated crops; and (3) contour and strip farming. While the movement is still at an early stage, it may now safely be said that proper methods of prevention and restoration are known, that essential co-operation of farmers is increasing, and that the problem of soil erosion is now definitely on the way to solution. A factor working strongly with the conservation movement will be the progressive increase in meat consumption and the accompanying growth of the livestock industry, which necessitates an expansion of grass culture and at the same time provides essential fertilization.

Scientific agriculture can enormously increase yields per acre.

As was pointed out in Chapter I, the mechanical revolution of the nineteenth century greatly reduced the cost per unit of agricultural products, but did not appreciably affect the yield per acre. Scientific agriculture, directed toward increasing yields and improving the utilization of food products, belongs to the twentieth century, particularly to the period since World War I. As already indicated, much progress has been made in recent years by means of humus accumulation, balanced fertilization, improved methods of tillage, better control of plant and animal pests and diseases, and the development of superior plants and livestock through selective breeding and hybridization.

As yet, however, a mere beginning has been made in realizing the potentials along these lines. Even though commercial fertilizers are relatively inexpensive and the results obvious, their use, especially in the proper mixture, is still comparatively limited. Particularly great are the possibilities of nitrogen compounds. In the words of a prominent chemist, who is also a practical farmer, the high pressure synthesis of ammonia from nitrogen if applied consistently to the soil in the form of cheap fertilizers would prove comparable in terms of increased output "to the discovery of a sixth continent."[7] Equally important with commercial fertilizers is the development of abundant organic material—in the interest both of soil structure and the absorption of moisture.

Until recently little attention had been given even in scientific circles to the importance of minor mineral substances in the soil. Many soils are basically deficient in some of these "trace elements," and all may become deficient through continuous heavy cropping. In consequence, both the yield and the nutritive quality of the produce may be low. An illustration of what may be accomplished is afforded by the remarkable results that have been obtained from the use of small quantities of boron in alfalfa culture. Among other important trace elements, cobalt, copper, magnesium, and calcium may be mentioned.

Only a small fraction of the farm population as yet makes any considerable use of the scientific knowledge now available. The dramatic success of hybrid corn has led to a rapid abandonment of the open pollinated varieties. But, on the other hand, the introduction of improved types of other plants and animals and the adoption of modern methods have been slow. This is due to a combination of factors: ignorance and ingrained conservatism; lack of capital and fear of losses; and sheer inertia and satisfaction with things as they are. The latter characteristic is aptly illustrated by the case of farmer Jones, who explained that he saw no point in attending a free course of lectures at the agricultural college when he wasn't using all he knew now. The traditional attitude of country people toward book learning is, however, rapidly changing as the demonstrated advantages of newer methods are brought to their attention through the activities of numerous types of agricultural agencies.

If the scientific knowledge *now* available were universally applied, present yields per acre could be increased at least 50 per cent. The best-operated farms commonly produce two or three times as much per acre as the representative farm. A few illustrations will serve to reveal possibilities:

The average production of butter fat for "reporting herds" (which are above the average) is about 185 pounds per cow annually. However, many individual herds run from 400 to 500 pounds. While some added feed is involved, the primary explanation of the increase is better balanced diets and herds of higher average quality.[8]

Farm pasture fields have traditionally been left to take care of themselves. The result is a low and declining production of grass of inferior quality. It has been demonstrated that the application of fertilizer will readily increase the livestock supporting capacity several fold. At a cost of a few dollars an acre the acreage is, in effect, greatly expanded. On the average farm, pasture lands have been the most neglected areas; and they offer perhaps the greatest possibility of increasing returns.

The cheapest feed is young and succulent vegetation. The problem, therefore, is to increase the number of months per year that such pasture is available. This requires the use of winter grains for late fall and early spring pasturage, and supplementary grasses and legumes for the hot summer months—sweet clover, Sudan grass, lespedeza, soybeans, etc. Such practices not only increase the total farm yield for the year, but also greatly improve the quality of the feed.

The elimination of waste in both production and processing is also of great importance.

Waste in production may be illustrated by reference to the curing and handling of hay. The basic requirement is to use the hay in as green a form as possible. While some compromise has to be made between obtaining maximum yield and maximum quality, it is essential that hay be cut well before the full-bloom stage, for two reasons: to retain the maximum of carotene, which supplies vitamin A; and to prevent the shattering of the leaves, which contain the principal food elements. Traditionally, the best values in hay have been lost by late-cutting, over-curing, and improper handling and storing.

Another type of waste is found in the lowly corncob. Recent experiments have shown that the food value in the cob of an ear of corn is equal to roughly one eighth that of the corn itself. When they are ground together, the wasted cob is consumed, and the value of the cattle feed is materially increased.

Great improvements are, moreover, occurring in the processing and marketing of foodstuffs whereby waste is reduced and food value increased. Mention may be made of dehydration, quick freezing, improved preserving and cooking methods, the use of refrigerated cars, and expedited transportation service by rail, highway, and air. New developments in electronics and ultrasonics suggest still greater improvements in the near future in food selection, processing, and marketing.[9] Storage facilities, at all stages in the distributing process, are also constantly being improved.

Numerous new discoveries of far-reaching importance have recently appeared on the horizon.

A late development of engaging promise is the artificial precipitation of rainfall. This is accomplished by dropping dry ice, or water, into clouds. The cost is low, but as yet control is highly uncertain. Among the discoveries since World War II, in the field of disease and pest control, are: *dithane*, to prevent a fungus disease of potato plants commonly called "late blight"; *benzene hexachloride*, to eradicate wire worm, a beetle larva that eats into potatoes and increases storage rot; D.D.T., which is already widely used in the elimination of orchard insects, flies, beetles, etc.; chemical preparations which kill weeds; *streptomycin*, derived from soil, and believed to be effective against such diseases as tularemia, typhoid, tuberculosis, and possibly contagious abortion.

The question may be raised at this point whether new pests and diseases do not appear at least as fast as old ones are eradicated. Does not the application of drugs and poisons render both plants and animals more vulnerable to other diseases? The answer, in historical perspective, is certainly in the negative. Science has brought, and, it seems highly probable, will continue to bring, net gains to mankind in its struggle with nature.

Other recent developments pertain to the utilization of waste agricultural materials. Demonstrations have been made of the practicability of using certain waste materials for fish food, making possible large-scale fish farming operations, the fish being used as protein feed for livestock. Fermentable farm wastes are now readily converted through certain bacteria and yeasts into food products high in proteins, fats, and vitamins. Conversion of waste materials from farm and forest into animal food possesses great potentialities.[10] It was the view of the unique genius, George Washington Carver, that plant chemistry is still in its infancy.

Abundant new food resources for the future may be provided by synthetic processes and radioactivity. Chemists are working on the production of artificial protein fibers—possibly from nonagricultural raw materials. Experimentation has already demonstrated some of the possibilities of developing synthetic meats and other foods from such fibers. While the cost is of course still high, once a substantial volume of output is obtained, the cost of production—if we may judge from the history of chemical manufacture—will be rapidly reduced.

There has also been much research in recent years into the processes of nature in the production of starches and sugars. This involves the direct action of sunlight, in conjunction with air and moisture, on the green coloring matter in plants—a process known as photosynthesis. The duplication of this process in the laboratory has not as yet been demonstrated as a possibility. However, if this process should eventually prove commercially feasible, limitless quantities of certain important foods would be produced without the use of soil.

The release of atomic energy is also leading to extensive experimentation in the field of plant nutrition and growth. Radioactive isotopes, or tagged atoms, provide the plant scientist with means of measuring the response of plants to fertilizer applications under varying conditions and also of tracing the course of the elements in soil solutions through plant tissues. Thus new knowledge of the process by which plants convert the sun's energy into life energy may be acquired. It is expected that atomic energy may also aid in the control of insect and plant diseases.

In summary, when one takes account of the possibility of increasing food producing areas, of expanding yields, of eliminating waste, and of soilless food production, it would seem that aggregate food production in the United States might readily be tripled during the course of the next century. The expansion required would vary widely with respect to the various types of farm products. In the case of wheat our present acreage and yields would be adequate—assuming no exports. The greatest required expansion would be in fruits and vegetables, and corn. The former could easily be achieved. Corn might, however, present some difficulty; but even here the problem could doubtless be solved by making greater use of substitutes.

In considering the potentialities of expanding agricultural production in the various ways here briefly sketched, one is prone to be skeptical when reflecting on retarding influences and the slowness with which increases in yields have thus far been obtained. But, when one thinks in terms of a hundred years, the possibilities appear very great. Scientific discovery appears to proceed at an accelerating tempo; it is only the application which lags. However, the agricultural colleges and experiment stations have been training ever-increasing numbers of future farmers imbued with the scientific outlook and acquainted with the new agricultural technology. Moreover, by means of agricultural bulletins, traveling exhibitions, farm demonstrations, the services of county agents, "farm-home weeks," special training courses, 4-H Clubs, and motion picture exhibits, even the rank and file of the farm population is steadily advancing in knowledge and in desire to adopt improved methods. When one contemplates the progress made in the last 25 years, the prospect for the next century can hardly be overestimated.

This vast expansion in food production would not involve diminishing returns.

The methods of increasing agricultural yields outlined above imply increasing returns rather than the reverse. That is, the increased yields are not obtained by applying disproportionate amounts of labor and capital. Even where yields are not being increased, the use of power machinery serves to lessen the labor and the money cost of production. This, as shown in Chapter I, was a factor of primary importance in the last century. A considerable percentage of American farms are still using obsolete types of machinery and power, of the vintage of 1900. Since World War II new types of machinery comparable in importance from the standpoint of cost reduction to the tractor and the combine have been perfected—such as corn pickers, silage conveyors, one-man hay balers, manure loaders, and airplane sprayers.

Since new machinery and new methods are introduced in order to eliminate labor and reduce units costs, the process involves increasing not diminishing returns. It is highly probable that continuing technological progress in agriculture during the course of the next century would permit a tripling of food production without any appreciable increase in the total population engaged in agriculture.

III. SHELTER AND HOME MAINTENANCE

The second most important element in consumer satisfaction is the provision of housing facilities and the furnishing and upkeep of homes. In 1946 this category accounted for over 20 per cent of aggregate consumer expenditures. The outlays, by principal classes, were as follows:[11]

	Billions
Dwelling facilities, owned and rented (gross rental values)	$12.7
Household operation (fuel, public utilities, domestic service)	8.0
Furnishings and equipment	10.0

As the plane of living rises, the increase in outlays for such purposes is much greater than for foodstuffs (see page 205 above). As with food and nutrition, however, the increase in expenditures would not mean a proportional increase in the quantity of materials used in the construction of homes and the equipment and maintenance of households. Here again as income rises, the larger dollar outlays reflect in part a selection of better qualities of materials, especially in furnishings, but also a much greater outlay for services, which bear little relation to the using up of materials. Without pretending to any precision, we may assume that multiplying expenditures for shelter and home maintenance by *sixteen* might mean, in quantity terms, multiplying the use of materials by perhaps something like *eight*.

Residential construction materials are altogether adequate.

Materials for construction of residential buildings are of many kinds, of which the most important are wood, brick and tile, cement, stone, cinders, glass, aluminum, and steel. In the case of stone, brick, glass, cement, and cinders, the raw materials are virtually unlimited. Even in the case of wood, systematic reforestation on an extensive scale can furnish abundant supplies perpetually. In addition to these materials, plastics and other synthetic products, already extensively used, may well come to play a role of major importance. The only real problem here relates to steel and other metals. Since these materials are not of primary importance in residential construction, they may more appropriately be considered in relation to other needs. In any case, it is apparent that so far as basic construction materials for houses, as distinguished from industrial structures, are concerned, a vast expansion is readily possible.

Residential construction is subject in a striking way to the law of diminishing costs. The production of building materials, both in the raw and fabricated stages, lends itself to the application of machine and mass production methods. In recent years, moreover, it has been demonstrated that phenomenal reductions in cost can be achieved in the actual construction of buildings. In this field, however, traditional conceptions and methods, together with restrictions imposed by labor organizations, seriously impede the process of cost reduction. As compared with the automobile industry the residential building trades remain in a primitive stage.

The principal items of material in household *operation* are fuel and light. The adequacy of fuel and energy resources in general will be discussed in Section VIII below.

The category—household furnishings and equipment—includes a wide range of items such as furniture, floor coverings, draperies, bedding, pictures, tableware, cleaning utensils, kitchen and bathroom installations, and refrigerators. The supply of such raw materials as glass and wood has already been discussed. Textile materials will be considered in the next section and metals in Section VII. Mention should be made here, however, of synthetic substitutes in the field of household equipment.

Hundreds of synthetic substitutes for fibers, wood, and metals are now being produced. They are moulded by heat and pressure into rods, sheets, sections, and contours of any desired shape or thickness. Moreover, by applying waterproof plastics to thin layers of cloth, paper, or plywood and thus bonding them, materials of great strength, toughness, and resistance are produced. Synthetic materials are already being made that will not split, warp, shrink, or expand, that have a dependable strength and uniformity of structure, that are flexible and yet crack-proof, and that are resistant to acids and are fire-proof, rust-proof, and termite-proof.

A very great expansion in the supply of materials required for shelter and home maintenance was suggested on page 205 above. It seems clear that there is no danger of running short of the necessary raw materials or of encountering increasing unit costs. Certain types of materials are virtually unlimited, and better and cheaper synthetics for use in home construction and household equipment are constantly being created. We seem to be at the mere beginning of such developments.

IV. ATTIRE AND PERSONAL CARE

Scarely less important than shelter and home maintenance in the family budget are the outlays for attire, adornment, and personal care. These items aggregated 24 billions in 1946, or 16 per cent of total family expenditures. The most important articles are clothing and footwear (18 billions), jewelry and time pieces (1.4 billions), and toilet articles (1.2 billions). In attire and personal care the service element becomes important (2.3 billions). This includes cleaning, repairing, storage, and services of barber shops, beauty parlors, baths, etc.

The projected increase in expenditures for attire and personal care was something like twentyfold. Here again, the *quantity* of materials required would not increase proportionately. For example, a dress costing $100 might use no more materials than one costing $20. The higher price is primarily attributable to more expensive design, display, and marketing. There would, however, be a great increase in the number of dresses, suits, shoes, etc. in the wardrobe of the average person. Changes in style, of course, also affect the quantity of materials used. Having in mind a doubling of the population and the increased number of articles of clothing purchased by each person, it would seem that something like six to ten times the quantity of materials might be required.

The supply of materials for attire and adornment is virtually inexhaustible.

For clothing and footwear man has in the past relied primarily upon natural textile fibers such as cotton, wool, silk, and leather from animal hides. The supply of such materials in the future will depend upon the productivity of our agricultural resources. In general their availability will be governed by the same factors that were discussed in connection with food: better methods of cultivation, more effective fertilization, selection of superior seeds, improved storage and processing methods, etc.

The supply of leather goods and fabrics may, however, be enormously expanded through synthetic processes. Many varieties of artificial leather have already been produced, having been stimulated by the great demand for automobile upholstering. The manufacture of synthetic fabrics is now well established, with rayon and nylon conspicuous examples.

Synthetic fibers involve the use of four principal elements—oxygen, hydrogen, nitrogen, and carbon. These are derived from water, air, and coal—which occur virtually without limit in nature. As time goes on, the carbon (which we get from coal) might also perhaps be secured from the carbon dioxide constantly being exhaled by all forms of animals. Synthetic fibers using other base materials are constantly appearing. Some employ rubber, some casein, some glass, and some agricultural waste materials or litter, such as corn cobs and husks, bean pods, and peanut shucks.

The ultimate sources of the raw materials upon which clothing and other articles of apparel depend are thus practically inexhaustible. Moreover, in the light of the rapid advances being made in agricultural and industrial chemistry, there is every reason to believe that the unit cost of such materials will continue to decline.

V. EDUCATION AND HEALTH

Expenditures for education and health represent both public and private outlays. That is to say, these services are in part paid for directly by the beneficiaries and in part indirectly out of public treasuries. In the case of education, public expenditures now represent something like 80 per cent of total outlays. With medical care, however, government expenditures account for less than 20 per cent of the total, though the proportion is steadily rising. From the standpoint of the amount of materials and supplies required, it is of course immaterial whether the expeditures are made by individuals directly or from taxes paid to the government.

In these fields the draft on material resources would not be heavy.

The table on page 205 above indicated that if the population were doubled and the plane of living octupled, expenditures for health and education would expand something like thirtyfold. It should be observed, however, that a large part of this increase would be for services which involve a relatively small use of physical materials. These include the services rendered by doctors, nurses, teachers, and administrators. Leaving out of account buildings and equipment (which are considered in Section VII), only about 25 per cent of present expenditures on health and education go for the purchase of materials. Moreover, as the standard of living rises, the percentage will decline. Thus a doubling of the population and a thirtyfold over-all increase in expenditures for education and health would mean something like a five or sixfold increase in drafts upon material resources.

The materials consumed in the field of education and health include chiefly textbooks and other school supplies, ophthalmic and orthopedic appliances, medicines, bandages, funeral and burial supplies, etc. The supplies of materials available for medicinal purposes are in general abundant—though there are a few exceptions. However, where natural materials are scarce, or natural drugs unsatisfactory, synthetic processes are being increasingly used to supply substitutes. Light-weight synthetic materials are proving serviceable for orthopedic and ophthalmic appliances. School supplies depend largely upon wood-pulp; and a recently developed chemical process, whereby paper is made from quick growing southern pine, has made it possible to increase the supply of this product almost indefinitely. Thus it seems clear that no difficulties would be encountered with respect to the resources available for the suggested expansion in the field of health and education.

VI. RECREATION AND TRAVEL

The largest projected rate of increase in consumer outlays is in the broad field of recreation and travel. These expenditures take two principal forms: *charges* in the form of admission fees, fares, etc. for recreation and travel facilities; and *purchases* of tangible commodities such as musical instruments, books, and automobiles. The expenditures for services rendered aggregated about 10 billions in 1946 out of a total of 21.5 billions of private and public expenditures for recreation and travel as a whole.[12]

Outlays for recreation and travel make heavy drafts upon mineral resources.

There are a few exceptions to the generalization just made. Admission fees go in large part to cover salaries of artists and directing personnel, and hence impose no direct draft on material resources. With parks and playgrounds the land area requirement is insignificant, and much of the land so employed has no other important use. Expenditures in connection with organized outdoor games run into large figures, but the amount of physical materials used is relatively small. The same is true with respect to such activities as fishing, boating, hunting, hiking, and skiing. However, the bulk of the outlays for the use of transportation facilities goes to cover the costs of metal and fuel resources used in railroad trains, street cars, buses, taxicabs, and airplanes.

As much as one third of the total expenditures included in this general category in 1946 went for private automobile transportation. As incomes expand, the percentage spent on automobiles may be expected to show a strong relative increase. Such expenditures constitute direct outlays for steel, rubber, and other materials used in the construction and maintenance of cars, and for gasoline and oil required for their operation. The railroads, highways, buildings, and other physical structures involved in the provision of all types of recreational facilities would likewise impose direct drafts upon underlying mineral resources. The adequacy of our metal and mineral supplies and fuel and energy resources will be considered in Sections VII and VIII below. The other materials involved are considered here.

In recent years, many automobile accessories formerly made of natural materials are being replaced by synthetic products. How far this process of substitution can be carried will depend largely upon relative cost trends, which will doubtless progressively favor the substitute materials. Under the impetus of war necessity, large quantities of synthetic rubber tires were produced in this and other countries. While not yet as satisfactory as those made from natural rubber, it is contended by some that in time they may be superior—"non-skid, puncture-proof, and good for 100,000 miles."[13]

The materials used in books, magazines, newspapers, sheet music, musical instruments, boats, plants and flowers, etc., present a less difficult problem. Newsprint, as already indicated, can be indefinitely expanded.[14] Pleasure boats are already being built of waterproof synthetic materials that will not warp, scratch, or splinter, the compound curves of which are prefabricated in convenient sections. The costs here are still high, but should gradually decline as synthetic processes are improved. Plastic materials are also now being used extensively in connection with musical instruments, and with improved results. Musical instruments over the centuries had been severely circumscribed in form and tonal combinations as a result of limitations imposed by the use of natural substances alone. Freed from such limitations by synthetic materials, the music of the future can be adapted more readily and completely to satisfying recreational and aesthetic desires.[15] Developments in radio, television, and other electronic instruments are also contributing to the fuller satisfaction of such desires.

VII. METAL AND MINERAL RESOURCES

Discussion of the underlying metal and mineral requirements for so vast an expansion of production as that under contemplation was postponed in earlier sections in order that the entire problem might be considered in one place. Fabricated metals are required in a large way in the production of certain types of consumer goods, such as automobiles, houses, and household appliances. The greatest use of these metals, however, is in capital goods, such as industrial plants, commercial structures, industrial and agricultural machinery, and transportation and public utility equipment. These metal products require the use of iron, lead, copper, zinc, and magnesium ores, and a wide range of lesser metallic minerals. Nonmetallic minerals such as sulphur and phosphorus are also extensively used by industry. Would the underlying mineral resources, or substitutes therefor, be adequate to meet the indicated requirements?

Numerous minerals are found in great abundance in the United States. Among these are molybdenum, magnesium, calcium, sodium, potassium, sulphur, and phosphorus. The unique deposit of molybdenum in Colorado will last hundreds of years. Magnesium is now commercially available from sea water—an inexhaustible resource. Calcium, sodium, and potassium salts are found, in seemingly limitless quantity, in beds deposited by the sea. Sulphur is closely associated with such sedimentary deposits and seems plentiful enough for all probable needs. Huge quarries of phosphate rock likewise appear ample to meet both industrial and agricultural requirements for phosphorus.

Present deficiencies in certain important minerals can be surmounted.

In the case of a number of important minerals, the United States is substantially dependent upon foreign sources of supply. Among these are nickel and tin, used in alloys and in electroplating; manganese, indispensable in deoxidizing, desulphurizing, and recarbonizing steel; cobalt, essential in the manufacture of high heat—and corrosion-resisting steels and other alloys; and asbestos, used for heat-resistant purposes in many products.

Such important metals as copper, lead, and zinc may

be placed in an intermediate category. The United States once seemed adequately supplied with these minerals, but two world wars exacted a heavy toll. Accordingly, in recent years we have been partly dependent on foreign sources of supply.

Looking forward, several means of overcoming present deficiencies should be borne in mind:

First, *systematic exploration* will still undoubtedly disclose important new sources of supplies within the United States. This is the view of the Geological Survey and the Bureau of Mines, which point out that only a small part of the ore-bearing regions has thus far been thoroughly explored.

Second, *imports* from other countries may continue to meet our needs. Fortunately, adjacent Canada is one of the world's richest ore-producing regions and is even now the greatest metal-exporting country in the world, ranking first in the production of nickel and platinum, second in uranium and asbestos, third in cobalt, copper, mercury, silver, and zinc, and fourth in lead. The far north of this continent, including Labrador and Alaska as well as Northern Canada, appear, on the basis of preliminary surveys, rich in promise with respect to such metals as iron, tin, tungsten, lead, chromium, mercury,[16] and titanium. New mineral discoveries are also being made in South America.

Third, *technology* in laboratories and pilot plants is constantly developing methods for producing manganese, chromium, titanium, and other metals from low-grade domestic ores. Moreover, scientific advances are making possible the ready substitution of one metal for another, as aluminum for copper and steel, and manganese for nickel, and the development of new alloys, such as titanium with aluminum, magnesium, and iron.

Fourth, *chemical discoveries* make possible the substitution of synthetic materials for natural mineral substances. It has been demonstrated that most of these synthetic products are as satisfactory as natural minerals, while in some cases they are distinctly superior.

We do not wish to suggest that no difficulties will ever arise with respect to one or more of the mineral products here under discussion. There is, however, good reason for believing that the combined results of systematic exploration, technological progress in the mining and use of materials, and chemical advances, can furnish a vast expansion in the supply of these materials, without increasing unit costs.

The crucial problem is the adequacy of iron and steel resources.

Modern industrialism has been built primarily on foundations of iron and steel. The chief mineral involved is iron ore, though coke and limestone are also important. Since the supply of limestone is abundant it requires no special consideration here. The United States has been self-sufficient with respect to iron ore and coke. However, because of the enormous consumption in recent decades, and especially since 1940, much concern has been expressed over the possibility that existing reserves might be nearing exhaustion.

To the end of 1943 as much as 2,125 million tons of high-grade ore—containing as much as 50 per cent iron—had been mined in the United States, chiefly in the Mesabi range of the Lake Superior region. The remaining "measured and indicated" reserves of such ore are estimated at 1,626 million tons. Meanwhile, the production of medium-grade ores—25 to 35 per cent iron—had amounted to 488 million tons, and the remaining reserves of this quality ore are estimated at 2,097 millions. These combined reserves of measured and indicated ore would last for about forty years at wartime rates of production.[17]

The Lake Superior ranges also extend into Canada, and substantial reserves of nearby ore are thus available to the United States on an import basis. More important has been the recent discovery of iron ore in the Labrador region, which is believed to rival that of the Lake Superior area both in quantity and in quality. Here, transportation costs will present a real problem.

We are not, however, dependent upon ores that are very rich in iron content. As already indicated, considerable quantities of ores containing from 25 to 35 per cent iron have already been mined. In the Lake Superior region alone there are stupendous deposits of lower-grade ores which have not as yet been drawn upon. Such ores, called taconite, would last at current rates of consumption something like 600 years.[18]

Taconite requires a different processing from high-grade ore, and new plants will be required for crushing and agglomerating operations. Although such preparation of the ore would add somewhat to the cost, it is contended by some that this would be offset largely if not wholly by economies in subsequent stages, flowing from the fact that the concentration is in purer form.[19]

Since the extraction of iron involves an extensive use of coke, consideration must be given to the potential supply of coking coal. So long as the supply of high-grade coking coal was abundant, no attention was given to the possibility of utilizing substitutes. It was not until the excessive demands of World War II arose that experimentation was begun in the use of lower-grade coals for coking purposes. Metallurgical coke is now to some extent being made from non-coking coals and from mixtures of coal tar and petroleum pitch. Economies are being obtained by blending low-volatile with high-volatile coals to produce an improved type of coke. It is believed that "increased application of processes now in use, such as washing, blending, and separation of non-coking fractions, could render at least 10 per cent of the non-bituminous reserves suitable for conversion to metallurgical coke."[20]

Of greater potential importance is the possibility of using other materials than coke in the extraction of iron. A high-hydrogen gas derived from lignite has already been employed in the direct reduction of iron ore without the use of coke. It has been demonstrated that so-called sponge iron—much purer than pig iron—can be made from low-grade ore without coking fuel.[21] Here, as in other fields, necessity may be expected to be the mother of invention, and its seems highly probable that as the need arises, some new process will be discovered for the separation of iron from its oxides on an economical basis without coke.

Other materials may be extensively used as substitutes for iron and steel.

Cement, glass, and other earth materials, as previously noted, are widely employed in the construction industry. Of 57.5 million tons of materials used in this industry in 1946, as much as 45 million tons were of cement, brick, and building blocks, as against only 6 million tons of steel. Synthetic materials can also be substituted for steel, especially in household equipment. It is reported, moreover, that synthetic materials may soon be made of such strength that they can displace structural steel.

Other metals, when combined with iron, produce alloys which greatly economize the use of the heavier metal. New alloying processes provide a tensile strength much greater than that of ordinary structural steel. It is significant that the larger part of the current expansion in steel-producing capacity has been in the field of alloy steels. Another new factor is the development of electronic testing devices which make it possible to meet strength requirements while using but a fraction of the structural steel formerly thought necessary.[22]

Aluminum and magnesium have become very important substitutes for iron and steel in a wide range of uses. In the last few decades difficulties formerly encountered in the production of these light metals have been overcome, and in consequence output has been enormously expanded and unit costs very greatly reduced.

Prior to 1920 the cost of magnesium was prohibitive, but as a result of subsequent technological developments, especially during the Second World War, a very great future for this metal now seems assured. Magnesium, the supply of which is virtually unlimited, can be used for many purposes as a substitute for aluminum.

Aluminum until recently was produced chiefly from high-grade bauxite. Thirty years ago it was assumed that aluminum could not be made from bauxite containing more than 2.5 per cent silica. But by 1940 new processes had made it possible to use bauxite containing 7 per cent silica, and further developments during the war extended the limits to as much as 15 per cent. It is thus now possible to extract, and at no increase of cost, alumina from bauxite which was formerly regarded as of no value. These developments have served to multiply 100-fold the world's supply of available bauxite.

The United States possesses limited quantities of bauxite, and imports large amounts from Canada, Trinidad, and the Guianas. Other potential sources of importation in the Western Hemisphere are Haiti and Jamaica, the reserves of which are larger than those of the United States, and Brazil, which has very extensive deposits.

We are not, however, dependent for aluminum upon bauxite. Recent experimentation has made it possible to obtain aluminum from bauxitic and high-alumina clays. This country possesses enormous quantities of such aluminiferous materials.[23] While the processing of such materials is still in the experimental stages, it is believed by experts in this field that when and as needed they can be utilized on an economical basis.

Titanium is another metal of great potential importance. Though the chemical element has long been known, it is only recently that methods have been developed for extracting the metal from sands and rock in usable amounts. Its commercial feasibility seems assured as soon as production can be undertaken on a volume basis. It is said to combine in an extraordinary way the qualities of strength, lightness, and resistance to rust and heat. It is found in such widely scattered areas as Florida, Virginia, Arkansas, Wyoming, Oregon, and Quebec in North America, and in Norway, Russia, China, and India. In 1948 extensive deposits were found in northern Canada. In terms of quantity titanium ranks behind only aluminum, iron, and magnesium.

In concluding this discussion of metal and mineral resources one general observation remains to be made. It is possible that so great an expansion in the use of mineral resources as is here under contemplation might in some cases increase costs at the raw-material stage. As an offset to this possibility, however, it should be noted that very great production economies are possible in the processing and manufacturing stages. Thus even though the extraction of minerals might, here and there, involve rising costs, there would still be reason for believing that the cost of finished products might be universally reduced.

Under modern capitalism, do not physical capital requirements increase relatively to output?

In this section of the analysis we have been concerned, primarily, with capital goods—the production instruments which make possible a rising plane of living. In the language of economists, capitalism grows constantly more complex; we make machines to make machines, to make still other machines in the ever-increasing roundaboutness of the processes of production. Would it not appear, therefore, that so enormous a rise in the level of production as is here under contemplation would impose a more than proportional draft upon our physical resources?

The answer to this question is clearly in the negative. An increase in the number of *stages* in the processes of production does not necessitate a greater quantity of capital equipment to produce a given final product. Indeed, this specialization process owed its origin to the production economies it made possible.

While the spread of mechanization naturally means

using increasing quantities of capital, the essence of technological progress is found in the improving quality, or efficiency, of the added units of capital. The increase in output is progressively greater than the increase in the physical quantity of capital employed.[24] Moreover, the increase in output may be greater than the increase in capital as measured in dollar values. First, a new machine, costing no more may, because of improved design, be more efficient than the one it replaces. Second, the more efficient machine may actually cost less because its construction requires less material. Third, it may cost less simply because of technological progress in its production. Between 1923 and 1937, a very great increase in man-hour output in American manufacturing industry occurred without any increase in aggregate dollar investment.[25]

It should be noted, also, that the physical quantity of metals required commonly does not increase in proportion to the expanding size of industrial plants. A plant covering four acres does not require in walls and superstructure four times as much iron and steel as a plant covering one acre. Moreover, the efficiency of equipment, as already noted, is not merely a function of size: the horespower of a generator or engine is not directly proportional to the pounds of metal employed.

Finally, it should be remembered that increasing manhour output flows from improvements in organization as well as from increases and improvements in capital equipment. Mass production methods, better technical layout, scientific management, improved industrial relations—all may contribute to the final goal of greater output per unit of physical capital employed.

VIII. FUEL AND ENERGY RESOURCES

Fuel and energy resources are required at every stage in the production process, and at the same time they are heavily involved in many forms of consumption, as in travel and household operation. We are dependent upon such resources for light, heat, motive power, and lubrication. Industrially, the latter two are of primary significance: Without motive power the wheels of industry could not start; without lubrication they would stop. The adequacy of our resources of fuel and energy is thus of decisive importance in the potentials of the next century.

The primary resources involved in the production of fuel and energy are running water, coal, oil, gas, and the special elements used in the creation of atomic energy. Minor sources of fuel and energy include the wind, the tides, and the sun's rays. The wind and the tides are too erratic or intermittent to meet requirements. The sun's rays may possibly some day be focused and relayed to the earth in a satisfactory way. In the following discussion, however, we shall confine ourselves to the primary sources of energy mentioned above.

The sources of electric power are superabundant.

Electric power is derived from two principal sources —running water and steam. The rapids and falls of minor streams were among the earliest sources of power used by man, the millrace supplying a crude form of mechanical power. With the development of modern science and engineering, it became possible to harness the immense energy resources of rivers for the creation of hydroelectric power. During recent decades the construction of huge dams and reservoirs and a great increase in the size of water turbines have made available, for industrial, transportation, and agricultural uses, enormous supplies of electric energy.

Looking forward, a great expansion of hydroelectric power may be expected, and at decreasing costs. Progress is still being made in reducing the cost of transmitting power long distances, which serves in effect to bring the resources of great river and mountain courses nearer to industrial and urban markets. At the same time, advances in hydraulic engineering are making possible the regularization of water flow in turbulent and unruly currents. The costs of generation in these more powerful water courses will be much lower than in the lesser streams and gentler rivers which have been harnessed first. It is certain that the water-power resources of the future will be many times the amount thus far developed and be available on a low-cost basis.

At present about two thirds of the electric current used in the United States is generated by steam, which is produced chiefly by combustion of coal. The cost of steam power compares favorably with that of water power. While the cost of *generating* hydroelectric energy is somewhat lower, this advantage is offset by the fact that hydroelectric power commonly has to be transmitted substantial distances to reach the centers of industry. Experience has shown that beyond a few hundred miles the cost of transmission has been such as to tip the balance in favor of steam power generated locally. Large supplies of steam power for the future seem assured because of the abundance of our coal resources.

The possibility of using atomic energy to produce electricity remains to be noted. It is not believed that such energy is adaptable for use in small units but would be restricted to large installations in the generation stage. This method of generation might prove particularly important in supplying current in areas remote from water power and coal resources.

[The possible use of atomic energy for other industrial purposes is not considered in this treatise. Until the costs involved in producing such energy, and especially in adapting it to the special requirements of industry, are determined, its future must remain a matter of engaging speculation. It is possible also that a dearth of essential minerals might prove a limiting factor.]

Reserves of coal are practically unlimited.

The huge expansion in coal consumption which accompanied the development of our industrial system naturally occasioned much discussion as to the adequacy of our coal resources; and prior to 1920 genuine concern was often expressed. Several factors have operated since that time, however, to change the outlook completely. First, new explorations have unearthed vast quantities of additional coal. Second there has been a steadily increasing economy in the use of coal resulting from improvements in the efficiency of furnaces and engines. Third, new scientific developments have made it possible to use coal of lower-grade quality. Fourth, there has been a phenomenal expansion in the use of substitute forms of fuel. As a result of these developments, instead of the expected rise in coal prices as the richer seams were exhausted, we have had, until the war boom of the forties, falling prices and a "sick industry." All concern with respect to the adequacy of our coal resources has disappeared; it is now believed that the coal supply will last thousands of years.

This abundance of coal is of paramount significance because of the varied services which this mineral may perform. We think of it first and foremost as a raw heat-producing fuel used in stoves and furnaces. But it is also used in the production of other forms of fuel, notably gas, oil, and electricity. Moreover, it is one of the primary bases of synthetic chemistry.

The potential supplies of natural and synthetic oil appear adequate.

Oil has two primary industrial uses—as lubricant and as fuel. It began to be employed in a large way as a lubricant with the development of machine industry in the early nineteenth century. Its extensive use as fuel waited upon the development of the internal combustion engine near the close of the century. Since lubrication is a vital requirement in the operation of machinery, oil has a priority; and if necessary, it could be conserved for this particular purpose. As we shall see, however, the potential supplies appear adequate for both lubricating and fuel purposes.

The supply of oil for the future will depend upon three factors: (1) the extent of the oil resources; (2) the efficiency with which oil is extracted and used; and (3) the development of synthetic substitutes. Separate consideration must be given to each phase of the problem.

Much confusion with respect to oil resources has resulted from the current practice of identifying reserves with the volume of petroleum in tested pools. By dividing the "proved reserves" by the current rate of production, some writers have arrived at the alarming conclusion that we have only 10 to 15 years of oil left in the United States. Such *proved* reserves take no account of the possibility of new discoveries or of obtaining larger supplies from existing pools by improved methods of extraction. As noted in an earlier chapter, the amount of proved reserves has steadily increased despite the enormous expansion in the consumption of oil.[26]

With respect to undiscovered oil, a special committee of the American Petroleum Institute stated in 1936:

> The oil to be discovered in the future is so concealed from observation that an estimate of ultimate reserves is obviously impracticable. However, we do have a definite, although incomplete, knowledge . . . of geologic factors which are favorable to the occurrence of oil. This gives reason to expect that ample discoveries will be made to meet national requirements for a period of indeterminate length.

At the same time, the president of the American Association of Petroleum Geologists, after reviewing recent developments in stratigraphic analysis, concluded that: "The day of geology, as applied to the practical problem of discovering a continuing oil reserve for our nation, is just dawning."[27]

The soundness of these observations has been evidenced by the vast new oil resources which have been opened up in the last decade. Important new fields have been discovered in various parts of the United States, and old fields have been greatly extended. Moreover, extensive deposits have been disclosed off-shore, under the continental shelf of the Atlantic and Pacific oceans and the Gulf of Mexico.

The supply of oil is also constantly being increased, in effect, by technological developments in extracting, refining, and utilization. New methods of extraction make possible great extensions of existing fields, both horizontally and vertically. Some of the greatest pools have been opened at a depth of four miles. Improved refining processes and conservation practices serve to increase the quantity and improve the quality of gasoline and other high-grade fuels. Improvements in engine design make a given amount of fuel go much further. The new gas turbines, developed during World War II, have been characterized as perhaps the most important discovery in this field since the steam engine. These highly efficient turbines require much less fuel, and they can also use a cheaper quality. Thus far, they have been effectively used only in large installations. When materials have been developed which will resist temperatures of from 2,000 to 3,000 degrees, it is believed that small gas turbine engines—the size of a dial telephone—may be used in automobiles.

Finally, oil and gasoline may be derived synthetically from other sources than petroleum deposits. By chemical processes, involving catalytic cracking and the recombination of molecular structures, they are now being made from such materials as natural gas, coal, oil shales, and tar sands. In view of our enormous coal resources, here is a vast new source of oil supply—of good quality. Shales containing oil are also plentiful—though the oil obtained thus far is of low grade.

As yet the cost of these synthetic products is, in the main, higher than that of extracting and refining petroleum. It has, however, been demonstrated that gasoline and diesel oil can be produced from natural gas on a competitive basis. The economical conversion of coal to gasoline seems assured in the not distant future—for costs are being constantly reduced and are at present not far above the competitive level. It may well turn out that progress in the production of synthetic oils will be so rapid that many high-cost natural petroleum deposits, now counted as reserves, will be left in the ground.[28]

When all these developments are taken into account, abundant supplies of oil and gasoline seem assured for many generations to come. The situation has been summed up by an eminent oil geologist, as follows:

> It may be argued that this process of multiplication must have limits and cannot proceed indefinitely, yet it is hazardous to set bounds to a force so dynamic, so rich in past accomplishment, and whose potency has been so enormously stimulated by the emphasis of the war upon technological progress. Conservation procedures, in turn, make possible the fuller application of the fruits of technology, guarding the benefits against the inroads of waste and intemperate development. . . . While the sources of oil are restricted by nature, the availability of oil is subject to almost indefinite extension under the impact of dynamic techniques.[29]

Natural gas has come to be an important supplementary fuel.

Gas is used as a substitute for oil and coal both in households and in many industrial activities, especially where intense heat is required. Because of certain advantages, manufactured gas, made from coal and oil, has long been extensively used for household purposes. At the same time, until after World War I the supply of available natural gas was restricted.

Since 1920 very large natural gas deposits have been discovered, in conjunction with oil-drilling explorations, especially in the South and Southwest. Meanwhile, the rate of gas consumption has been only half the rate of discovery, in consequence of which huge reserves have accumulated. It should be noted, moreover, that the deeper the level at which gas is discovered the greater is the quantity per cubic foot of space. Recent improvements in pipelines have made it possible to transmit gas, on an economical basis, from the Southwest to either coast.

It has already been pointed out that natural gas is used not only as a raw fuel but can also be refined into gasoline. It thus becomes a substitute for petroleum in the production of high-grade motor fuel. Moreover, so-called "natural gasoline" can be extracted from unrefined gas, and is now extensively used in conjunction with gasoline derived from oil.

In combination, our potential resources of power, fuel, and lubrication appear clearly adequate to support an expansion in production and consumption such as is here under consideration.

IX. THE SIGNIFICANCE OF ELECTRONICS

Recent developments in the realm of physics are of far-reaching significance in relation to the future of industry and the satisfaction of human wants. These developments include atomic fission, ultrasonics or inaudible sound, and a wide range of phenomena comprehended in the term "electronics." (Atomic fission is touched upon elsewhere.[30]) Since supersonics is commonly dependent upon electronic devices for effectiveness, it will be given no separate consideration here.

The term "electronics" relates to the phenomenon of

electrons passing through space in a vacuum tube. Illustrations are found in such commonplace instruments as the radio, the talking picture, television, neon signs, the electric eye, and radar. These devices provide one of the most important sources of consumer satisfaction, and they have also come to play a role of vital importance in industry, aviation, navigation, communication, and a host of trade and household operations. It has been said, with pardonable extravagance, that electronic science has taught the electron to see, feel, smell, taste, hear, remember, calculate, and beat and tell time.

Electronic devices are already highly important in industrial production.

By such devices imperfections in metals, such as in sheets that pass through the rolling machine, can be immediately spotted, a signal given to indicate their appearance, and their location accurately indicated. The heat of molten metals is now precisely controlled by chemical analysis and the electronic recording of the light given off. By another electronic gadget the worker can be protected while at his machine so that if his hand, for example, gets into a danger area the machine stops.

Another development has to do with induction heating and resistance welding. The heat thus produced is so nearly instantaneous that it can be limited to a small spot on a piece of metal, producing a white heat in a fraction of a second, while but a few inches away the metal remains cool. This is particularly useful with metals like aluminum which melt instead of welding under the old methods. Electronic welding consists of sharp thrusts, up to nearly 2,000 a second, and thus acts as if stitching the pieces together.

By electronic vibration studies, the fatigue of metals can be precisely measured and the lifetime of a machine part accurately determined. In time, it will thus be possible to use much less material to obtain a given result, and to build much less cumbersome factories, office buildings, industrial equipment, and automobiles. The X-ray is used in finding cracks and blow-holes in metal castings and in exploring the completed welds for possible defects.

The ignitron will instantaneously convert alternating to direct current, not only in huge installations such as are required in the refining of aluminum and magnesium, but also to a particular machine in the industrial plant, where the insertion of a small electronic tube, no more difficult to put into place than an ordinary incandescent lamp, will convert to the type of current needed at the exact point of use. Still other electronic controls have been developed to ensure exact speeds in an electric motor in place of the crude controls provided by rheostats.

The services of electronic science to society are manifold in character.

Applications forecast by recent developments include: the creation of new chemical compounds; the mixing and drying of paint; increasing the yield of plant seeds; the production of smoother milk, ice cream, mayonnaise, and other food products; the sterilization of food; the acceleration of the aging of wines and spirits; and the preservation of food, drugs, and flowers. Some of these results involve the use of ultrasonic waves.

Modern long-distance telephone service would be impossible without electronics. A vacuum-tube repeater amplifies the current at intervals as the impulses grow too faint after miles of transmission; and newly-developed electronic carrier systems convey simultaneously many voice channels over the same wires. Since World War II, electronic calculating machines have been developed which are of revolutionary importance in industry, in government, and in military science.

By means of electronic devices, fruits and vegetables are sorted, picked over, and accurately counted. The fluoroscope is employed in detecting foreign substances, spoilage, and shortages in food packed in tins. By electronic induction heating, foods are dehydrated, and tobacco cured. Ordinary cooking and roasting of meats can be reduced to a matter of seconds by means of the electronic stove—though as yet the units are too costly for use in the home.

The importance of electronic devices in the field of health and medicine has long been established. The best-known applications are in connection with the X-ray and the fluoroscope. An electronic precipitron has been invented which removes dust and smoke from the air. Another device disinfects the air and kills bacteria. Electronic microscopes 100 times as powerful as the best lens microscopes have been constructed. Ultrasonic waves are being experimented with in connection with surgery.

Electronic instruments of superhuman sensitivity increase human efficiency many-fold. In time, electronic devices will doubtless make it possible to relieve the worker of most routine labor and at the same time secure a performance immeasurably better than anything unaided human skill can achieve. These developments in the realm of electronics are in striking contrast to the simple division of labor, or specialization in hand tasks, which Adam Smith regarded as the basic principle underlying progress in the arts of production.

A striking feature of these electronic instruments is that the enormous gains are achieved without appreciable drafts upon material resources.

In concluding this discussion of the many ways in which scientific discovery and invention can, in the next century as in the past, continue to yield progressively increasing returns through an ever more effective utilization of the resources of nature, it may be observed that some, perhaps many, of the engaging developments that have been noted may not materialize or prove economical. Yet there can be little doubt that the onward sweep of science and technology as a whole is such that in one way or another scientific advancement as applied to the processes of production could yield results of the magnitude projected at the beginning of this chapter.

The actual future of the United States will of course depend both upon the peace of the world and on our ability to maintain the conditions essential to rapid economic progress. The considerations involved in the latter will be discussed in subsequent chapters.

CHAPTER VIII

CERTAIN UNDERLYING REQUIREMENTS

The purpose of the preceding chapter, as indicated, was to gauge in a rough way the economic possibilities of the next century. The discussion was focused throughout on the question: Are the resources of nature so limited as to preclude the possibility of another century of expansion comparable to that of the last hundred years? It should be emphasized that we were not seeking to judge the future by the record of the past; we were concerned with possibilities only. Nor in the remainder of the book shall we attempt to forecast the rate of economic advancement or to estimate the probable level of national income at any particular date in the future. The entire discussion will be centered on the question: What is involved in promoting steady and progressive economic development—what principles, methods, or policies must be pursued in order to realize in fullest measure our national economic goals?

The analysis in earlier chapters served to disclose the principal factors responsible for the great economic advancement of the last century and also to indicate some of the retarding influences. It thus furnished criteria useful in formulating the underlying requirements for continued economic progress. In the present chapter we shall attempt to summarize these requirements as a basis for the discussion of economic problems and policies in following chapters.

I. PROTECTION OF NATURAL RESOURCES

The optimistic conclusion with respect to the adequacy of natural resources reached in Chapter VII was predicated on the assumption that such resources will be systematically conserved and fostered. While some attention was there given to the conservation problem, our soil, water, forest, and mineral resources are so indispensable that their protection requires emphasis at this place.

Any neglect of our natural endowment would undermine the very foundations of economic progress.

Many areas in the world have suffered severe economic retrogression in consequence of soil depletion resulting from erosion and excessive cropping without replenishment of essential elements. Indeed, great civilizations have declined and perished with the deterioration of the soil which nourished them. It is a striking and disquieting fact that in only a few areas in the world has diversified agriculture been permanently sustained—in river bottoms and in regions where rainfall is characteristically gentle and evenly distributed, as in western Europe. The richly endowed United States has been peculiarly vulnerable because of torrential rains and the susceptibility of our soils to sheet erosion. Even the great prairies, produced by thousands of years of decaying vegetation, have in a short century of cultivation been severely depleted by erosion and soil-robbing practices.

Conservation of the soil and of the moisture content by contour and strip farming, by improved rotation, and especially by greater concentration on grass culture, is thus an indispensable requirement. Fortunately, it is not too late to save and even to improve the soil resources of the United States. Since the requisite knowledge is available, the problem is chiefly one of educating the agricultural population and of stimulating conservation practices.

The preservation and reproduction of timber resources is closely related to soil protection. That is, forests are essential not only to ensure adequate supplies of wood but also as a means of checking excessive water run-off, thus conserving moisture and soil.

Systematic conservation of minerals is no less important. Wasteful practices should be eliminated in connection with all types of mineral resources and the supplies of scarce minerals should be protected by the use of substitutes wherever possible. Our mineral resources, supplemented by synthetic substitutes, may appear adequate for a century to come, but we are obliged to think not in terms of centuries merely but of millenniums.

II. INCREASING PRODUCTIVITY

A rise in the general plane of living is dependent on increasing efficiency in production—that is, per-capita consumption cannot expand unless per-capita production expands. It was of course the phenomenal increase in productivity which accompanied the development of the modern industrial system that made possible the progressive improvements in living conditions over the last century, and also the progressive reduction in hours of labor.

Since increasing productivity is commonly measured in terms of *man-hour output*, it is sometimes assumed that the gain is directly attributable to an increase in efficiency on the part of labor itself. It is true that output may be increased by more efficient performance on the part of workers; but the factors of primary importance have been the provision of more abundant and efficient tools, and improvements in industrial organization and management.

Science and technology are the fountainheads of increasing productivity.

Scientific discoveries laid the foundations, as we have seen, for what may be described as the continuous industrial revolution of the nineteenth and early twentieth centuries. It is of the first order of importance, therefore, that we continue to expand the bounds of scientific knowledge and to provide opportunity for the exercise of inventive genius. In the light of history this seems so obvious a fact as scarcely to deserve mention; yet it is necessary to emphasize the point because of the persistent or at least recurrent fear that science and technology will inevitably lead to overproduction and chronic unemployment. As late as the 1930's there developed in the United States a great national program designed to restrict the volume of output and restrain technological advancement, in order to maintain a satisfactory balance between supply and demand and to prevent the accumulation of chronic surpluses of goods.

Scientific training and scientific experimentation become ever more time-consuming and costly as the range of knowledge widens and the complexity and magnitude of scientific instruments and mechanisms increase. What has come to be involved may be indicated by the fact that a single scientific instrument nowadays may cost a million dollars, and that the government's annual budget for research and development in the field of atomic energy exceeds half a billion dollars. The larger industries spend hundreds of millions of dollars annually on scientific research. It should be emphasized that engineering research is quite as important as research in what is called "pure science," because it is through engineering that the results of science and invention are translated into effective instruments of production in the form of plant and equipment.

The use of capital equipment must be universalized.

It has been the progressive substitution of machinery, especially power-driven machinery, for hand labor in virtually every field of production that has lifted mankind from the drudgery and poverty of earlier centuries to the comparatively easy labor and material comfort of the present age. In all the major branches of industry, every worker has been provided with many thousand dollars worth of machinery and tools. In railroads, for example, the value of the capital equipment at the present time is equal to approximately $20,000 per man employed. In industry, and even in agriculture, the hours of work required to achieve a given result have been continuously reduced, so that one man becomes able to do the work of two, five, ten, or even a hundred in some types of operation.

Since mechanization has provided the cutting edge for increasing productivity, it is obvious that the use of efficient capital equipment should be universalized if we are to achieve the largest possible output of goods and services with a given expenditure of human energy. The relative economic advancement of nations reflects principally the extent to which machine production has replaced hand labor. There may possibly be objections to machinery or industrialization on aesthetic grounds, because of the monotony of highly specialized tasks, or even because of moral and social dangers associated with too much leisure; but there can be no argument on grounds of economic efficiency.

Obsolete plant and equipment must be rapidly replaced.

In the preceding paragraphs emphasis was placed on the initial substitution of machine for hand methods. Of equal importance is the continuous replacement of existing capital equipment with better capital equipment. This principle has, of course, always been recognized in a general way, but its full import is not usually clearly understood. The problem may be illustrated by accounting practices.

When a new capital installation is made, it is recognized that the initial book value must be written down annually in order to take account of depreciation or physical wear and tear. In setting the annual rate of depreciation it is necessary to estimate the probable life of the equipment. In doing so, the primary question is that of physical durability. Some consideration will be given to the fact that the time will come when the cost of repairs will be prohibitive, and some allowance will ordinarily be made for the possibility that it might be wise to replace the machine by a better one before it is completely worn out.

In a period of rapid technical progress, capital equipment may become obsolete long before it has suffered any appreciable physical deterioration. American industry affords countless illustrations of this fact. Indeed, a large percentage of our industrial equipment is older than the life estimated in the depreciation accounts. The very high percentage of obsolete equipment in Europe has long been recognized. The moment it can be shown that the reduction in cost made possible by a new, more efficient, machine is sufficient to offset the loss involved in scrapping the old equipment, the replacement should be made. In a dynamic technological age it can frequently be demonstrated that a new machine can within a very short time absorb the loss from scrapping the old machine and pay for itself.

The process of change is, however, commonly delayed by failure to think sharply and to see the true situation as to loss and gain, by difficulties in financing the initial cost of the new equipment, and by sheer inertia. One of the greatest drags on the wheels of progress has been the tendency to continue to use capital equipment that has been rendered obsolete by advancing technology. In recent years, however, the shift to improved equipment, which saves labor cost, has often been expedited by advancing wage rates.

Organization and management policies may greatly increase productivity.

The emphasis placed upon the creative role of physical capital has tended to obscure somewhat the significance of organizational and managerial policies and procedures which affect productive efficiency. Many developments have occurred in modern times which have a very important bearing on man-hour output. Some of these relate to the industrial plant and others to the individual worker.

Among the factors pertaining to the plant the following may be mentioned: (1) location, in relation to sources of raw materials, markets, available labor, transport facilities, etc.; (2) internal layout, with a view to eliminating waste motion and facilitating a steady flow of materials and continuous production; (3) specialization of tasks, to obtain increased operating skill; (4) reduction of the number of types or brands of products; and (5) development of interchangeable machine parts. These methods are commonly referred to by such general terms as the elimination of waste, the promotion of efficiency, standardization, and rationalization of industry. The term mass production is commonly employed to describe an operation of such size as to permit a maximum of specialization and a minimum of lost motion.

On the personnel side, mention may be made of: (1) the improvement of working conditions by attention to sanitation and the provision of rest periods, recreational facilities, medical care, and counsel on personal problems; and (2) increasing individual efficiency by means of special training, aptitude tests, and placement, and "time and motion" studies. The terms personnel management, scientific management, and human engineering are often used to describe such developments as these.

Workers' attitudes and union policies frequently affect man-hour output adversely.

The attitudes of workers toward their jobs are a reflection of many factors—some pertaining to the nature of man and others to the environmental circumstances by which the individual is surrounded. Man himself appears to be subject to widely divergent, even conflicting, influences, and of course individuals show the greatest diversity of qualities. In general terms it is often stated that nearly everybody likes leisure and works only because it is necessary. On the other hand, emphasis is frequently placed upon the instinct of workmanship and the sheer love of activity as motivating influences. Perhaps the truth is that nearly everyone likes some work, but most people feel they are obliged to work too hard or too continuously. In any case, it is clear that the easier jobs are the preferred ones, and that shorter work days are always welcomed.

Prevailing ideas or conceptions may also strongly condition workers' attitudes. Perhaps the most pervasive is the thought that the amount of work available is limited and that the harder one works the less time the job will last. In many cases this result reflects the laborer's own experience; he has often been laid off because a specific job was finished. Even where the employment is supposed to be continuous, he may be laid off occasionally or periodically because of a lack of orders. And in times of general depression he hears his plight attributed to overproduction.

Another source of confusion arises from the fact that under modern industrial conditions the connection between the amount of work done and the amount of pay received is not an obvious one. That is, the relation between cause and effect, and *effect* and reward, seems remote and dubious. The worker is thus prone to assume that he gets a fixed sum per day or week more or less regardless—with any gain from speeding up accruing to the employed as profits. It was to overcome this attitude that the "piece rate" system was devised. But this system met with opposition for two principal reasons: it appeared that it would the more quickly exhaust the available work; and it was often regarded as a device for exploiting labor, the assumption being that rates for piece work would be reduced as output increased.

In general it may be said that the capitalistic system, under which payments for services are made in money rather than in commodities, has served to obscure the controlling importance of expanding physical output. Attention centers on the fairness of the division of existing money income rather than on the significance of increased production. The elementary fact that consumption is restricted by the supply of physical goods tends to be overlooked.

These conditioning factors serve to explain the basic policies of labor organizations. Collective bargaining—the heart of union policy—is designed to strengthen the position of labor in obtaining a satisfactory share of the income. In order to be strong in the bargaining process the supply of labor must be scarce relatively to the demand. Hence it appears good policy to restrict membership and also to reduce individual output. The nearer the union can come to a monopoly position the stronger will be its bargaining power. The fear of periodic overproduction, plant shutdowns, and permanent technological unemployment reinforces the union conception that labor welfare necessitates not only a reduction in hours but in hourly performance.

The varied ways in which unions seek to make work for their members have been summarized as follows: (1) limiting daily or weekly output; (2) indirectly limiting the speed of work; (3) controlling the quality of work; (4) requiring time-consuming methods of doing the work; (5) requiring that unnecessary work be done or that work be done more than once; (6) regulating the number of men in a crew or on a machine or requiring the employment of unnecessary men; (7) requiring that the work be done by members of a given skill, craft, or occupation; (8) prohibiting the employers or foreman from working at the trade; and (9) retiring, or probiting the use of, machines and labor-saving devices.[1]

The effects of these work restriction policies cn output vary widely in different industries and in different types of productive operations. The result will depend in part upon the strength of the labor organization and in part upon the nature of the task. In operations where the machine sets the pace there is little chance for malingering on the part of the individual workers; hence emphasis has to be placed on preventing the use of the machine or restricting its speed or hours of operation. In some industries the desired result is achieved by means of so-called "feather-bedding" practice. This is illustrated by union rules in the railroad industry which provide, among other things, that trainmen shall still be paid for the same number of hours that were required a generation ago to cover the distance between division points even though the travel time is now only half as long.

Extreme illustrations of the effects upon workers' performance may be cited as follows: Since 1940 the number of bricks a mason may lay in a day has been reduced from 1,000 to less than 500.[2] Where formerly 2,600 sacks of sugar were loaded by a 16-man gang of longshoremen in a day, restrictive rules reduced the performance to 850 sacks.[3] Such reductions were the result not of a shorter work week but of less work per hour. While in many lines of activity the worker's performance cannot be measured accurately, testimony is abundant that there has been for many years a persistent decrease in labor efficiency. In some types of operations the machine governs the pace of labor; but by and large the workers can in large measure still set their own pace. The less the competition for jobs the greater appears to be the tendency to take it easy.

If we are to have maximum economic progress, there must be efficient performance on the part of labor as well as rapid improvements in capital equipment and in industrial organization. If individual labor efficiency simply declines in proportion to improvements in capital equipment and management, it is obvious that no general advance in living standards is possible. On the other hand, if technological progress were matched by a corresponding improvement in labor's performance, the rate of expansion in production would be very greatly increased.

The greatest single requirement at the present juncture, both in the United States and in other countries, is a progressive increase in the efficiency of workmen. Concretely, a universal increase of 20 per cent in output through better labor performance would mean close to a 40 billion dollar increase in American national income. Such an increase in output, generally speaking, would impose no real hardship. We are not thinking of longer hours, of a driving pace, of the sweatshop, or the lash; we are speaking simply of greater assiduity on the job. The increased output would come chiefly from a decrease in malingering in its various forms.

Even with so moderate an increase in labor efficiency as 20 per cent, most of the difficult economic problems which now confront us would become easy of solution. Simultaneously, real wages could be materially increased, the returns to capital could be enlarged, and prices to the consuming public could be lowered. Moreover, the expansion of real national income would gradually alleviate the very difficult fiscal burdens of the present time. It cannot be too strongly emphasized that the real solution for our economic problems is to be found in improving performance on the part of the masses of workers. All that is required is a clear perception of the primary requirements and an appropriate emphasis in the guiding philosophy and policies of labor organizations.

In concluding this brief discussion of productive efficiency, it should be emphasized that adequate incentives must be maintained for both labor and capital if the desired results are to be achieved. Labor incentives may take a variety of forms, such as piece-rate pay, a sliding wage scale, a bonus system, or profit sharing. On the management side, the basic incentive is the chance to retain some share of the gains resulting from the technical advances. Special incentives designed to promote rapid installations of new capital equipment include patent protection, liberal depreciation policies with respect to new plant and equipment, and other tax concessions. There must also be at least a fair degree of assurance with respect to the perpetuity of the private enterprise system.

III. NECESSITY FOR LARGE-SCALE ENTERPRISE

There has been much discussion in economic literature of the appropriate size of business establishments, and much concern has been manifested over the giant proportions of modern corporations. The view is often expressed that we would be much better off if the present industrial organization were "atomized" into something akin to the small-scale producing units of former times. It is possible that corporations may become so large as to be unwieldy, and there may be serious doubt as to the economic advantages of huge consolidations of a large number of companies under a single overhead management.[4] But it can readily be shown that under modern conditions considerations of efficiency require operating companies of great size.

Several factors combine to necessitate large business enterprises.

The most striking feature of the modern economic system is the magnitude of the physical instruments employed in production and the physical space required for their utilization. The continuing industrial revolution has brought the development of implements and tools of ever-increasing size and complexity. Only the word "giant" is adequate to describe the greater part of present-day capital equipment. Diesel engines, leviathan liners, cargo planes, bulldozers, electric turbines, generators, cranes and conveyors, and the huge stationary installations within industrial establishments are familiar examples. The increasing magnitude and complexity of capital instruments is a characteristic of all branches of industry, and it is becoming true of agriculture as well.

Considerations of efficiency often make it necessary for a single company to operate a number of smaller plants rather than a huge central unit. Transportation and marketing requirements may dictate the location of operating units in more than one center. In the interests of stability, diversification of product may be desirable. In some types of business, moreover, the nature of the market is such as to necessitate the production of a number of related products. Indeed, the determining factor in arriving at the most efficient size for the enterprise may be found in what is necessary to ensure the steady flow of materials into the manufacturing operation, or to ensure the most effective absorption of the output through adequate distributive channels.

The small business is definitely limited in the character of its operations. It is usually confined to the making of a single product and parts or small assemblies for larger companies. This does not mean that small business units have no significance in the scheme of things. However, it does mean that they can contribute little toward technological advancement—for the simple reason that they do not possess the requisite resources with which to carry out basic and applied research programs.

The magnitude of the resources required in modern industry may be illustrated by reference to the assets of the thousand largest manufacturing corporations in the United States in 1945. As many as 107, many of which were independent companies, had assets in excess of 100 millions; 88 had between 50 and 100 millions; 167 from 25 to 50 millions; and 382 were in the range of 10 to 25 millions. Any manufacturing company with assets of less than 10 million dollars has come to be regarded as a small-scale enterprise.

IV. MONETARY STABILITY

Among the factors emphasized in Chapter I as contributing to the great economic expansion of the nineteenth century was the stability that had been achieved in the realm of finance. The bimetallic standard had been gradually replaced in all important countries by a single monetary unit, and national budgets had been brought into satisfactory equilibrium. Hence businessmen could enter into the credit operations involved in large-scale capitalistic enterprise with reasonable assurance that the risks involved would be confined to the ordinary hazards of business. If we are to realize the economic potentials of the ensuing century, the financial needs of business will continue to necessitate both short and long-term borrowing transactions on a vast scale; and financial stability will be as indispensable in the future as in the past. In this section consideration is given to the monetary aspect of the problem, while discussion of the maintenance of fiscal stability is reserved for the following section.

The essential requirement is a fixed, unchanging, monetary unit.

As pointed out in Chapter I, the establishment of a monetary unit of definite quantity and purity by the leading nations of the world laid the basis for the national and international credit operations which made possible the phenomenal world-wide expansion of the nineteenth century. Since 1930, as noted in Chapter III, there has been a universal abandonment of the gold standard so far as domestic transactions are concerned and a substantial suspension of the use of gold in international transactions. The United States suspended the convertibility of paper currency into gold in 1933 and subjected gold exports to a license system. In addition, the weight of the monetary unit was reduced and made subject to periodic modification with a view to controlling the general level of commodity prices. Since February 1934, however, the weight of the monetary unit, and hence the price of gold (which means the number of dollars paid for an ounce of gold), has not been changed.

Under the system as it exists today, American citizens can obtain gold from the Treasury for export to meet international obligations. Similarly, foreigners can obtain gold for export by purchase at the United States Treasury. Thus on the international side we operate on a gold standard basis—paying out gold as needed for international trading and financial operations. The only limitation is that licenses are required in order to ensure its use for designated export purposes.

On the domestic side, however, paper currency has not been redeemable in gold since 1933. Thus, strictly speaking, the United States is not on the gold standard in its internal financial operations. However, the fact that paper currency is not redeemable in gold no longer causes the general public any uneasiness with respect to the acceptability of such currency in every-day financial transactions. Whereas in earlier times we were so accustomed to the use of gold that we were gold-minded and distrustful of paper that was not immediately convertible into gold, we have now become habituated to the use of paper currency. We are not interested in using gold as a medium of exchange, and since the various types of paper currency are interchangeable, we do not even bother to determine what forms are in our possession—all are "money" to the average person. If paper currency were again declared redeemable on demand, it is doubtful whether any appreciable volume would be converted into gold. In the light of present conditions and attitudes, a restoration of the principle of convertibility would be of no practical importance. Since little, if any, would return to private hands, the reserve position of the banks would scarcely be affected.

The basic requirement is to refrain permanently from altering the weight of the monetary unit (the dollar price of gold)—either up or down. This is because any change in the dollar affects its value in relation to foreign currencies, and thus the prices of exports and imports, thereby unsettling international commerce and financial relations. In view of the dominant role of the United States in the economic life of an unstable world, the maintenance of a stable dollar unit is of fundamental importance. Gold is still the basis for fixing parity relationships among national currencies, under provisions of the International Monetary Fund, and the gold dollar is the ultimate point of reference. Any change in the weight of the dollar unit would thus react upon the currencies of all countries and complicate still further the difficult problem of ultimately re-establishing international financial stability.

V. FISCAL STABILITY

The problem of maintaining fiscal stability is closely interrelated with that of maintaining monetary stability. Tampering with the monetary standard, through its repercussions upon business enterprise, inevitably complicates the fiscal situation; and, similarly, a persistently unbalanced budget and mounting public indebtedness imperil the maintenance of a stable currency system.

Sound fiscal policy necessitates keeping the public debt within manageable proportions.

During the hundred years from the Napoleonic Wars to World War I finance ministers everywhere sought to keep the public debt within safe bounds. While it was not regarded as necessary to pay off public indebtedness altogether, it was deemed imperative to keep it well within revenue possibilities. Adherence to this policy over a century of comparative peace and economic expansion served in most countries to remove all concern over public debts.[5] In the United States the substantial debt resulting from the Civil War was virtually eliminated before the end of the century. The First World War left a federal debt of over 25 billion dollars, and this was reduced to approximately 16 billions by 1930. But large annual deficits during the decade of the thirties increased indebtedness—from 16 to 40 billions—and served to make the public debt a subject of vital interest and controversy.

The economic vicissitudes of the depression and stagnation period of the 1930's led some to conclude that it would be impracticable in the future to achieve and maintain a balanced budget. Indeed, the theory developed that since the wellsprings of expansion under private enterprise appeared to have dried up,[6] it would be necessary henceforth to employ public credit on an ever-expanding scale in order to sustain employment at an acceptable level. The leaders of this school of thought held that the growth of an internal public debt, contrary to traditional views, need not be a matter of concern. It was argued that an internal debt "has none of the essential earmarks of a private debt"—that it "is in fact so different from what we commonly think of as debt that it should scarcely be called a debt at all." The explanation advanced was that "taxes will be collected to service the bonds, and when interest or principal payments are made on them the money is merely shifted about within the economic system."

This same observation may of course be made with respect to the debts of states and municipalities and private corporations and individuals. The money paid out by the debtors is income to the receiving creditors and thus is merely shifted about within the economic system. Such borrowers may, however, undermine their credit position if their indebtedness expands beyond their capacity to pay out of current revenues.[7] The essential requirement for any borrower, public or private, is to keep debts well within the capacity to meet the carrying charges.

In periods of great national emergency such as a war or an acute depression, deficits in the federal budget are unavoidable. In a time of war the rapidly mounting financial requirements of the government can as a practical matter seldom be fully met, immediately speaking, from increased tax receipts. During a depression revenues fall off sharply, and at the same time the government is called upon to relieve distressed institutions and suffering groups in society. It is precisely because of such periodic deficits that surpluses and debt reduction are necessary in periods of business expansion. In short, the essence of sound fiscal policy is to reduce public debts substantially in good times in order to provide an adequate margin of safety for periods of adversity.

Fiscal stability cannot be achieved with a level of taxes that destroys business incentive.

It is theoretically possible to balance the budget

either on a high-expenditure, high-tax basis or at a low-expenditure, low-tax level. Historically, the United States operated on a very low basis of public expenditure and a correspondingly low level of taxation. A comparable level of taxation in any near future is of course impossible in view of accumulated indebtedness and the greatly increased responsibilities of government. But it does not follow that it is immaterial at what level of taxation the budget is balanced, so long as it is balanced.

The balanced federal budgets of 1947 and 1948 were made possible because of the continuance of taxes (apart from the excess profits tax) at almost the wartime level during a period of unprecedented peacetime economic activity. It should be understood that the volume of tax revenues is highly sensitive to changes in general economic conditions. Even a moderate recession, reducing national income by as little as 10 per cent would mean a reduction in tax revenues of 7 to 8 billion dollars, while a 20 per cent decline would involve a drop in tax receipts of 16 to 18 billions. A situation in which only a modest surplus is realized in a period of intense boom, and which could be replaced by huge deficits with only a slight decline in economic activity, affords no adequate margin of safety and imperils long-term fiscal stability.

It is, moreover, virtually impossible to maintain indefinitely a wartime level of income tax rates. The masses of the people soon become insistent that the burden of taxes be alleviated; and no political party can long ignore such demands. As soon as such reductions are granted, it becomes necessary either to forego the possibility of debt reductions, or to increase the tax load on the upper-income classes or on business enterprises. When the taxes on the wealthy classes already absorb the larger part of their incomes, little leeway exists; and in any case such taxes may trench upon the supply of "venture" capital essential to the expansion of business enterprise.

If added levies on business are of the type that can be shifted—such as sales taxes—the burden remains on consumers in the form of higher costs of living. If they fall directly upon business concerns, they may so reduce profits as to imperil the continuance of employment and especially to destroy the incentive to make new commitments for future expansion. One says *may* so reduce profits because the weight of the impact will naturally depend upon the magnitude of the tax load and the degree of prosperity existing at the time. At best, even under favorable business conditions, only a very few billions of added revenues could be realized from this source.

The conclusion seems clear that sound fiscal policy necessitates that the budget be balanced on a comparatively low rather than a very high tax level. To state the matter in extreme terms, there can scarcely be any question that the private enterprise system would function more vigorously with a tax system that absorbs, say 10 to 15 per cent of the national income than under one that absorbs 25 or 30 per cent.

Term programs, involving limits, are necessary for the maintenance of fiscal stability.

Traditionally, fiscal procedure has involved first a determination of expenditure requirements and then the formulation of a tax program, or an adjustment of tax rates, to yield the necessary revenues. So long as expenditure requirements were modest and taxable capacity well above revenue needs, this procedure could involve no serious difficulties. But in view of the effects upon public finance of the epochal developments of the last two decades, such a procedure is no longer tenable. For the future a new approach is necessary; taxable capacity has now come to limit expenditure possibilities.

For reasons indicated in preceding paragraphs, the federal budget situation has become precarious; and the same is true of many state and local governments. If long-term fiscal stability is to be maintained, it is indispensable that definite limits be set with respect to both revenues and expenditures. In the case of the federal government, it is necessary to view the problem, not merely in annual terms, but in terms of four-year periods corresponding with the presidential term of office.

A four-year fiscal program could take account of possible fluctuations in business activity; that is, it could deal with the fiscal problem in average or normal terms and not merely in relation to *prospectively* good or bad years. Each new administration should thus assume the responsibility of formulating a four-year fiscal program. Concurrently, and independently if desired, the appropriate committees of Congress should consider the problem in similar perspective—for in the end it is Congress which must set the essential limits. It is not intended that annual *budgets* would be supplanted; the suggestion is, rather, that the annual budgets would come within the limits set by the four-year program.

On the revenue side, the limit is governed by taxable capacity. This cannot be precisely measured—for the amount of taxes that can be raised is determined by psychological as well as economic considerations. Experienced tax officials know, however, within reasonable limits what level of personal income taxes is feasible; and they also have a fair idea as to the yield of other forms of taxes under ordinary conditions. The formula should be to set the over-all tax limit for the federal government as a percentage of the national income that can reasonably be expected over the four-year period. There would naturally be much divergence of opinion as to the prospective level of national income, and the estimates arrived at would necessarily be in the nature of compromises. Nevertheless the estimates finally agreed upon would constitute the foundation for control of aggregate expenditures.

On the expenditure side it would be necessary to set the limit in terms of aggregate dollars. The volume of expenditures should be fixed somewhat below the projected revenues—for two reasons: first, to furnish a margin for debt retirement over the four-year period; and second, to provide leeway for revenue deficiencies in the event of untoward economic developments. The besetting weakness of our present system is that, in making specific appropriations, Congress does not have before it a clear picture of aggregate commitments; and the difficulty of controlling the total is enhanced by the practice of making deficiency appropriations. Only if there is an agreed-upon grand total of permissible commitments—an upper limit—can genuine control be exercised.

The problem of maintaining fiscal stability is complicated by three considerations that require emphasis at this place. The first is the prevalent view that there is little which the nation cannot afford—or to put the matter in popular language, that the nation cannot afford *not* to provide the services essential for the public welfare. For example, it is held that we cannot have too much education, or too good health, or too much security against the vicissitudes of life. Even if it were agreed that the provision of such services by government is in line with the primary goals of our national life, the question whether unlimited services of the types indicated can be provided, without undermining the financial stability upon which the very life of the economy depends, would still have to be faced.

The second factor deserving mention is that some of the insurance and pension plans involve, automatically, a rising level of expenditures over a long period of years. Similarly, many of the welfare programs follow what may almost be called a law of expansion. Thus, decisions currently made tend to have a vast forward thrust, heavily mortgaging potential revenues decades hence.

Third, it should be noted that the prevailing conception that money income derived from government expenditures, or to use the more euphonious and euphemistic phrase, "the government's contribution to purchasing power," involves an elemental fallacy from the tax point of view. While individuals who are employed by government may pay back a portion of their salaries in the form of taxes, non-revenue producing government enterprises cannot contribute to the support of government. The percentage of the total income derived from procreative private enterprise has been steadily decreasing as the range of governmental activities has widened. Thus the burden to be carried by the private sector of the economy continuously increases.

A program involving limitations on taxes and expenditures over a four-year period cannot of course be expected to meet fully the extraordinary requirements of war emergencies or of acute business depressions. Such a program should, however, ensure fiscal stability in normal periods and gradually restore some margin of safety with which to meet the needs of great national emergencies.

VI. PROGRESSIVE EXPANSION OF MASS PURCHASING POWER

In a specialized economic society the great bulk of the goods produced is sold in commercial markets. Buyers are sought not only for each particular product but also for the aggregate of goods and services which can be turned out by the producing establishments. Since manufacturing enterprises are operated on the basis of week-to-week or month-to-month plans, current production is necessarily adjusted rather closely to current sales, or orders. If adverse developments check or retard the flow of orders, production schedules will be curtailed. Hence if the economic system is to function effectively, consumptive demand must at all times be strong. Emphasis is placed upon the demand for consumer goods because it is the demand for these final products that provides the stimulus for the expansion of capital goods.[8]

The unfulfilled desires of the masses constitute the great potential markets of the future.

As has been pointed out in preceding chapters, the incomes of a large percentage of the population, even in the United States, are still very low; indeed they are inadequate in many cases to meet the requirements for health and efficiency. Beyond this lie vast desires, the satisfying of which would furnish the principal markets for the enormously expanded production suggested in Chapter VII. It will be recalled that we were there raising the question whether our fundamental economic resources were adequate to permit a doubling of the population and something like an eight-fold rise in the plane of living.

If we are to realize the economic potentialities of the future, if we are to have reasonably steady, sustained, progress toward the higher levels of living which our natural resources and our technological genius will permit, there must be a constantly broadening distribution in the income annually generated by our producing establishments. An increasing proportion of the expanding total income must go to those in the lower levels of income, where consumption wants are least satisfied. The greatest single problem with which we are confronted is how to achieve such a distribution of income. The complicated processes involved will be given detailed consideration in the following chapter.

CHAPTER IX

THE DISTRIBUTION OF NATIONAL INCOME

The analysis in Chapter VII of future economic potentialities was based on the character and expansibility of consumer demands as revealed by studies of family expenditures at different levels of income. That is, production requirements were gauged by potential demands for the major categories of consumer goods—food and nutrition, shelter and home maintenance, attire and personal care, health and education, and recreation and travel. It was assumed that the unfulfilled desires of the consuming public for such goods and services could be translated into effective market demands. It will be observed that this expansion potential is not primarily dependent upon the development of new industries. While many new types of products and new industries will doubtless emerge as a result of continuing technological advances and of changes in consumer tastes and habits, fundamentally the growth will take place in already existing lines of production. In any case the underlying requirement is seen to be a progressive expansion of income and buying power among the great masses of the population whose wants and demands constitute the ultimate motivation for production.

In earlier chapters the bearing of income distribution upon economic progress has been discussed in general terms. In this chapter we come to grips with the problem more specifically, and consider the way in which an expanding national income has been distributed in the past and the bearing of methods of distribution upon the functioning of the economic system.

In economic literature the traditional approach to the problem of income distribution has been to analyze the forces, or so-called laws, which determine the relative size of the shares accruing to each of the "factors of production"—that is, land, labor, capital, and management—in the form of rent, wages, interest, and profits. The analysis concluded that under free competition the amount received by the several producing factors tended to approximate closely their respective contributions to the aggregate product. However, the amount of the respective contributions and shares would vary with changing conditions, affecting the supply and demand and the productivity of each factor. Thus the competitive system appeared to be self-regulating and to assure an equitable division of the income produced. In line with this analysis the benefits of technological progress would automatically accrue to the masses of consumers as a result of declining prices brought about by the competitive process.

However valid this analysis of the laws of income distribution may have been under the conditions prevailing in the early stages of the capitalistic competitive system, it was inevitable that it would not be permanently acceptable as a just and equitable system. The explanation is largely psychological. Rents obtained from the possession of superior pieces of land, especially if the holdings were large, and especially where inheritance was involved, seemed to enable fortunate individuals to reap where they had not sown.[1] Similarly, when capital accumulations became large, profits naturally appeared exorbitant as compared with the meager returns to labor.

Moreover, the possibility of receiving higher real incomes as a result of price reductions is a difficult concept to understand, and at best it appears as a roundabout, uncertain process. What labor naturally desires is higher *money* income—for more dollars in the pay envelope can be counted, and they appear as tangible evidence of an improving position. Thus the stage was inevitably set for the development of labor unions and for the wage conflict.

The distribution of income in modern society, however, involves much more than the struggle of labor for higher money wages. Salaried officials, professional persons, farmers, laborers, and capitalists are equally interested. Each of these groups, to be sure, is to some extent a hybrid; wage earners and salaried individuals are also property owners; business enterprisers receive salaries as well as interest and profit; and farmers are property owners, business enterprisers, and laborers all in one. Yet this broad classification is highly significant because these are the groups who compete, so to speak, for the national income. Labor unites to strengthen its position at the bargaining tables, and also to gain the support of government in its struggle for higher incomes. Employers create associations to advance the interests of industry, commerce, and finance in manifold ways. Farmers organize to protect and improve the position of agriculture—both directly and by means of government aid. Even investors sometimes organize for the purpose of protecting property rights. The salaried and professional groups alone have done little through joint action to safeguard and promote their interests.

The struggle over the distribution of income inevitably thus became the basis of class conflict and hence of social and political instability.

I. WAGES AND PRICES IN HISTORICAL PERSPECTIVE

The technological progress which occurred over the course of the nineteenth century made possible, as noted in Chapter II, a progressive increase in man-hour output and a corresponding rise in the plane of living. Were the benefits of such improvements in the arts of production realized by the consuming public in the form of lower prices, or were they garnered by labor in the form of higher wages?

Increasing wage rates were more significant than price declines in the nineteenth century.

The diagram on page 278 shows the movements of wholesale prices and weekly wages over the course of the nineteenth century.

It will be observed that there were two sharp upward movements of wholesale prices—during the second war with Great Britain and the Civil War. In between wars the general trend was downward, and over the century as a whole the decline was over 50 per cent. There were, however, moderate advances during periods of prosperity, such as the middle 1830's and the early 1880's. During the forty years from 1820 to 1860 the general trend was slightly downward, and there was a substantial downward trend from 1872 to 1895—the bulk of which occurred during the long depressions of the late seventies and the early nineties.

The rise in weekly wages was more pronounced than the fall in wholesale prices. While there were numerous fluctuations in the wage line, the upward trend is very

WHOLESALE PRICES AND WEEKLY WAGES, 1801-1900[2]

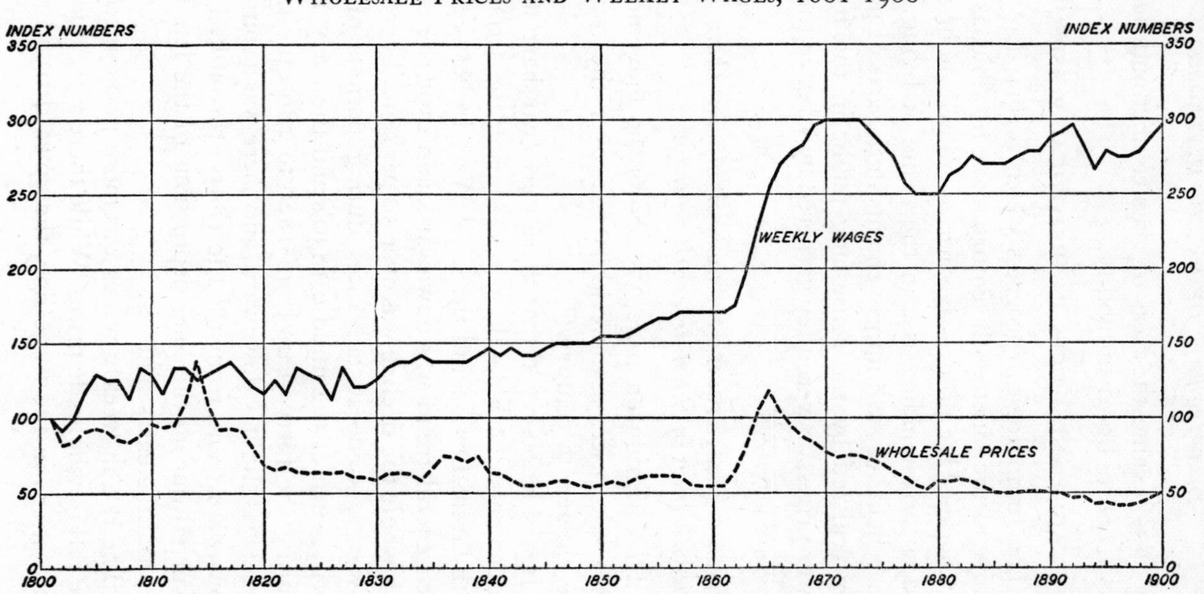

evident. The increase from 1801 to 1860 amounted to 70 per cent, and the rise was fairly uniform after 1830. Moreover, the wage decline following the War of 1812 was much less pronounced than the decline in prices. During the Civil War period wages increased considerably more than prices, and the subsequent downward adjustment through to 1880 was less marked in the case of wages. Thus if we compare 1860 with 1880 we find little change in the level of prices and a great rise in the level of wages. During the two succeeding decades the wage trend was upward, while that of wholesale prices was downward.

Over the century as a whole both the price reduction and the wage increase methods contributed to rising purchasing power, as indicated by the spread between the wage and price lines shown on the chart. However, the wage increase method was the more important. It is of interest to note that the spread increased most rapidly in periods of business depression, when the decline in prices was distinctly greater than the decline in wage rates.

Between 1900 and 1930 wages increased relatively to prices.

For the period since 1900 it is possible to present more adequate data. The chart on page 280 shows the movements of average hourly wages, wholesale prices, and productivity, or man-hour output, in manufacturing from 1900 through 1947.

During the comparatively stable period from 1900 to 1915 both hourly wages and wholesale prices in manufacturing industry increased, with the former showing a slightly greater rise. In the war years wages rose more sharply than prices, while the subsequent de-

Wholesale Prices, Hourly Wages, and Productivity in Manufacturing, 1900-47[3]

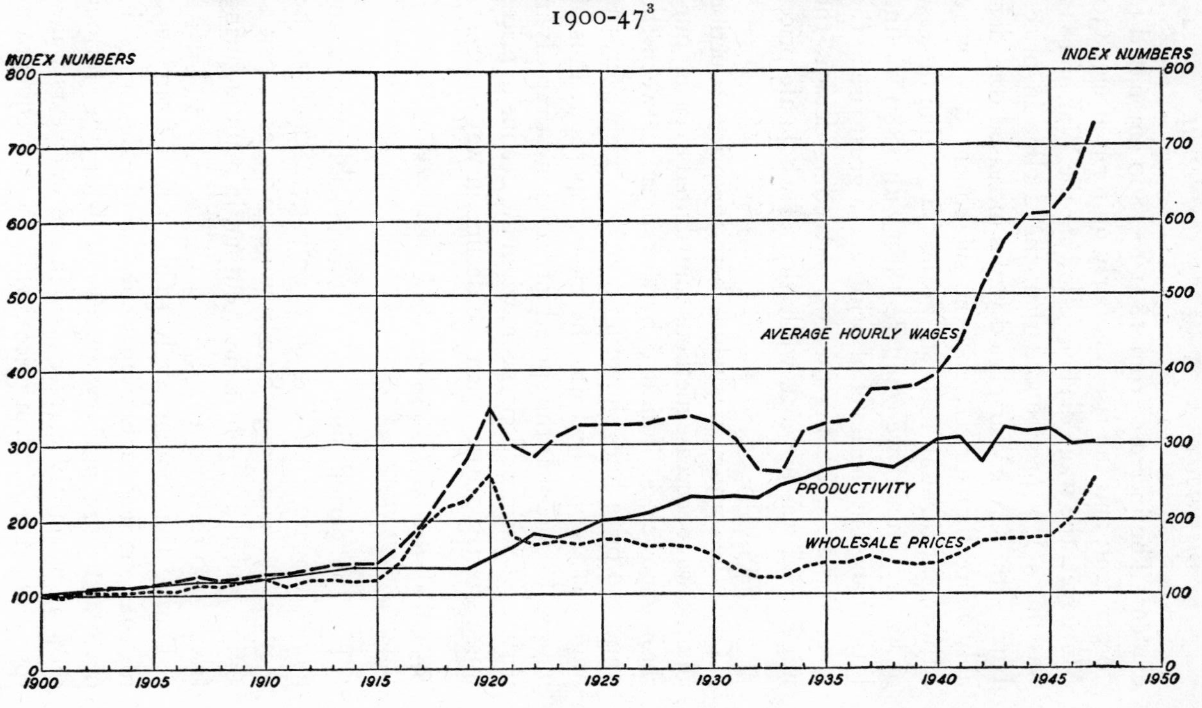

cline in wages was distinctly less marked. Hence the wage and price lines which were fairly close together in 1915 were far apart in 1920. During the prosperity period 1923-29 wages rose somewhat while prices showed a moderate decline. Comparing 1915 with 1929, prices show an increase of about 37 per cent, as compared with an increase of 137 per cent in wages. The wage decline in the great depression of 1929-33 was somewhat greater than the decline in the prices of manufactured products. But at the bottom of the depression the wage index (1900 = 100) stood at 264, while the price index was only 123.

After 1933 wages rose sharply as compared with prices.

During this period both lines moved upward, but the wage line shows a much more rapid rise both during the thirties and the forties. The very steep advance in 1933-34 is attributable largely to the code agreements under the National Recovery Administration. The persistent climb reflects the combined influence of powerful labor organizations, government support, and the labor shortages occasioned by the Second World War. Prices recovered substantially from the low levels reached in the years of acute depression, but again declined somewhat in the late thirties. The upward trend was moderate during the war period, but since the close of the war it closely parallels the rise in wage rates.

Increases in productivity have not kept pace with wage advances.

During the decade of the twenties man-hour output increased faster than hourly earnings, thus making possible some reduction in prices. But from 1933 to 1947 the hourly wage index rose from 264 to 728, while man-hour output increased only from 246 to 303. In consequence there was a strong pressure from the cost side to increase prices. Had it not been for the economies realized from capacity operations since 1941, the upward pressure on prices would of course have been very much greater.

It is apparent that over the century and a half under review labor has been increasingly successful in garnering the benefits of technological progress by means of wage increases. The fact that prices as a whole declined during the nineteenth century suggests that the general increase in productivity was more than sufficient to meet the increasing cost of wages. During the first three decades of the twentieth century the increase in wage rates ran a little ahead of the increase in man-hour output. Since 1930 it may be said that wage increases anticipated and greatly exceeded the rise in productivity.

II. THE DIVISION OF CORPORATE INCOME, 1929-47

Thus far we have been concerned with the relative movements of wage rates and prices—that is, with the mechanism by which the benefits of technological progress are distributed as between the workers on the one side and the consuming public on the other. We now consider the division of corporate income among the groups who participate in the productive process and are remunerated in the form of wages and salaries, interest, and profits. Satisfactory data are available only for the period since 1929. These are presented in the chart on page 283.

The share of corporate earnings going to labor has steadily increased.

Aggregate wages and salaries were of course greatly reduced during the years of acute depression; and throughout the decade of the thirties they remained be-

DIVISION OF CORPORATE INCOME, 1929-47[4]

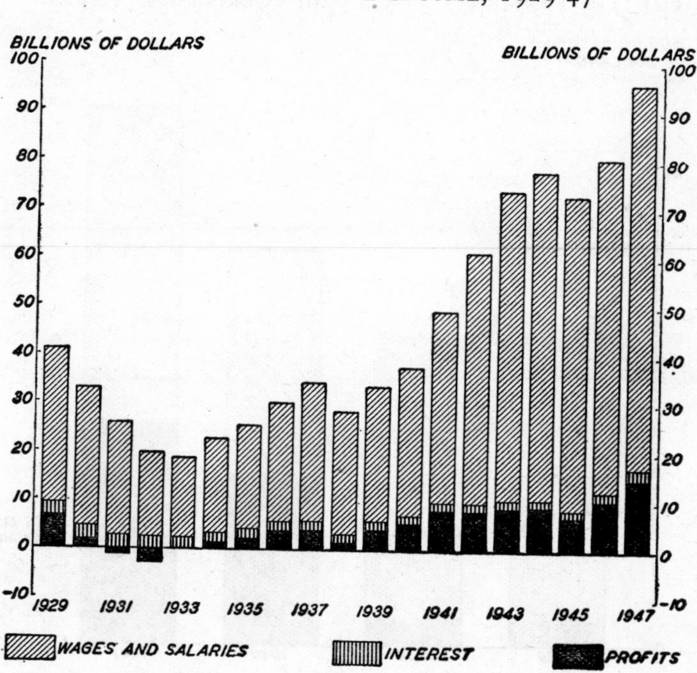

low the level of 1929. But from 1939 to 1947 they increased roughly 200 per cent.

The interest item it will be noted remained practically stable and was slightly lower in 1947 than in 1929.

Profits show wide fluctuations. There were net losses in 1931-32 and very high earnings in 1947. It should be pointed out that the profit figures include inventory gains and losses which are substantial in periods of rapidly fluctuating prices. In 1947 the actual realized profits were some 5 billion dollars less than the nominal figures.

THE GOVERNMENT "TAKE" OF CORPORATE EARNINGS[5]

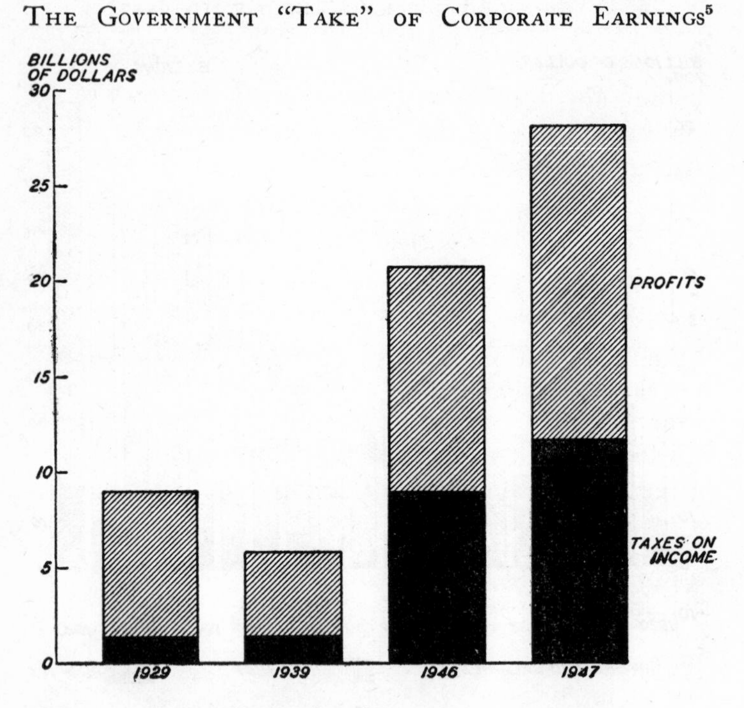

Government has been absorbing a constantly increasing share of corporate earnings.

The earnings figures used in the accompanying chart represent the income available for division before payment of corporate taxes to federal and state governments. Since 1929 increasing corporate tax rates have taken an ever-larger proportion of gross earnings. The chart on page 284 shows corporate profits before and after taxes for selected years.

The proportion of corporate taxable income taken by government has increased from 15.5 per cent in 1929 to 43.3 per cent in 1946. It is obvious that the income absorbed by government is not available either for profits or for wage increases. Moreover, the possibility of extending the benefits of technological progress to the consuming public in the form of lower prices is thus restricted.

III. THE CHANGING DISTRIBUTION OF PERSONAL INCOME SINCE 1929

Thus far we have been considering only special aspects of income distribution. Our ultimate concern is with the division of the total national income among the population as a whole irrespective of their classification as wage earners, farmers, entrepreneurs, or property owners. In this section we shall consider first the changing character of income distribution in the United States since 1929.

There has been a vertitable revolution in income distribution.

It should be recalled at this place that prior to 1929, and especially in the decade of the twenties, the distribution of income in the United States was becoming increasingly concentrated. That is, while the income of all groups was expanding, the growth was more rapid in the higher levels. Since 1929 the situation has been strikingly reversed. This is due in part to a vast upthrust of families to successively higher levels of income, and in

THE RISING LEVELS OF INCOME AMONG THE MASSES[6]

Percentage of Families in Major Income Groups and Percentage of Income Received

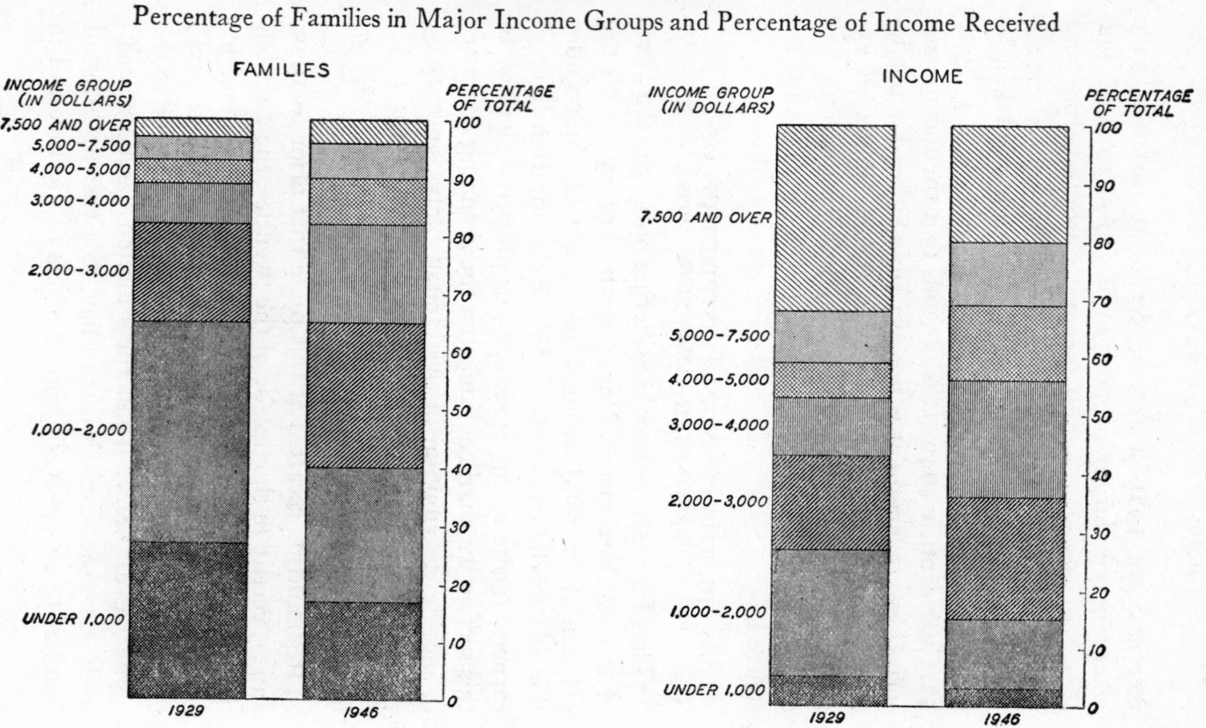

part to the effects of the increasingly progressive income-tax system. It is necessary, therefore, to consider the two aspects of the problem separately.

The chart on page 286 shows for the years 1929 and 1946, respectively, the proportion of families (and single individuals) in the principal income groups and the proportion of the income received by each group. These years afford a good comparison because both were years of high business activity and, moreover, prices were at approximately the same level. The figures represent income received—without adjustments for personal income taxes.

The changing distribution of income is most clearly revealed by the increase in the proportion of the population in the moderate-income groups, that is, from $2,000 up to $5,000. In 1929 about 10 million families—28 per cent of the total—had incomes in this range, while by 1946 this group included 23 million families, or about 50 per cent of the total. The rise is also strongly manifest in the increasing number of families with incomes of from $5,000 to $7,500. Looking at the situation in a reverse way, the percentage of families with incomes of less than $2,000 shows a sharp decline—from roughly 65 per cent in 1929 to about 40 per cent in 1946.

When we study the income columns, we find a marked increase in percentages of total income received in all the intermediate groups from $2,000 up to $7,500. There is a corresponding decrease in the percentage received by those having incomes of less than $2,000; and there is also a decrease in the percentage received by those with incomes in excess of $7,500. In aggregate dollar terms the families in the $2,000 to $7,500 groups in 1929 received 38 billions, as compared with 111 billions in 1946.

The extraordinary rise in the incomes of the masses of the people since 1939 is explained by three principal factors. The first was the vast expansion of production arising out of the war, which virtually eliminated unemployment and increased the number of employees per family. The second was the increase in wage rates as compared with the cost of living. The third was the rise in farm incomes resulting from the extraordinary demands for American farm products which coincided with a period of favoring weather and good harvests.

The tax system has meanwhile effected a great *re*-distribution of income. That is, by means of steeply graduated income-tax rates, the government has come to absorb a large portion of the higher incomes, thereby greatly reducing the *disposable* income available for current consumption and for individual savings. In 1929 federal personal income taxes amounted to 1.2 billion dollars, or 1.5 per cent of the aggregate money income of individuals; in 1946 such taxes aggregated approximately 18 billion dollars, absorbing 10.6 per cent of the income.

In 1929 a family of four having an income of $5,000 paid a federal income tax of 75 cents:[7] a family with an income of $10,000 paid $26; one with $25,000 paid $644; and one with $1,000,000 slightly over 20 per cent. For purposes of comparison we here use the year 1948, in order to take account of postwar tax revisions. The minimum effective rate on 1948 income was 16.6 per cent—which was applicable to the first $2,000 of the taxable income of a single person and $4,000 for married couples. The maximum effective rate was 82 per cent and applied to all taxable income above $200,000 for a single person and $400,000 for married couples. The following table shows the amount of federal tax for 1948 payable at various levels of income by a family of four persons:

Income	Income Tax		Income After Tax
	Amount	*Per Cent*	
$ 2,000	$ 0	*0.0*	$ 2,000
3,000	50	*1.7*	2,950
5,000	349	*7.0*	4,651
7,500	732	*9.7*	6,768
10,000	1,167	*11.7*	8,833
25,000	4,640	*18.6*	20,360
50,000	14,019	*28.0*	35,981
100,000	39,317	*39.3*	60,683
500,000	317,612	*63.4*	182,388
1,000,000	687,186	*68.7*	312,814

The changes in income distribution have modified the consumption-savings ratios.

As a result of the vast shift of families from lower to higher income groups since 1940 and the progressive increases in tax rates, the division of income between consumption and savings has undergone considerable change. Instead of a rising percentage of savings as total national income increases we have had an actual decline in the percentage saved. As noted on page 124 individual money savings declined from 11.7 per cent of the national income in 1941 to 6 per cent in 1947.

The rapidly rising level of family incomes provided the basis for a great postwar expansion in demand for nearly every type of consumer goods. The effects of this enhanced buying power in the hands of millions of families was felt all along the line, notably in better quality meats and other foods, in household furnishings and supplies, in textiles, in a wide range of luxury goods and services, and even in high-priced durable consumer goods. This in turn furnished the stimulus for a great increase in productive capacity.

The expansion of industry, together with the high level of operating costs after the war, required a vast increase in financial resources. The funds required were obtained chiefly from the following sources: (1) accumulated business reserves; (2) undistributed earnings; (3) loans from financial institutions; and (4) the flotation of securities in investment markets.

In the aggregate, business has been able to obtain the funds required—as is evidenced by the fact that existing plants on the whole, have operated at or near capacity, while at the same time new plant capacity was being constructed. However, the sources of funds and the methods of financing employed underwent much change. Accumulated reserves were in due course exhausted, making necessary larger recourse to outside sources of funds—financial institutions and the securities markets. In obtaining funds from the investment market, industrial corporations for a time relied heavily upon common stock flotations; but later preferred stocks and bonds came to play a larger role.

The supply of "risk" capital is becoming meager.

The trend toward preferred stock and bond financing is a reflection of changing conditions in the investment market. By 1947 a critical situation existed with respect to the flotation of common stock issues. The amount of so-called "equity" money had become inadequate to absorb the volume of equity securities that were currently being offered. Numerous issues were very slow in being absorbed, and many contemplated flotations were abandoned.

This situation apparently resulted not from any dearth of investment funds but from a shortage of a particular kind of money savings. The savings of the masses were increasing, but such funds flow chiefly into savings institutions and insurance companies, which are restricted by law to the purchase of seasoned bonds and preferred stock. The deficiency was in that type of investment money that finances new enterprises and the expansion of old ones—commonly referred to as risk capital. The explanation of the comparative scarcity of risk capital is found in three related factors: (1) the restriction of the savings capacity of the middle- and higher-income groups, caused by the steeply graduated tax rates; (2) the fact that tax-exempt securities may yield a higher net return than stocks in new enterprises, where both corporate income and stockholders' income are subject to high tax rates; and (3) the apparent necessity under "prevailing conditions" of emphasizing safety first in the matter of investment.

IV. METHODS OF MODIFYING THE DISTRIBUTION OF INCOME

We are now in a position to analyze the relative merits of the principal methods of modifying the distribution of the national income in the interest of making the economic system function more effectively. Some of the methods affect the *initial* distribution of income, that is, at the points of origin in producing enterprises. Others involve a *re*distribution—after the income has been paid out as wages, interest, dividends, etc. It will be convenient to consider the redistribution method first.

The redistribution method involves on the one side the tax machinery, and on the other the allocation of public expenditures. The system of progressive taxation is based on the principle of ability to pay and is thus by its nature designed to impose heavier taxes on the wealthy than on the masses. Similarly, many types of expenditures are for the express purpose of raising the plane of living and welfare of the masses of the people. This is illustrated by the various forms of relief and security payments and by a wide range of free services designed especially for the benefit of those who cannot afford to pay for them. In recent years this type of redistribution has been broadened to include subsidies of various kinds for the support of selected groups.

The fiscal system can play a significant, though limited, role.

Within limits, the system of progressive taxation is defensible and effective. Beyond a certain point, however, it dulls incentives, and may destroy the principal source of funds for new enterprises involving exceptional risks. Thus the opening up of new fields of production, employment, and income is prejudiced.

Within limits, also, public expenditures to raise the plane of living of the underprivileged and to underwrite and provide free services to the public may be justified. The fundamental problem is to keep aggregate commitments within bounds—that is, within the limits of taxable capacity, and at a level that does not imperil financial stability. A factor already noted is that such programs commonly involve commitments which heavily mortgage future revenues on an expanding scale over a long future. This is notably the case with pensions, social insurance, and educational and health services. Starting from the proposition that all such programs are essential to national welfare, it is easy to argue that we cannot have too much education, health, or security. It is equally easy to forget that such services compete with other national activities for available funds and also for available resources and man power. The over-all limits to the supply of goods and services are set by national productive capacity, which is in turn determined by the factors affecting the expansion of wealth-producing power.

A serious complication, inherent in the fiscal method, is the opportunity afforded special interests to obtain government largess. Such expressions as the "pork barrel" and "feet in the trough" serve to convey the low nature of the process. Such a method cannot be expected—except perhaps in the case of relief—to apportion government outlays in any true relation to the respective merits or needs of the groups involved.

Legislation to increase the income of favored groups tends to destroy economic flexibility.

It has long been the policy of major economic groups to seek legislation designed to protect their special interests or to improve their relative income status. The protective tariff, first on manufactures and subsequently on selected agricultural products, is perhaps the earliest and most familiar illustration. In due course agricultural interests sought and obtained the aid of government in supporting agricultural prices and income at favorable levels, under what is known as the "parity" principle. In effect this policy is designed to maintain former relationships between the prices of agricultural and manufactured products, irrespective of relative changes in demand or in costs of production. Thus the gains resulting from technological advances in agriculture would accrue solely to farmers.

Labor has also sought and obtained the support of government in its struggle for higher wages. First, legislation has been passed which established minimum wage rates for many types of work. Second, labor's policy of establishing a standard work week and requiring overtime rates of pay for extra labor has been given legal sanction. Third, the government, by various means, has strengthened the bargaining power of labor.

This group-pressure political-action method of improving income status gradually results in the destruction of flexibility in the economic system. Reliance is placed on group and government support to prevent the readjustments made necessary by changing demands and changing costs. To the extent that these groups are successful in achieving the ends sought, the market mechanism, by which shifting demands and prices guide the allocation of productive resources, is abrogated.

Profit reductions would yield meager results.

In recent years much emphasis has been placed upon reducing profits as a means of increasing the share available for labor or for the consuming public. It requires only a brief analysis to show that the potentialities in this method are very limited.

The aggregate profits of all industrial, railroad, and public utility corporations in the United States in the exceptional year 1947 were 14.9 billion dollars. Of this sum, however, 5 billions represented inventory gains resulting from rising prices; and were thus not real profits available for distribution. Many corporations had such meager profits that nothing could be taken from them without serious repercussions upon production and employment. At the most, only a few billion dollars earned by the more successful corporations could possibly have been diverted; and this would curtail the funds available for expansion.

Aggregate wages and salaries paid by industrial corporations in 1947 amounted to 79.1 billion dollars. Hence a diversion of as much as 4 billions of profits to labor would have permitted an average increase of only 5 per cent in the level of wages. But since profits are earned very unequally by companies, such a diversion could not raise wages generally; the increase would be confined to the successful companies.

Moreover, the amount of labor employed varies widely in different industries and bears little relation to the profits earned. For example, in the oil refining and chemical industries, profits aggregated $2,030,000,000 in 1947, and the number of workers was 926,000. By contrast, in coal mining and railroading where the number of workers was 2,074,000 aggregated profits amounted to only $560,000,000.

Similarly, the sacrifice of profits in order to reduce prices would not yield significant results. To understand this aspect of the problem, it is necessary to compare the dollars of profit earned with the aggregate sales price of the commodities sold. The dollar sales of all industrial corporations in 1947 aggregated 319.5 billion dollars. The *complete* elimination of 10 billions of real profits would have permitted on the average only a 3 per cent reduction in selling prices. Since the character of productive operations differs widely in different industries, there are naturally wide variations in profit margins—ranging from 1.2 per cent in meat packing to more than 10 per cent in textile products. The possibilities of price reductions would vary accordingly.

The basic problem with which we are concerned pertains to the dissemination of the benefits of technological progress by means of a constantly broadening distribution of currently produced income. The benefits of increasing productive efficiency may be passed along through the medium of increased wages; they may be distributed by means of price reductions which enlarge the buying power of consumers; and the two methods may of course be used in combination. What are the relative merits of the wage-increase and price-reduction methods?

Many hold the view that the simplest and most effective means of promoting continuous economic progress is by passing all of the net gains from increasing productivity to the pay envelopes of workers. It is assumed that the enhanced buying power in the hands of labor will, through generating increased demand, furnish stimulus for further industrial expansion. It should be noted that we are here concerned with progressive increases in wage *rates* in line with increases in productivity rather than with increases in *aggregate* wages resulting from a general expansion of employment such as occurs in times of war or in periods of great boom.

Does the wage increase method generate increased demands and sustain employment?

In seeking the answer to this question it must be noted, first, that increases in productivity do not occur simultaneously throughout the economy. They occur in individual producing establishments at varying times and in differing degrees. The fact that productivity may be said to be increasing at a rate of 2 or 3 per cent a year does not mean that the increase is universal. It may be 5 or 6 per cent in some lines, negligible in others, and even declining in some sectors of the economy. Moreover, in any given industry it may be occurring in some plants and not in others. The analysis of the problem must, therefore, begin with the individual plant where an increase in efficiency occurs.

Let us assume that in a given manufacturing establishment productivity has increased by 10 per cent, and that in consequence the same volume of output can henceforth be produced with 1,000 fewer workers. The discharge of 1,000 workers no longer needed would mean a pay-roll saving of say, $1,000,000 a year. By hypothesis this sum is added to the wages of those remaining in employment. Would this process generate a general increase in purchasing power?

The arithmetic is that a *plus* one million in purchasing power (in the hands of the employed laborers) is exactly offset by a *minus* million of purchasing power (in the hands of the discharged laborers). The increasing productivity thus furnishes no net addition to the national purchasing power. It will be noted also that the money costs of production are not lowered, since the economies resulting from the decrease in labor are completely absorbed in raising the wages of those who continue to be employed.

Since total purchasing power is not increased, no new employment either in this industry or in other industries has been *generated* as a result of the increase in productive efficiency. If those thrown out of employment still have some purchasing power, it would be because they are supported either by relatives, friends, charitable organizations, or the government. In the former cases, the purchasing power of their supporters would be reduced by the amount of the support given; and in the latter case the nation as a whole through tax contributions would have to provide the wherewithal.

In summary, this process results as follows: (1) total wage disbursements remain unchanged; (2) prices remain unchanged; (3) the volume of output remains stationary; (4) the national income remains unchanged; and (5) the volume of employment *decreases*. All that has happened is that employed labor has gained at the expense of those displaced. No direct stimulus to employment either in this or other industries would thus be given.

Where wage agreements are consummated on an industry-wide basis and horizontal increases are called for, the process is further complicated. There are wide variations in the efficiency status of individual plants, and the more efficient may be able to pay the added wages, while the less efficient cannot. When this is the case, prices are of necessity raised to protect the profit margins of the higher-cost producers.

The complications are of course still greater when the wage increases in industry A become the more or less enforced pattern for general increases throughout all industry. The inevitable result is a general rise in prices which, in turn, leads to demands for compensating wage increases. Moreover, under the farm parity principle the rise in industrial prices must be matched by a corresponding increase in the prices of agricultural products. The ultimate result of this distortion is to weaken the income position of unorganized workers, of salaried professional classes, and of those living on fixed incomes. These groups, who comprise many millions of people, suffer a positive reduction in real income.

The price reduction method generates a general expansion of demand.

Starting with the same assumptions as above with respect to the increase in efficiency and the saving of labor power, the million dollars of savings would permit a reduction in the price of the commodity being produced. Thus *inducement* is offered to consumers to buy more of this company's product, the lowering of the price being a *positive* measure calculated to bring an immediate stimulus to demand—thereby tending to sustain employment.

It is possible that the demand for the product of the particular industry in which the increased productivity had occurred might not be sufficiently stimulated by the price decline to call forth an additional increase in output sufficient to maintain employment in that industry. It will be noted, however, that if all the increased purchasing power were not spent for the products of this industry it would be available for purchasing other commodities, stimulating employment elsewhere. Thus in either case the total demand would *tend* to be maintained, thereby preventing displacement of labor.

To guard against misunderstanding, it should be emphasized that in a complex industrial society the process which we have been describing cannot be expected to work with automatic precision. A reduction in price may not always bring an immediate stimulus to demand either in the particular industry or elsewhere. Adverse factors in the general business situation may complicate the problem. There can be no doubt, however, that the *positive inducement* which the price reduction method offers to consumers generally is a direct and immediate stimulus to increased output. The consuming public of course includes the labor population.

It should be recalled at this place that the data pertaining to price and wage movements from 1800 to 1947, presented in the charts on pages 278 and 280, indicates that the sharpest increases in the real income of the masses occurred as a result of readjustments in the price-wage ratio during periods of depression. In virtually every case the price index declined more than did the wage index. In consequence, there was a more or less universal rise in the buying power of wage earners; and as a result there was a general stimulus to demand.

The price reduction method of passing along the benefits of technological progress serves to disseminate the gains to society as a whole. Through the play of market demand, it helps to maintain a flexible economy, responsive to the wants of the masses. It promotes a balanced society, and reduces class and group conflict. The social benefits can, of course, be fully realized only when the practice is followed in all sectors of the economy—in agriculture, transportation, and trade, as well as in manufacturing, mining, and public utilities.

Granted that the foregoing analysis is sound as a matter of logic, it may still be contended that some place must be given to money-wage increases. Since the worker in any given establishment may consume little or none of its product, a price reduction appears of no value to him. What he desires is more dollars with which to buy more of whatever goods or services he may desire. In view of this readily understandable psychology, if wage rates were never increased, there would be a dulling of labor incentive, and some of the potential reductions in costs would not be realized. For these reasons both methods have a place. A compromise has to be worked out by each individual business enterprise through discussions and negotiations with its own workers.

Sharing company profits offers another means of increasing labor income.

A share in profits resembles wages in that it is received in the form of money income. Since it is contingent upon earnings, it cannot be counted on for sure and can only be paid periodically. It has an advantage over wage increases in that the supplementary payments do not become a part of the cost and price structure.

Profit-sharing schemes of various kinds have long been employed by numerous companies, and on the whole with satisfactory results. The idea has been, however, strongly opposed by labor leaders and also by prominent industrialists. The opposition of labor leaders appears to be based, first, on the fact that the role and prestige of the labor leader is greatest when he can claim credit for obtaining increases in the weekly pay check, and, second, on the knowledge that profit-sharing plans tend to draw employers and employees closer together and to emphasize the mutuality of interests. Another objection is that a share in profits is uncertain at best and may be made an excuse for never granting wage increases. On the other hand, a wage-rate increase becomes a definite contractual obligation which can be counted on.

The opposition of employers is based on a simple

principle. It is contended that exceptional profits are due to exceptional management; and since the contribution of labor is no greater in the exceptional plant than in the ordinary or marginal plant, labor is not entitled to a share. All companies should pay the market rate of wages, but should not be expected to give to labor a share in the gains that are directly attributable to management. In the writer's view this conception fails to take account of one significant phase of the problem. Experience suggests that the incentives which profit sharing provides for the workers may make possible the procurement of superior workmen, a reduction in rate of turnover, and an improvement in industrial relations generally.

In conclusion, attention is again called to the paramount importance of continuously increasing the amount of national income available for distribution. Unfortunately, the struggle of competing groups which has come to be the dominant feature of modern capitalistic society rivets attention upon getting a larger share of current income, and thus the importance of producing an ever-larger total to be shared tends to be forgotten. The impression is created that the interests of the various groups are basically conflicting, whereas they are essentially mutual. In fact, the policies pursued often serve positively to lessen man-hour productivity and hence the volume of income available for distribution.

CHAPTER X

CAN DEPRESSIONS BE PREVENTED?

The widely divergent theories that have been advanced as to the cause and cure of business depressions were discussed in an earlier chapter. The analysis there given ended with the conclusion that there was no single cause, that the highly complex economic system is subject to numerous types of maladjustment, that it may get out of gear sometimes at one place, sometimes at another. In the present chapter we shall attempt to answer the question whether any of the devices for controlling the business cycle that have been suggested can be relied upon to eliminate or at least greatly mitigate the severity of recessions in business activity.

We shall consider in turn the possibilities of control by means of: (1) banking and credit policy; (2) fiscal policy; (3) other government stabilization measures; and (4) business policy. In each section the analysis will involve two more or less distinct phases of the business cycle. The first question is whether by restraining or controlling the antecedent expansion a break can be avoided; and the second is whether a recession once begun can be checked in its early stages—in time to prevent extensive paralysis of the economic system.

I. BANKING AND CREDIT POLICY

The reserve reservoirs established in central banking institutions were originally conceived chiefly as a means of meeting financial stringencies and drains on the resources of individual banks—tiding them over dangerous situations and thus preventing financial panics with their disastrous repercussions on business. But in due course these institutions came to be regarded as agencies which might through appropriate credit policies stabilize the economic system as a whole. The credit control machinery as it has developed may be said to have a threefold objective: first, to restrain "dangerous" business expansion; second, to prevent banking panic in case acute financial tension should develop; and, third, to stimulate recovery in the event of a substantial business recession.

The rate of interest has been regarded as the key to central bank policy. According to the theory, the amount of credit outstanding and the volume of money in circulation should be restricted in periods of great business activity and be increased in periods of dull business. This result could be achieved, it was believed, by alternately raising and lowering the interest rate at which banks could borrow from the central institutions, which in turn would affect the rates charged business borrowers.[1] It was reasoned that if the cost of borrowed money increased, businessmen would borrow less, and vice versa. The efficacy of *central bank* control is supposed to lie in the fact that interest rates may be raised or lowered quickly—without waiting upon the slow-moving processes of market adjustment.

The record shows that central banks have nowhere been able to prevent depressions.

In the nineteenth century, as pointed out in Chapter II, depressions in European countries, where central banking institutions had been established, were similar in character to those in the United States with its defective banking organization. The relatively high interest rates existing in periods of prosperity did not effectively restrain expansion; and similarly the very low interest rates of depression periods resulting from the changed conditions of supply and demand in the money market did not bring quick recovery. In the 1870's, for example, in both Europe and the United States interest rates remained at unprecedentedly low levels for several years; and the eventual business recovery is directly traceable to other factors.

Under the Federal Reserve System, established in 1913, the first disappointment came with the acute business collapse and severe depression of 1920-21. The view nevertheless continued to prevail that some progress had been made—since this depression was not ushered in or accompanied by a run on the banks or a general breakdown of the currency system, and moreover proved to be of relatively short duration. The collapse was regarded rather as a sort of inevitable aftermath of the war and early postwar inflation period. It was still believed that under more normal conditions the Federal Reserve Board would be able to restrain undue expansion and bring about a high degree of stability. Such hopes were, however, rudely shattered by the coming of the great depression of 1929.[2]

The interest item is a negligible factor in the outlook for profits.

Profits depend upon the relation between costs and selling prices. Costs in any given enterprise depend upon outlays for wages, raw materials, transportation, etc., as well as for interest. It is, moreover, a truism that unit costs are markedly affected by the volume of production and the extent to which plant capacity is being utilized.

Under modern conditions interest is an insignificant item among the elements of cost. The simplest means of revealing the inconsequential character of the interest factor is by comparing interest with wages and salaries in the major divisions of industry. The figures given in the following tabulation show interest and wages and salaries as percentages of total costs in 1947.[3]

	Interest	Wages and Salaries
Manufacturing	0.4 per cent	26 per cent
Construction (contract)	0.2 per cent	56 per cent
Mining	0.8 per cent	54 per cent
Railroads	4.4 per cent	59 per cent
Electric and gas utilities	11.4 per cent	32 per cent
Trade	0.2 per cent	20 per cent

The sector of the economy that is of dominant importance in relation to business fluctuations is manufacturing industry. It should be observed here that in addition to disbursements for wages and salaries manufacturing enterprises incur large costs for raw materials, transportation, fuel, etc.—in which again the wage element is a major component. Changes in any of these cost items are of vastly greater significance than changes in the rate of interest. The business system does not revolve about the least important element of cost.

It should be noted also that added interest costs, if significant, might be passed along in the form of higher prices. It is always taken for granted that in a period of expansion increases in wage and raw material costs will be added in whole or in part to selling prices; but, curiously, it is always implied by interest-rate theorists that higher interest costs cannot be shifted but must be absorbed by the producer. In this connection it may prove illuminating to see how much of a price increase in manufacturing industry would be required to offset a 100 per cent increase in the average rate of interest—say from 3 to 6 per cent. The answer is—less than half of 1 per cent. By contrast, a mere 10 per cent increase in wage rates throughout industry and transportation would, other things equal, necessitate an increase of something like 7 per cent in price.

In short, the primary sources of rising industrial costs in a period of expansion are higher wages and higher raw material prices. Since the banking authorities have no control over these elements of cost, they can exercise no restraining influence. They have no voice in the wage contract, which governs the amount of pay for a given amount of work.

It is sometimes contended that the impact of higher interest rates is felt in marginal situations—that high-cost producers would be forced to curtail operations. With reference to this observation three comments are in order: First, the interest item among marginal establishments remains a minor element of cost; such companies are much more vulnerable to increases in the cost of wages and raw materials. Second, the interest rate would be raised in periods of prosperity, that is, at the time when even the least efficient companies make good profits—thanks to high volume and high prices. Third, in a highly developed, concentrated industrial economy business trends depend almost entirely upon the outlook as gauged by the managements of large enterprises; marginal establishments are of negligible importance in this connection.

The housing field is commonly cited as one in which the interest item is very important. As the foregoing table indicates, it is scarcely a factor for the building contractor. For the individual home owner also, interest is a factor of minor importance. Where houses are financed out of accumulated savings, the interest item obviously does not bulk large in the figuring. Where houses are purchased on the installment plan, interest is included in the aggregate monthly payments. The simple question in the mind of the potential buyer is whether he can meet the combined monthly payments for amortization, interest, and insurance. Any moderate increase in the rate of interest would be less important than comparable increases in monthly charges resulting from high costs of construction, or from a decrease in the time allowed for amortization of the loan.[4]

At best higher interest rates may exert a psychological influence.

The theory that the interest rate is a powerful instrument of control has become so deeply imbedded in economic and financial thinking that an increase in the rate may possibly produce the desired result even though its direct effects upon costs and profits would be negligible. In other words, faith in the theory may shake business confidence and thus bring about retrenchment; a rise in the interest rate may be regarded as a sort of forecast that trouble lies ahead.

In former times—before the accumulation of abundant centralized reserves—an increase in the interest rate was evidence of a growing scarcity of loanable funds and hence was regarded as a forerunner of positive curtailments of loans. This conception tends to persist even though the money market situation has fundamentally changed, with reserves superabundant. While it is difficult to weigh the significance of this psychological element, at any given time, one can only conclude from the historical record that it has never served to check expansion before the crisis stage was reached.

This psychological factor does not operate in a period of depression. That is, declining interest rates have seldom been looked upon as harbingers of recovery. This is because interest rates have commonly been at a low level for a long period before recovery occurred and remained low for some time after the recovery process had been under way.

A restriction of loans would check expansion, but at the cost of depression.

Credit control by means of higher interest rates, it should be observed, is not supposed to freeze the credit situation; some additional loan expansion would be permitted providing borrowers are able and willing to pay the added cost. We have now to consider the effects of positive *restrictions* on credit expansion and also of outright *contractions* of outstanding loans.

In a period of business prosperity, accompanied by expanding volume and rising wage and other costs of production, business constantly requires an increasing supply of operating funds. In the year 1947, for example, the gross national product increased by 22 billion dollars, higher wage and salary disbursements accounting for roughly 10 billions of the expanded national disbursements. If no additional credit expansion for operating purposes had been permitted, sufficient funds would not have been available with which to meet the increased pay roll and other disbursements. Hence it would have become necessary to contract the volume of production. At that juncture the problem of the banking authorities would have been not how to check further expansion but how to prevent widespread curtailment of business activity and general depression.

It is often assumed that the problem thus posed need present no real difficulty because a restriction of credit expansion would merely serve to prevent further increases in commodity prices, without affecting the physical volume of production. Similarly, it is assumed that a positive reduction of credit would not affect production but would reduce commodity prices. Thus conceived, credit restriction is also deemed an effective means of control. This line of reasoning implies that there is no connection between the supply of goods produced and the supply of money and credit—that they are independent variables.

This underlying assumption is not in accord with the actual processes by which production is carried out in a *pecuniary* society. Industrial production involves in every phase money costs, and the profit obtained is the dollar difference between the financial costs and the sales price. The additional borrowed money made necessary by higher financial commitments enters the channels of trade through the disbursements of business enterprises in connection with current productive operations.

To give concreteness to this analysis let us suppose that in the year 1949 there should be a general increase in wage rates amounting to 10 per cent. This would mean commitments to disburse something like 12 billion dollars of additional pay-roll money during the course of the year. The initiating factor in this situation is the wage contract and not an independent expansion of bank credit. The increased demand upon the banks for operating funds is a direct result of the antecedent increased commitments with respect to financial cost of production. If under such conditions the banking authorities were to prevent any further expansion of bank credit, business would be unable to meet its commitments and a curtailment of production with accompanying unemployment would ensue.[5] Since the credit authorities have no control over the factors which determine wage rates, they must either allow the essential credit expansion to occur or take the responsibility for disrupting contractual agreements and productive operations.

In concluding this discussion, it should be noted that in former times, before central reserve reservoirs were established, positive restrictions on loan expansion often became necessary because of the exhaustion of lending power; that is, the gradual reduction of the reserve ratio served as an automatic check. When the reserves reached the irreducible minimum, it was necessary to restrict loans even though the obvious result would be to precipitate depression. But with the superabundant, concentrated, reserves of the present age, the restriction or curtailment of loans has to be the result of positive action by the central banking authorities. To make such a policy effective, it is necessary to reduce the lending power of member banks, which can be accomplished only by increasing the reserve requirements. Since Federal Reserve officials have not been vested with power to modify reserve ratios, except within prescribed limits, a positive loan restriction or curtailment policy would necessitate congressional action and presidential approval. For this reason quick action would be impossible.

Under present conditions, moreover, the Federal Reserve is not in a position to control all the sources of funds available for business enterprise. First, many corporations possess marketable bonds which can be liquidated. Second, they may float bonds or stock in the investment market or "place" serial notes with insurance companies. Finally, the individual banks may procure additional reserve money by the sale of government bonds to the Federal Reserve Banks—the latter being obliged to purchase such offerings lest the government bond market be undermined. All of these methods of obtaining funds have, in fact, been utilized. Thus a mere increase in reserve requirements will not automatically prevent expansion in working capital funds as required to meet rising costs.

This analysis leads to the conclusion that bank credit control, either through the medium of interest rates or by loan restriction, cannot be relied upon. The interest factor is of negligible importance, and this is the only element of cost which Federal Reserve policy can directly affect. The aggregate volume of credit required to conduct the nation's business is dependent upon the physical volume of production and also upon the level of financial costs—as governed by wage and other cost-determining factors. The banking system may check speculative tendencies by conservative loan policies; but it cannot refuse increased loans to meet rising operating costs without disrupting business and causing depression.

In the foregoing discussion, no reference has been made to consumer installment credit. Here the problem is essentially different because such borrowing is not directly connected with the productive process itself. This retail credit extension merely makes it possible for consumers to purchase more final products than would otherwise be the case. In this field reliance is placed not on increasing interest rates but on requiring larger down payments and shorter maturities on the loans. Restrictions on installment credit, however, can have but small effect upon aggregate consumer demand. A 20 per cent, or 2 billion dollar, decrease in the course of a year in the aggregate volume of installment credit outstanding would be regarded as a great achievement. Such a decrease could be completely engulfed by increases elsewhere—rising money wages, larger profits, and expanding farm income.

II. FISCAL POLICY

The failure of bank credit policy to prevent depression and to bring about quick recovery eventually resulted in shifting attention from the Federal Reserve Banks to the Treasury as the agency for control. This shift, it may be observed, constituted a fundamental departure in policy, for it had hitherto been believed that the control of private finance and business should be divorced from public finance. To this end the Federal Reserve Banks had been made independent of the Treasury; and the members of the Federal Reserve Board had been given long-term appointments. It was feared that budgetary difficulties and political considerations might prevent the exercise of independent judgment with respect to requirements in the realm of private finance and business.[6]

The new view held that it was the responsibility of government to alleviate the distress and suffering wrought by depression and to promote recovery. In due course it was conceived that the Treasury, through alternately expanding and contracting its net disbursements, might become a balance wheel in the whole economic system, decreasing purchasing power in flush times and expanding it in periods of recession. This method came to be known as "compensatory" fiscal policy.

The Treasury possesses one great advantage over the Federal Reserve Banks. The latter, as we have seen, must work *indirectly*—seeking to induce private lending institutions to expand loans in periods of depression and to deter them from increasing loans in periods of great business activity. The Treasury, on the other hand, can put money directly into the channels of circulation—by means of relief payments to distressed individuals and institutions, by subsidies, and by disbursements for the construction of public works. Such funds may be borrowed as required either from private individuals and institutions or indirectly from the government-controlled reserve banks.

The fiscal authorities do not control the most important pipe lines.

Attention must first be given to the problem as it presents itself in periods of great business expansion. Money income flows to the people chiefly as: (1) wage and salary payments by private industry and government; (2) interest and rent disbursements both private and public; (3) business profits (including dividends and retained earnings); and (4) net proceeds from farm operations. The relative magnitude of these disbursements may be indicated by the figures for 1947:

Wages and salaries	118 billions	Business profits	42 billions
Interest and rents	11 billions	Farm proceeds	16 billions

Of the wage and salary total, government disbursements accounted for only about 17 billions, of which 8 billions were paid out by state and local governments. The interest item amounted to roughly 4.4 billions, of which about 400 millions were state and local. Government payments to farmers amounted to less than a billion dollars.

In a boom period the Treasury is powerless to control the flow of funds through the principal conduits. The volume of wage and salary payments in private industry is determined by general employment conditions and the rates of pay stipulated in the wage agreements. The amount of profits depends upon the volume of business and the relation between costs and selling prices. Farm proceeds reflect conditions of supply and demand in the markets for agricultural products. If in a boom period prices of raw materials and the rates of wages constantly rise, the flow of funds through the major pipe lines will increase. At the most, fiscal policies can have a slight *indirect* influence upon the flow of funds through these major pipe lines.

The ultimate source of an expanding supply of money income flowing through private pipe lines in the form of wages, profits, etc. is the commercial banking system. As indicated in the preceding section, as wage rates or other costs increase, the additional operating money involved commonly requires an expansion of borrowing from commercial banks. The Treasury has no direct control over the policies of commercial banks. The Treasury and the Federal Reserve Board find difficulty in co-operating because the fiscal authorities and the banking authorities have divergent interests. The primary responsibility of the Treasury is to preserve fiscal stability, which may involve borrowing at low rates of interest, whereas the primary concern of the Federal Reserve authorities is to raise interest rates in the hope of curtailing credit expansion.

It should be observed at this place that the use of public funds in controlling business expansion would require the aid of Congress which appropriates the essential funds. Theoretically, Congress might co-operate in severely restricting certain types of expenditures in a boom period. But in view of the pressures to which that body is subject, such co-operation cannot be counted on; for example, in the 1947-48 boom congressional appropriations for public works, housing, etc. were substantially increased. To meet this situation, it has been suggested that Congress should give the Treasury, or other administrative agency, discretion with respect to the *timing* of expenditures. In view of the constitutional responsibility that has been placed upon Congress with respect to the expenditure of the people's money, it may well be doubted whether Congress would ever consent to transfer to an administrative agency the power that has been suggested. In any case, the administrative branch of the government is scarcely less subject to pressures for the continuance of expenditures deemed in the interests of the people.

Fiscal control involves taxation as well as expenditures.

Thus far we have been considering only expenditures. Tax revenues are regarded as equally important because they also affect the *net* fiscal situation and hence the volume of funds available for expenditure by the people. The amount of a deficit measures the extent of the government's so-called "contribution to purchasing power," and, in reverse, the size of a surplus measures the government's subtraction from purchasing power.

The volume of tax revenues is partly the result of

the scope and character of the federal tax system, partly the result of tax rates, and in substantial measure the result of the degree of business prosperity. It is difficult to gauge the prospective yield of taxes because an increasing volume of business, accompanied by rising levels of money wages and profits, will greatly increase aggregate revenues, while a moderate slump in business will produce sharp curtailments in tax receipts. Since a twelve-months' budget has to be approved well over a year before the end of the period covered, a relatively long forecast of the trend of business is necessarily involved. If the forecast proves seriously in error, the fiscal situation will be materially altered. If a boom unexpectedly develops, a prospective deficit may be converted to a surplus by a resulting sharp increase in government revenues, together with a possible decline in expenditures. Or if a depression occurs, an expected surplus may be converted into a heavy deficit because of shrinking government receipts and increasing government expenditures.

In this connection it may be recalled that the government's "net contribution to purchasing power" (deficit financing) was extolled as the decisive factor in the business recovery and prosperity period of 1936-37. But, thanks to the increase in tax receipts resulting from the recovery movement, the deficit was wiped out by the spring of 1937—long before the goal of full employment was reached. Then during the severe recession which followed, the deficit again automatically expanded. The government's "net contribution to purchasing power" thus tended to follow rather than lead changes in the business situation.

Such changes in the net fiscal situation cannot concurrently be offset by modifications in the tax system for two reasons: (1) the effects of changes in the tax rates under fluctuating business conditions cannot be accurately appraised, and (2) the results would manifest themselves too late to be effective. Precision and speed are emphasized because business expansion or contraction proceeds daily and weekly; hence if there is to be real "compensatory" action, the change in the net fiscal situation would have to be closely geared to the reverse changes in the private sector of the economy. This is the very essence of the theory. In a boom period, when the compensatory principle requires the maintenance of if not an increase in existing tax rates, there is insistent demand from the public for tax reductions. Whatever the eventual outcome in the way of tax legislation may be, months of time elapse before new legislation can be passed. Moreover, the schedule for tax collections cannot be closely articulated with changes in the flow of purchasing power through private channels.

Fiscal policy cannot control price inflation.

The checking of commodity price advances, or inflation, is regarded as an integral part of the problem of controlling business expansion. Indeed, the view is widely held that price control is the only means of curbing a boom and preventing depression. Tied in with this conception is the belief that rising commodity prices are directly caused by an increase in the national money supply, and that this in turn is primarily due to government fiscal policy. Concretely, it is contended that when the government has a deficit, it pumps money into the channels of circulation, which raises prices, and that when it has a surplus, it subtracts money from the channels of circulation and lowers prices. Accordingly, the obvious way to control inflation would appear to be to replace a budget deficit by a surplus.

The fallacy in this conception lies in the fact that the Treasury controls neither the principal pipe lines by which money gets into circulation nor the principal price motivating factors. Money enters the hands of the people, as we have seen, through the medium of wage, salary, interest, rent, and dividend payments; and the amount of such payments is governed chiefly by wage and other contractual agreements. An increase in wage rates, unaccompanied by an increase in output, naturally involves paying out more money for the same volume of goods produced. On the one side this means that the money cost of production has increased, which commonly necessitates an advance in prices in order to preserve the margin of profit. On the other side, the higher money incomes received by workers enable them to purchase the higher-priced goods. All this lies wholly beyond the control of the fiscal authorities. The determining contractual agreements are made in the realm of business; and the additional money needed to finance the expanding requirements is obtained chiefly from bank credit expansion.

Emphasis has been placed in the foregoing analysis upon the relation of increasing money wages to the inflationary process because of the vast importance of industrial wage payments in the national economy. However, important price movements may also be rooted in agricultural conditions. For example, the very sharp advance in commodity prices in the second half of 1947 and early 1948 was directly traceable to subnormal foodstuff production in this country, coupled with abnormal needs abroad. While the European aid was ultimately financed through the Treasury, *deficit* financing was not involved.

The evidence shows conclusively that there is no correlation between changes in the net fiscal situation and the movements of commodity prices. In the prosperity period of the twenties there were substantial government surpluses every year, but the trend of prices was only slightly downward. In the early thirties there were large deficits, yet the price trend was sharply downward. From 1934 to 1936 the deficits increased and prices rose somewhat. In the prosperity period of 1936-37 the budget was virtually brought into balance, yet prices advanced. From 1938 to 1940 deficits again increased, but the price level remained virtually stable. The vast deficits of the war period were accompanied by rising commodity prices. A deficit of nearly 18 billions in fiscal 1946 was replaced by a surplus of roughly 7 billions in fiscal 1947 and 9 billions in fiscal 1948, yet prices rose sharply. The most rapid advance in prices occurred in the first half of fiscal 1948, at the very time when the budget surplus was reaching maximum proportions. During fiscal 1949 the extent of the surplus was being rapidly reduced and prices were receding.

Before concluding this discussion, it should be pointed out that while the government cannot, through fiscal policy, prevent inflation in a boom period it may, on the other hand, accelerate the inflationary process. By passing legislation establishing higher minimum wage rates, or by otherwise supporting demands for higher wages, the government may assist the spiraling process. By increasing its expenditures for public enterprises, such as public works, highways, housing, etc., the government may contribute to the tension in both labor and commodity markets. Such an increase in government outlays does not, however, necessarily involve deficit financing; for example, the government expanded its expenditures along the lines indicated in the fiscal year 1948 out of a large available surplus. Similarly, the government might restrain business activity by increasing taxes; but the result would not be contingent upon obtaining a budget surplus.

Depressions are not necessarily dependent upon antecedent inflation.

The methods of control which we have been discussing, both bank policy and fiscal policy, are predicated on the assumption that depressions are solely the result of inflationary booms—that if the latter can be prevented business stability would automatically ensue. As pointed out in Chapter II, numerous types of maladjustment within the highly complex economic structure may be responsible for recessions in business activity. The historical record clearly shows, moreover, that depressions are by no means always preceded by boom conditions—involving capacity production full employment, and rising prices.

This is true, for example, of the severe depression which began in 1893, of the moderate depression of 1913-14, of the great depression of 1929-33, and of the depression of 1937-38. In the late twenties commodity prices had been tending gradually downward, there was much unused plant capacity, and there was considerable unemployment. The recession of 1937 followed a very short period of recovery and occurred long before plant capacity was fully utilized and when there was still a vast amount of unemployment. On the basis of the record it cannot even be said that depressions which follow inflationary booms are more severe than other depressions.

Neither banking nor fiscal policy can promptly check an incipient depression.

The analysis to this point has been focused on the possibility of preventing a break in the flow of production and distribution. We now turn to the question whether a recession once under way can be quickly arrested by means of government financial policies.

It may be observed first that the shrinkage in the flow of funds through private channels in a period of contracting production commonly proceeds in a cumulative fashion. Wage and salary incomes fall as overtime pay ceases and the volume of employment declines; and as soon as wage *rates* are reduced, the shrinkage in labor income is accentuated. Concurrently, there occurs a sharp decline in business profits and farm incomes.

All that the *banks* can possibly do in this situation is to be lenient in the matter of loan payments and reduce interest charges on renewals or future loans. The latter would be of inconsequential importance; the former would be helpful only in permitting hard-pressed borrowers to postpone, and possibly escape, bankruptcy.

The *Treasury* can affect the situation *directly* only by giving financial assistance to distressed institutions; and such aid is only alleviatory. Main reliance has to be placed upon the *indirect* influence of the Treasury—through increasing its expenditures for relief and for public enterprises. But at the beginning of a recession such expenditures cannot be expanded with sufficient speed to check the general decline. Whereas the shrinkage in the private sector proceeds daily, some time must elapse before a corresponding expansion in public disbursements can take place. In 1937, for example, the government sought to arrest the recession by means of increased outlays for: general relief, transient relief, rural relief and rehabilitation, student aid, old-age assistance, dependent children, aid to the blind, Civilian Conservation Corps, Civil Works Administration, Works Progress Administration, Bureau of Public Roads, Public Works Administration, and self-liquidating projects of the Reconstruction Finance Corporation. Despite this vigorous and extensive effort to arrest the recession, the decline proved to be very sharp—industrial production falling by one third in the first seven months and by as much as 38 per cent in a year. The volume of unemployment increased by several millions, returning to the level of 1935.[7] The rate of decline was in fact more rapid than in 1929-30 when the shrinkage in industrial production was about 30 per cent in the first twelve months. There was no significant recovery until the war preparedness program was launched in late 1939. Government outlays performed a useful function in alleviating distress; but as the record shows they did not prevent the *recession* from becoming a severe depression.

The sheer volume of contraction in the private sector may well greatly exceed any practical possibility of expansion in the public sector. Starting from a high level of national production, employment, and income such as prevailed in 1948, a 30 per cent slump would quickly reduce the rate of flow of money income by something like 60 billion dollars a year.

III. POLICY UNDER THE EMPLOYMENT ACT

Consideration must now be given to the Employment Act of 1946 as a more comprehensive approach to the depression problem. It may be recalled that the original sponsors of this law contended that the government should be *required* to maintain or provide full employment, thereby eliminating or "outlawing" depressions. As finally passed the term *full employment* was dropped and instead of a mandatory provision it was declared to be the

> . . . continuing policy and responsibility of the federal government . . ., with the assistance and co-operation of industry, agriculture, labor, and state and local governments, to coordinate and utilize all its plans, functions, and resources for the purpose of creating and maintaining . . . conditions under which there will be afforded useful employment opportunities . . . for those able, willing, and seeking to work, and to promote maximum employment, production and purchasing power.

To facilitate the carrying out of this policy of doing everything practicable to maintain a high level of business activity and employment, the act created a Council of Economic Advisers to assist and advise the president. In brief, it is the responsibility of this Council to analyze and interpret economic developments and trends, both current and prospective, for the purpose of determining whether a recession is in the making; to appraise the various programs and activities of the federal government in relation to current trends; and to recommend to the president policies designed to avoid economic fluctuations. The president is required to present in January of each year an Economic Report to Congress. The act also provided for a joint congressional committee to review the president's economic report; to make continuing studies of problems therein raised; and to consider means of co-ordinating programs in furtherance of the general policy laid down by the Employment Act.

This approach to the problem is commendable in that it abandons the conception that business stability can be achieved by some single device or simple formula. It comprehends both banking and fiscal policy, along with other federal government programs such as public works and relief payments; and it also seeks to enlist the co-operation of state and local governments and of private industry, labor, and agriculture.

The possibilities of this plan are severely limited by several practical considerations.

In the first place, the analysis and interpretation of current economic trends, as the history of business forecasting has amply demonstrated, remains a very hazardous enterprise. There is commonly wide disagreement both among professional prognosticators and business executives as to the probable trend of business; and it is a fact that depressicns have often broken quickly and unexpectedly. Psychological elements and political developments may at times be no less important than underlying economic factors.

Second, in view of the complexity and sensitiveness of the economic system, there are no adequate criteria by which to gauge the potential effects of the policies that might be pursued. Ill-considered actions, or even carefully conceived programs, may precipitate rather than prevent recession. As the Third Annual Report of the Council of Economic Advisers states the problem:

The principal limitations [to the functioning of the Council] are imposed by the fact that no collection of data can comprehend the enormous variety of economic relationships and no techniques of analysis can forecast with assurance the actions and reactions of a free people.

A condition which has given the Council great difficulty is the lack of criteria by which to determine the relationships among prices, wages, and profits which are workable, in the sense that they contribute in the largest possible degree to economic stability.

A third difficulty relates to the time involved before the stage of action could be reached. The Council's analysis prepared in December is made available to the Joint Committee of Congress some time in January. After conducting hearings, this Committee must submit a report not later than the first of March for the guidance of various congressional committees having jurisdiction over one or another phase of economic policy. Before these committees could complete their deliberations and a co-ordinated program could be achieved, several months would have passed. And it is pertinent to recall here the discussion in Chapter VI with respect to the inherent difficulties in evolving a truly co-ordinated national program. Ill-considered government policies might do more harm than good.

The only types of action that can be taken with considerable expedition are those for which congressional authority had hitherto been granted. As a practical matter action would have to be chiefly along the lines pursued, without effect, in 1937. (See page 323.) The most that could be hoped would be that government disbursements might be on a substantially greater scale; it is hardly conceivable that they could rapidly be increased by as much as 40 or 50 or 60 billion dollars a year. The volume of public works authorized and blue-printed is likely to be limited in view of the demonstrated reluctance of the government in good times to postpone such undertakings for an indefinite period. In any case much time is required to reach the stage of actual disbursement.

The fourth limitation derives from the fact that the law specifically states that government action shall be carried out "in a manner calculated to foster and promote free competitive enterprise." With this restriction it would not be permissible, for example, for the government to construct industrial plants with a view to offsetting reductions in private capital construction and continuing or accelerating the current rate of expansion.

It will be observed that if a government-financed industrial plant expansion program were undertaken the test of need would not be found in free competitive markets, reflecting consumer demands. The decision for expansion would be made by government officials in accordance with their conception of national needs. Thus would the private enterprise system be supplanted by a government planned economy. At this point it is pertinent to observe that the very effort to maintain prosperity by means of government actions which interfere with market adjustments and forecast direct government participation in industrial activities might prove the decisive factor in bringing on a depression.

In a later section we shall consider whether anything can be done by government, or by government and private enterprise jointly, to establish a depression floor and to expedite the process of recovery.

IV. BUSINESS POLICY

The alternating periods of prosperity and depression that have characterized the private enterprise system furnish sufficient evidence that business management has not been able in the past to stabilize production and employment. Nor is there reason for hope that businessmen can in the future prevent the occurrence of depressions.

It is difficult for individualistic enterprises to restrain expansion.

It is the task of each business manager to gauge the outlook for his company and to plan his production schedule accordingly. The future will depend in part upon conditions in his particular industry, and it will also commonly be affected by the general outlook for business as a whole. If the general economic situation is strong, nearly every type of industry will stand to benefit; and accordingly, each business executive will be inclined to expand his production schedule. An expansion movement thus begun tends to feed on itself, for each increase in output means an increase in purchases of raw materials, in wage disbursements, etc.

In a period of such expansion no business executive can risk reversing the general trend unless he is very certain that the general advance has practically run its course. It is the business manager's job to make profits for the stockholders, and as a practical matter he is under strong compulsion to make all the profits possible while the going is good. If the hired executive contracts production a year too soon, his very position is rendered precarious; thus even the cautious executive is constrained to go with the tide.

The question must be raised, however, whether wise business policy with respect to prices might not remove the possibility of depression. In a period of business expansion, when technological progress is occurring, would not price reductions serve both to check inflation and to sustain the purchasing power of the masses? For reasons set forth in other chapters, it appears essential that progressive reductions in prices should accompany advances in productivity—both in periods of prosperity and depression. But it does not follow that sound price policy can be depended upon to stabilize business conditions.

Consider first the operations of the price system in a highly competitive economy—in which prices are determined by the forces of demand and supply in free markets. Under the competitive principle, each individual business executive is expected to get the best price possible; and in a seller's market, which is characteristic of boom periods, one would expect prices to advance. It should be recalled in this connection that in the nineteenth century, when small-scale, non-monopolistic enterprise was in its heyday, prices advanced rapidly in boom periods. The individual enterprise system naturally works that way.

The possibility of restraining price advances is much better where business is conducted by giant corporations, which are in a position to formulate price policies designed to yield the best results over a period of time. If a few hundred major corporations, whose combined output is of overwhelming importance in the national economy, should pursue systematically a policy of reducing prices whenever technological progress permits, a stabilizing influence would be exerted. Certainly the results would be substantially better than if they followed a policy in boom periods of charging all that the traffic might temporarily bear.

It should be observed, however, that in a boom period labor may be able to appropriate the full benefits of technological advances. Indeed, because of shortages and the power of organization, labor may obtain increases in wages quite out of proportion to improvements in technology and the advantages obtained from capacity production. Under these circumstances prices must rise if the profit margin is to be retained. In short, the individual businessman finds himself inextricably involved in the general spiral of rising costs and prices.

In concluding this discussion, it should be noted that *concerted action* to check overexpansion and advancing prices does not appear to be feasible. Agreements to restrict production, which would involve a reduction of employment, would doubtless meet with the strong opposition of labor and of government. It is possible, moreover, that if any substantial curtailment in production schedules were made in major industries, the result might be not only to check expansion but to cause a recession which might get out of hand. In any event, concerted action either with respect to production or prices runs counter to the principle of free competition and would be in contravention of national antitrust policy.

Business enterprises, whether small or large, may contribute to stability in periods of prosperity by refraining from speculation in inventories. The accumulation of excessive stocks of raw materials and supplies in anticipation of price advances not only adds to market tensions and price distortions but gravely complicates the subsequent processes of readjustment. Understanding with respect to this problem has been growing in recent times, and improving inventory control offers promise for the future. However, prudential restraint along these lines cannot ensure that depressions will not occur—for, as we have seen in earlier chapters, numerous types of maladjustment can precipitate business reaction. It may be recalled in this connection that the 1929 depression had not been preceded by inventory accumulation.

Once under way a buiness recession cannot be halted by business management.

Once a business reaction begins the problem of the individual business manager is the reverse of that in a period of expansion. If he resists the downward tide and seeks to maintain or increase his production schedule, he courts disaster. As a practical matter he finds it necessary to trim sail to meet the changed situation. Again, the forces at work are cumulative in their effect, each curtailment resulting in a ramifying decrease in demand.

Granted that the individual business manager is helpless in the situation, could not the difficulty be met by means of group action? It was this thought that prompted the Hoover administration in 1929-30 to induce the railroad and public utility industries to continue, and even increase, their outlays for construction and equipment. The fact is that capital outlays in these fields in 1930 reached record levels. Whatever may have been the sustaining influence of such expenditures during the year 1930, they obviously were not powerful enough to prevent the collapse of 1931. (See pages 89-90.)[8]

In Chapter II attention was called to the *price rigidity* explanation of business depressions. In brief, this theory holds that recessions degenerate into depressions because of inflexible elements in the price structure—that if all prices and wages were promptly reduced, market demand would be sustained and equilibrium would be quickly restored. Those who hold this theory condemn the price and wage maintenance policies of big business and big labor organizations and extol the virtues of the price flexibility of a small-scale, highly competitive economy.

Unfortunately this conception finds no historical support. We had frequent, acute, and long depressions prior to the development of large-scale business enterprise and labor organizations in the late nineteenth and early twentieth centuries. (See page 40.) While adequate statistical indexes relating to the prices of manufactured products—and to wages—are not available for the nineteenth century, it is known that sharp wage and price cutting was characteristic of these earlier depressions.[9]

The explanation of the failure of price and wage cuts to halt the onward sweep of a recession is found in the fact that the price declines themselves cause business managers to postpone purchases in the expectation of buying more cheaply later. This *waiting* for prices to fall still further is primarily responsible for the continuing shrinkage of demand, and in production and employment.

V. IS IT POSSIBLE TO MITIGATE DEPRESSIONS?

If we cannot prevent the recurrence of depressions, is it not at least possible to lessen their severity and shorten their duration? Here we are disposed to believe that an affirmative answer may be given with some degree of assurance.

Traditional analysis assumed that business recovery could not occur until the "liquidation process" had run its course. In the view of some this meant until costs had been reduced to a "reasonable" level; to others it meant until normal commodity price relationships, temporarily distorted, were again restored. It was believed that automatic market processes, if allowed to operate freely, would in due course bring about the essential readjustments; and that any effort to start an upward movement before *bottom* was reached would be abortive.

However, as has often been pointed out, it is difficult to know when bottom with respect to costs has been reached. So long as business leaders believe that costs may go still lower or that certain elements of costs are still seriously out of line, they will continue to operate on a cautious, minimum basis. Prudent business policy requires waiting until the danger of further liquidation appears to have been rather definitely removed.

The difficulty with the conception that we must wait until normal price relationships are restored before recovery can proceed is that the pre-depression relationships may never be reached. There certainly appears to be no reason to assume that the particular price relationships existing at the time depression began were satisfactory and that their re-establishment would in consequence furnish a sound basis for recovery and expansion. In any case, the historical record reveals that recovery has often occurred at a time when the price structure was highly distorted, as gauged by former relationships. Then, after recovery was under way a considerable readjustment of prices occurred as a result of an exceptional rise in lines that had been most severely depressed.

One of the worst features of depressions is the exceptional declines in the prices of agricultural products. The explanation is that the production of these commodities cannot be quickly adjusted to changing conditions of demand; hence the markets for such products are demoralized and prices fall to levels which bear little relation to underlying economic realities. In turn, this extreme depression in the agricultural sector of the economy reacts upon the industrial situation and contributes to the general uncertainty over the future. It would seem, therefore, that government support of the prices of agricultural products at specified levels would be helpful in checking the general decline. Such price floors should be substantially above the levels which might otherwise be reached but should be substantially below the levels existing in the prosperity period.

The need is to establish confidence that a tenable bottom has been reached.

A striking characteristic of depressions has been the long-continued hesitation in making forward commitments, even after drastic liquidation has occurred. For example, in the depressions of the 1870's and the 1890's business remained severely depressed for several years. Since there is no assured rock-bottom level at which recovery will automatically occur it would seem that the essential requirement is to reach agreement at some stage in the decline that a sufficient readjustment has taken place to provide a satisfactory basis for recovery. Granted that some readjustment is essential to remove the distortions that develop in a boom period, a 50 per cent reduction in prices and wages hardly seems necessary to purge the economic system. Why would not a much less drastic readjustment serve equally well? In short, why should we wait for a "natural economic bottom" when such a bottom is not definable and can be recognized and identified only in retrospect?

Since a forward movement, once under way, tends to

be self-propelling, it would seem that an *initiating impulse* or push-off is the primary need. Such an impetus has often been provided by some fortuitous development. It would seem that it might also be provided by an agreement between government and industry that further liquidation is not necessary and that a feasible basis for recovery exists.

Such a plan was in fact formulated shortly after the First World War. For the first few months after the cessation of hostilities, business judgment as to the future was in a state of suspense. While no drastic liquidation occurred during the winter of 1918-19, business remained hesitant about making forward commitments on the prevailing level of costs and prices. The view eventually crystallized, however, that while prices *might* fall and doubtless *would* fall unless a forward movement was soon started, it would be possible to go forward on the basis of the existing level of costs. There were many discussions of the situation among business leaders and government officials, and the opinion was strongly expressed by some that the essential requirement was for leading producers to agree to go forward for the balance of the year.

While no formal agreements were consummated, certain leading industrial corporations announced in the spring of 1919 that they were going ahead with production programs. This change in psychology, accompanied by expanded commitments in important sectors of the economy, rapidly dispelled the existing uncertainty and led to a general forward movement. As noted above, a somewhat similar plan was pursued by President Hoover in 1929-30, though the agreements then reached were confined to the railroad and public utility fields.

To be effective such an accord would require the co-operation of all major groups concerned—government, industry, labor, and agriculture. In the interest of reaching a tenable bottom as rapidly as possible, thereby shortening the depression, voluntary readjustments of prices and wages might be necessary.

It does not appear possible to lay down a general formula by which to judge precisely when a tenable bottom has been reached. The degree of liquidation essential to establish a feasible basis for recovery would depend upon the extent of the antecedent inflation or distortion and the intensity and scope of the recessionary movement. While views as to whether and when a feasible bottom had been reached would doubtless vary widely, it should be remembered that recoveries have usually occurred at times when disagreements still existed as to whether the liquidation process had gone far enough. Fortunately, the history of depressions and recovery movements indicates that once some fortuitous development or combination of circumstances, economic or political, provides a sufficient forward impulse to restore business confidence, an expansion will occur irrespective of the severity and duration of the liquidation process. (See page 40 for the duration of American depressions.)

Such a co-operative effort to turn the tide of depression offers much greater prospect of success than does any conceivable single-handed government action. Government outlays as we have seen are largely confined to relieving distress and providing employment on public enterprises that are not of sufficient magnitude to offset the decline in the private sector. At best such expenditures can only indirectly provide a stimulus to private enterprise. Moreover, this pump-priming process is like a two-edged sword. Since the public enterprises are for the most part not self-supporting, procreative, and revenue producing, they involve an expansion in the public debt and an added tax load upon the private economy for the future, thus weakening business confidence. This method of promoting recovery was put to the test in the thirties, especially in connection with the recession of 1937-38, when, as we have seen, the government opened every faucet to enlarge the stream of purchasing power. Genuine recovery did not ensue, the private economy remained depressed, and unemployment continued on a vast scale. A much more comprehensive and direct attack upon this problem is therefore necessary.

We can hold out no assurance that a co-operative effort to turn the tide of depression such as has been suggested is sure to succeed. Certainly it provides no automatic machinery by which to start the wheels in motion. It might prove extremely difficult to reach accord with respect to the conditions requisite for recovery. Moreover, some depressions might be so far-reaching in their ramifications, nationally and internationally, as to make it impracticable to proceed with the desired dispatch. We suggest only that the approach here outlined is worthy of serious consideration.

In conclusion, it would appear that in view of the variety of forces operating within the economic system and the many potential sources of maladjustment which exist there is little reason to believe that perennial prosperity is a realizable goal. However, it does not follow from the fact that there is no panacea that there is no hope for improvement. Long experience has given us a somewhat better understanding than formerly of the sources of economic maladjustment that may develop in periods of prosperity; and the accumulation of statistical data in recent decades has made it possible to detect developments or trends much earlier than was formerly the case. With growing wisdom we may hope to lessen the amplitude of business fluctuations and especially the severity and duration of the depression phase of the cycle.

If, as the analysis of this chapter indicates, there is slight prospect that fluctuations in business activity can be altogether eliminated, does it follow that the private enterprise system must be abandoned in favor of state socialism or communism? Such a conclusion would imply that the only criterion of the merits of an economic system is its ability to provide continuous employment for the entire working population. It would forget the advantages of the creative and driving force inherent in the competitive system and ignore the stultifying effects of the destruction of individual freedom and initiative that characterize government-controlled and dominated societies. Free enterprise, despite its imperfections, weighs well in the balance.

CHAPTER XI

THE WORLD THEATER

The analysis of this volume as a whole has been concerned with factors and forces that are as germane to other countries as to the United States. Indeed, the discussion of the first two chapters was definitely cast in terms of world conditions and developments and that of the third in terms of international economic relationships. In subsequent chapters, however, the analysis was focused largely on American conditions, potentialities, and requirements. In this final chapter some comments appear necessary with respect to economic conditions and problems in the world at large and to the bearing of such conditions upon American economic life.

As we write, the threat of future war still enshrouds the world scene. In the nature of the case if war, or concentrated preparation for war, should continue to dominate the economic life of nations, there is little prospect of economic stability or progress. We can only hope that in due course mankind will find his way to enduring peace. The analysis which follows is based on this assumption.

I. THE EVOLUTION OF A WORLD ECONOMIC SYSTEM

As a preliminary to the discussion of the international situation today and the problems involved in re-establishing stability, it will be helpful to summarize very briefly the main factors responsible for the evolution of a world economic system during the nineteenth and early twentieth centuries. To give concreteness to the discussion, reference will be made to the developments which have occurred in one after another of the leading nations of the world.

Great Britain took the lead in becoming a nation with wide international economic relations. Its economic pre-eminence throughout the nineteenth century was due chiefly to two factors. The first was the momentum of an early start in the field of manufacturing enterprise, especially in the heavy industries. The second was the early development of a sound currency system which established universal confidence in credits payable in British sterling. From the Napoleonic era on, London banking houses financed much of the trade of the world, and well before the middle of the century the British people were extending long-term credits to and making direct investments in the United States, British possessions, the Orient, and South America. By the end of the century the economic and financial life of the island kingdom was closely linked with that of the entire world. As a part of the process of becoming internationally interdependent, Great Britain abandoned the protective tariff in the 1840's in order that cheap raw materials and foodstuffs, and hence low-producing costs, might give particular advantages to the export trade in manufactured commodities.

France began to make substantial investments abroad toward the middle of the century. By 1870 it had accumulated some 2 billion dollars of foreign investments, chiefly in England, the United States, and nearby European countries, a substantial part of which was liquidated in paying the German indemnity of 1870. Between 1875 and World War I, France gradually extended her foreign investments, particularly in Russia, and in her colonies in Africa and the Far East—the latter chiefly by the process of direct investment. Unlike Britain, France continued to maintain her agriculture as an important part of her economic structure.

Germany did not emerge as a great industrial and financial power until after 1875. The extraordinary expansion that occurred during the next twenty-five years was, however, the most striking European development of the nineteenth century. While the industrial revolution came somewhat tardily in Germany, once under way it flowered with astonishing speed. Despite restricted natural resources, except for coal and iron ore, German organizing genius and scientific aptitude quickly made the Reich a great manufacturing nation, purchasing foodstuffs and raw materials in other parts of the world and converting them into finished products for sale over wide geographic areas. She also became a great financial center, especially in connection with short-term trade and industrial credits extended to central and eastern Europe. Germany, like France, continued to foster agriculture. This great development was accompanied by a very rapid increase in population and also by a steadily rising plane of living which made Germany a large importer of certain types of manufactured products, especially from the countries of western Europe.

Other western and central European countries of course contributed to and shared in the general expansion. This was especially the case with Holland and Belgium, which possessed colonial empires, but it was also true of the Scandinavian countries, Austria, Hungary, and Italy. Russia, the Balkans, and Spain, however, remained largely agricultural.

The development of industrialism in central and western Europe, accompanied by a vast increase in urban population, contributed greatly to the prosperity of agricultural countries in far parts of the world. For example, the opening of the great interior of the United States to profitable agriculture was a direct result. In turn, these cheap foodstuffs and raw materials made it possible for European countries, with restricted agricultural resources, to sustain huge populations.

In the last quarter of the nineteenth century there began in the Far East another great economic development. As a matter of national policy, Japan isolated itself from the rest of the world from 1600 until the political revolution of 1868. Immigration and emigration were forbidden and virtually all trade relations with the outside world were proscribed. The population of the Japanese islands, with a productive area about equal to that of the state of West Virginia, had increased between 1600 and 1720 from roughly 10 to 30 millions; but for nearly a hundred years thereafter it remained practically stationary, being limited, not by birth control but by famine, disease, and systematic infanticide.

The revolution quickly transformed the hermit kingdom to a nation seeking universal knowledge of and trade with all the world. The rapid acquisition of scientific and technical knowledge, the establishment of a modernized internal economic and financial organization, and the opening up of extensive trade relations with the outside world, resulted in a doubling of the population and of the plane of living in a period of sixty years. The application of science and technology, both in agriculture and industry, rapidly increased man-hour output, and at the same time Japan was now able to specialize her productive efforts in the lines where she possessed the greatest relative advantage. She furnished raw silk to the industrial nations of the West, and she drew in turn upon the outside world for other raw materials. She imported raw cotton from the United States, Egypt, and India, converting it into finished products, not only for her own population but for export, especially to the Asiatic mainland. In due course the range of her industrial proficiency was extended to include metallurgical products and chemicals. Japan also furnished capital, largely in the form of direct investments, for the development of the resources of eastern Asia.

This complex, integrated, world system was in a state of balanced equilibrium.

The developments to which we have been referring proved cumulative in their effects—expansion in each particular nation or area contributing to expansion elsewhere. The process was furthered by the flow of investment capital from the wealthier states to the less developed areas, enabling the latter to increase productivity and thus to raise their standards of living. The system may perhaps best be characterized as one of financial and trade interdependence. This world-wide economic structure, it should be noted, was built up through the ordinary processes of trade and finance. With few exceptions governments played a minor role.

This world system was held in a state of equilibrium by a more or less balanced interchange of goods and services, supplemented by credit operations and international movements of gold. As indicated in Chapter III, the internal economies of each nation were adjusted to international economic requirements. That is, creditor countries received the income due from abroad through net importation of goods and services, while debtor countries met their external obligations from the proceeds of export surpluses. Such deficiencies as might exist at any particular juncture could readily be met by additional credits or by shipments of bullion and specie.

II. WORLD ECONOMIC DISORDER TODAY

As shown in Chapter III, the First World War thoroughly disrupted the economic equilibrium of the world, and the world depression continued the process of disintegration. The international monetary system, based on gold, was abandoned in the thirties, and the exchange and fiscal position of nearly every country was seriously weakened. Meanwhile, a vast network of economic controls, designed to protect and foster the trade and industry of each country, came into being.

The Second World War completed the destruction of world equilibrium. The economies of the enemy countries collapsed under the impact of war and ultimate defeat; and the condition of many of the occupied countries of Europe and the Far East was little better. Meanwhile, the United States had furnished aid to its allies on a scale vastly greater than that in World War I. This time, however, the aid was extended on a gift rather than a loan basis.

The United States assumed the leading role in providing relief and promoting reconstruction.

The devastation and ravages of the conflict were such that a continuance of American assistance to other countries for a year or more after the war was seen to be indispensable to the recovery of prostrate nations. The relief and rehabilitation program was extended to enemy-occupied countries as well as to our wartime allies. Such aid took a variety of forms and was administered by numerous agencies. While there was much confusion, ineffectiveness, and waste in their administration, these programs nevertheless served to alleviate human misery and also to bridge the gap between the cessation of war activities and the resumption of peacetime production.

The grave situation that would exist at the end of the war and the difficult problems of economic and financial reconstruction that would be encountered had been perceived by the governments concerned, and much advance planning had occurred. The Export-Import Bank, organized during the world depression to finance American foreign trade, was given an expanded role, in connection with the extension of credits for purposes of rehabilitation. Of more far-reaching and enduring significance was the organization by international agreement, in which the United States played a leading part, of the International Monetary Fund and the International Bank for Reconstruction and Development.

The basic purpose of the Monetary Fund was to help preserve stability in the international exchanges by enabling countries temporarily short of foreign currency to tide themselves over the crisis. Its focus was thus on the short-term credit situation. The International Bank for Reconstruction and Development, as the name implies, was concerned rather with long-term loans for the development of the productive resources of the countries concerned. Whereas the Export-Import Bank was a purely American institution, both the Monetary Fund and the International Bank were joint enterprises, sponsored, owned, and administered by a large group of participating countries.

It may be noted in passing that two other agencies, organized under the auspices of the United Nations, were designed to further international economic stability. The first is the Food and Agriculture Organization of the United Nations, concerned with stimulating general agricultural progress and stabilizing the prices of those agricultural commodities which are highly susceptible to fluctuations. The other is the International Trade Organization, whose purpose is to promote an expansion of reciprocal interchanges of commodities among nations.

These various plans and agencies were, however, unable to bring about a quick restoration of world prosperity or to stabilize the international exchange situation. The disorganization of economic life resulting from the war, the social and political instability of many countries, and the continuance of international tension combined to retard thoroughgoing economic reconstruction and recovery. These conditions, for example, made it virtually impossible for the Monetary Fund and the Bank to function in the ways intended.

In due course a co-operative stabilization program was evolved.

To appreciate the significance of the so-called Marshall Plan for the stabilization of Western Europe, inaugurated in 1947, it is necessary to summarize the sources of difficulty and the major principles deemed necessary for the successful operation of the plan.

The sources of disorganization included: (1) the direct effects of the war in dissipating assets and reducing productive capacity; (2) the disruption of trade relations; (3) acute shortages of certain *key* products, which limit the use of existing plant and equipment and impede production generally; (4) financial and monetary instability, destructive to business enterprise; (5) the continuance of government restrictions hampering the resumption of international trade; (6) the concentration, in previous aid programs, on *relief* to the neglect of *economic reconstruction;* (7) ill-conceived policies pertaining to postwar requirements, especially in Germany; and (8) the unsettled political situation.

The most fundamental and persistent source of difficulty was not the actual physical destruction of wealth but the disruption which had occurred in a closely interrelated producing, trading, and financial system, embracing all Europe and extending also to other parts of the world. Of particular importance was the great decline in European trade with Southeast Asia. Industrial production in many countries had shown marked improvement, but in others there was little or no increase in output. Moreover, in the case of certain commodities of crucial importance, production was everywhere still far below prewar levels.

The adverse consequences of these various factors reached a common focus in the international exchanges. Europe's loss of foreign investments and the destruction of shipping facilities reduced earnings hitherto available for meeting foreign payments. Similarly, low agricultural yields increased import requirements of food and certain raw materials. On the other side, the reduced output of industrial products and the disruption of foreign markets curtailed exports and hence the capacity to pay for essential imports. How to meet the deficit in the international accounts was thus the basic problem of postwar Europe.

The economic effects of these various factors also directly affected the fiscal situation in each country, serving in some cases to increase expenditures and in others to reduce revenues. Fiscal instability in turn contributed to the disruptions and maladjustments in industry and trade. Government policies, developed under stress and strain by inexperienced and insecure administrations, added to the complications.

The crux of the problem lay in helping the participating countries so to increase their productive power and exporting capacity as to restore a state of equilibrium or balance in their international accounts. Once this was reasonably achieved, the Monetary Fund and the World Bank, supplemented by a resumption of the flow of private credits, could presumably be depended upon to maintain exchange stability and promote further economic expansion. The focus was thus on an *intermediate period*—of something like five years' duration. Accordingly, a definite termination date and a tapering off of the program after the first crucial year or so was necessary. A permanent underwriting of European deficits by the United States government could of course not be contemplated.

Several guiding principles were involved.

1. Concentration on the quick restoration of production of key commodities was essential. Subnormal activity in industries of fundamental and ramifying importance means subnormal activity nearly everywhere; high-level production in these lines makes possible recovery and expansion elsewhere. For example, without adequate food, or fertilizer, or transport, no European state can recover prosperity and achieve stability. Coal is of far-reaching importance. It is vitally important in electric power, transportation, steel, and other basic in-

dustries, and it is an essential for agriculture because it is necessary in the production of nitrogen fertilizers.

2. If key industries are given a high priority, the extent of aid required elsewhere will rapidly be reduced. The concentration method is constructive and of ramifying importance; hence it is quicker and less costly.

3. The European aid problem included three principal categories of assistance. First, there were the urgent requirements for food and fuel for the rehabilitation of distressed populations. Second, and of a very different character, were the financial requirements for the restoration of stable currencies and the development of productive enterprises. Third, there were the needs for what may appropriately be called working capital—for industrial rehabilitation and the purchase of raw materials and supplies. Only the relief aspects of the plan should be on a gift basis.

4. A co-ordinated program was essential. A series of independent plans, designed chiefly to tide particular countries over immediate difficulties, would certainly be self-defeating.

Finally, the success of the plan would depend upon certain internal modifications of policy within Europe. Emphasis was laid upon four important requirements: (1) exchange stabilization; (2) monetary and fiscal reforms; (3) the reduction of trade restrictions; and (4) concentration on policies designed to increase production and exports. These various problems are closely interrelated, and none could be solved independently of the others. Nevertheless, concentrated efforts were necessary in the several directions simultaneously.

In view of these conceptions and principles of operation, it was apparent that an over-all figure of requirements covering a five-year period could not be determined with any precision. Changing conditions would inevitably call for modifications both as to amounts and types of aid required. Hence the plan set up rough estimates for the period as a whole, with annual appropriations adjustable in the light of subsequent developments.

A final part of the reconstruction program is the development of backward countries.

A final phase of America's far-flung program of world reconstruction was suggested by the president at the beginning of the year 1949, namely, systematic aid in the development of backward areas of the world. Highly developed industrial countries have long participated in the upbuilding of primitive regions. Private interests have seen in such expansion additional outlets for investment and new fields of enterprise; and governments have seen in colonial development new sources of essential raw materials and new markets for the future. Such conceptions constituted, indeed, the essence of so-called imperialism. The new program is essentially different in that it is conceived as an essential part of the program of restoring world prosperity and promoting universal progress.

The emphasis in this program is placed not on financial assistance but on guidance in the transformation of primitive economic regions. The fundamental requirement for rising standards of living is to increase the productive output of the average individual. This is as true of agricultural as of industrial economies. The new program builds on this premise and contemplates showing the people of such areas how to develop labor-saving devices and methods and to increase productive efficiency. Emphasis is placed on private enterprise.

This effort is altogether laudable in purpose, but it is beset with difficulties. To achieve significant results, it would be necessary in many cases to overhaul the educational system and build from the ground up. The first requirement is not guidance in the higher realms of technology, but elementary instruction in mechanical and industrial arts. Involved in the problem also are deeply embedded traditions and cultural attitudes. Even more fundamental in densely populated areas is the unceasing opposition to the introduction of labor-saving devices through fear of unemployment. This program can thus not be expected to yield results quickly. It must be regarded rather as a long-term program which here and there may serve as an impetus to expansion and may ultimately prove of universal significance.

Do the developments in the international realm thus briefly sketched forecast an early return of international economic equilibrium and stability—assuming the threat of war is somehow eliminated? Unfortunately, we cannot give a sanguine answer to this ultimate question. If the problem were merely one of restoring production and employment in the war-torn countries of Europe, we should be hopeful. The basic difficulty, however, lies much deeper. European countries, generally speaking, had a high level of domestic production and employment during the late twenties—but without achieving balanced economies. And Great Britain in 1937 at the very moment of impending crisis had full production and employment.

The basic sources of weakness are found in such intangibles as the dissipation of foreign investments, the loss of hitherto important sources of income from shipping and financial services, and especially the disorganization of former trade relationships and the restriction of international trade as a whole in consequence of nationalistic commercial policies and exchange instability.

Of paramount importance also is the continuing economic paralysis in the heart of the European continent. Our early postwar policy with respect to Germany—designed to destroy industrialism and to reduce the nation virtually to an agricultural status—was conceived in ignorance of the inescapable economic consequences to all Europe. The economic distintegration of Central Europe was further promoted by the Russian occupation and the continuing political difficulties. Even if an accord should be reached with Russia, one may still foresee a long period of difficulty, in consequence of the destruction of the network of commercial and financial relationships which nurtured and made possible the industrial Germany of former times. It should be emphasized that a restoration of the old level of iron and steel and armament production is not essential; indeed that concentration only served to distort the German economy and to limit the supplies of goods available for consumption. But a return to a well-rounded industrial system, operating on a high level of efficiency, with extensive international trade relations, is indispensable to the support of the German population and to the reestablishment of European equilibrium.

Similarly, a reconstruction of the economic life of Japan and of other parts of the Far East is essential to the restoration of world prosperity. The loss of producing and purchasing power in these areas restricts the markets there for the agricultural and industrial products of the Western world. Since the physical destruction of wealth was less in these regions and the economic relationships were on the whole somewhat simpler, the task of reconstruction should be easier than in Europe. However, because of restricted natural resources and great density of population, these countries face special difficulties of their own. The world as a whole thus appears to be faced with a long period of international instability, the ultimate outcome of which cannot be forecast. The United States cannot wholly escape the effects.

III. LIMITING FACTORS IN WORLD EXPANSION

In Chapter VII an effort was made to indicate the potentialities of the United States over the next century as gauged by basic natural resources. This chapter may well be concluded by a brief discussion of the controlling factors in economic development in other parts of the world.

In discussing world potentials it is desirable, first, to look at the problem globally—without reference to individual countries. The question is whether the resources of the earth, if systematically and scientifically developed, are adequate to permit an increase in production and living standards comparable to that projected for the United States.

The resources of nature, globally viewed, could support a vast increase in world living standards.

With respect to food, it may first be noted that only 3.5 million out of a land surface of 57.5 million square miles are now used for cultivated crops. It has been estimated by agricultural specialists that by irrigating some areas and draining others, by better adaptation of crops to soils, and by new methods of cultivation, the tillable area of the earth might readily be doubled.[1]

The possibilities of bringing additional land under cultivation are perhaps greater elsewhere than in the United States. The land resources of arctic and tropical areas may be made highly productive. The former would involve chiefly a greater use of short-season crops and the employment of refrigerating methods for accelerating germination.[2] The available land area of the tropics has been estimated at roughly 7.5 million square miles.[3] Opening of the tropics to cultivation depends upon the control of disease and insect pests and the provision of drainage facilities. While phenomenal progress has been made along these lines in recent years, one must be cautious in appraising the potentialities of such areas. Not only might the cost of subjugation prove prohibitive, but leaching of the tropical soil often leaves serious mineral deficiencies.

Nevertheless, when one takes into account reclamation possibilities in the tropics, the arctics, the deserts, and the oceans, the over-all expansion of tillable areas appears very great. Moreover, the development of these additional resources need not entail diminishing returns in relation to capital and labor employed. Thanks to the efficiency of modern power machinery, most of such land might well be brought under cultivation on a relatively low-cost basis.

The application of science to agricultural production in the manifold ways discussed in Chapter VII above would, in other countries as in the United States, result in greatly increased yields per acre. In most parts of the world farming is still comparatively primitive. Even where intensive agriculture has long been practiced, there is opportunity for much improvement in methods of land use.

Mineral resources considered as a whole are widely distributed over the face of the globe, and most of the important minerals are found in many parts of the world. The amounts available in different areas, however, vary widely, and every region is deficient in particular mineral products. Hence, extensive trade in minerals is indispensable to a universal expansion of industrialism.

Extensive resources of rich iron ore formed the basis of the industrial civilization of western Europe and the United States. As has already been noted, vast resources of iron ore have in recent years been disclosed in Canada and Labrador.[4] Extensive deposits exist in South America, large mines have been opened up in Soviet Russia, and important discoveries have been made in Africa. The Far East was formerly regarded as being deficient in iron ore resources, yet the supplies which became available to Japan in Manuchuria, Korea, North China, and the Malay Peninsula proved sufficient to found a high-powered industrial empire.[5] If we bear in mind the feasibility of using low-grade ores and the possibilities of substituting other metals for iron and steel in a wide range of uses,[6] we can only conclude that the world as a whole appears at least moderately well supplied with iron resources.

Such minerals as copper and lead are also widely distributed. While world resources are perhaps less abundant than is the case with iron ore and coal, the possibilities of substitution are very great. We have in mind especially aluminiferous clays and the magnesium supplies of the ocean.[7]

The deposits of coal are very extensive in many parts of the world, the reserves being adequate to meet requirements for centuries to come. As already noted, the vital importance of this basic resource is illustrated in its many uses as raw fuel, as coking material in the manufacture of iron and steel, and as a source of synthetic gasoline and other high-power gaseous and liquid fuels.[8]

Petroleum and natural gas are also found in extensive pools in many parts of the world. In recent times some of the greatest discoveries have been made in the Caribbean area, in Russia, and especially in the Near East. Moreover, exploration in other parts of the world has thus far been less intensive than within the United States. When account is taken of the potentials of synthetic products, it would appear that a vast increase in production and living standards would not be limited by inadequate supplies of oil and gas.

Power resources are equally abundant. There are vast untapped sources of hydroelectric energy in many parts of the world. Similarly, power derived from coal can be generated wherever coal is found.

Energy derived from atomic fission may be developed in other countries as well as in the United States. Electronic and supersonic forces are universal in character and, potentially, may be applied anywhere in the world.

However, very great difficulties stand in the way of realizing these world potentials.

The world situation is of course enormously complicated by the existence of many separately organized countries. The spirit of nationalism constitutes a powerful barrier to the systematic development of world resources. The requirements for national defense and the desire for a wide diversity of economic activity within each country lead to restrictions with respect to trade and also to the flow of capital and labor across national boundaries.

Moreover, the degree of scientific knowledge, organizing ability, and industrial aptitude varies widely in different countries. In some areas, where natural resources are adequate and the existing population is comparatively sparse, the lack of capital and managerial experience can be surmounted, in substantial degree, by utilizing foreign capital and experience in conjunction with local labor. But even with complete mobility of capital, managerial talent, and labor throughout the world, certain factors would combine to restrict the rise in living standards everywhere.

In economically primitive countries with dense populations, such as China and India, it is extremely difficult to get started on the road of technological advancement. On the one hand, the excessive supply of workers causes stout resistance to the introduction of labor-saving devices. At the same time, the cost of unskilled labor is so very low that there appears scant inducement to install labor-saving machinery. The dense populations of such countries as China and India are virtually fixed as to location, because of economic, climatic, racial, religious, and social considerations which keep them from migrating. In any case, extensive emigration from such areas would probably not solve the difficulty there because the vacuum might soon be filled by an increase in the rate of population growth.

Reference has been made to vast areas in the tropics, the arctics, and the deserts where food production could be enormously increased. But the distribution of world population is such as largely to divorce the development of these resources from the people most in need of greater food supplies. Even if American capital, with Chinese or Indian labor, were to produce food in the tropics or the arctics, this food could not be sold to the vast populations remaining in China and India, because of the lack of producing, and hence buying, capacity there. It may be noted that this would be largely true even under a single world state.

The possibilities for universal economic progress are thus greatly restricted by the conditions which exist in certain areas of the world. In some instances the limiting factors are found in a dearth of natural resources, but more often they arise from economic, cultural, and political complications. Even with world peace assured, the road to universal economic advancement would still be difficult.

The essence of this volume as a whole may be succinctly stated as follows: The achievement of economic progress is everywhere dependent upon the combined influence of: (1) natural and human resources; (2) scientific discoveries and inventions; (3) engineering applications; (4) business organization and management; (5) the economic system; and (6) the governmental system. Scientific discoveries would not yield practical results if we did not have invention; patented technological devices would be impotent without engineering applications to productive processes; engineering can function in a private enterprise system only in conjunction with a business organization able to appraise the commercial feasibility of new developments; individual business enterprise in turn will be thwarted if the economic system is defective; and, finally, the functioning of the economic system is dependent upon the character and the administration of the governmental system. Thus scientists, inventors, engineers, business managers, and professional students of economics and government co-operate in a common objective—that of increasing the capacity of the people to satisfy their wants.

As a result of a combination of developments summarized in Chapter I these several contributing forces came to work together so effectively as to give us a century or more of phenomenal economic progress. The natural endowments of the earth are such as to permit a vast rise in world standards of living over a long period of time. Whether we can achieve the potentialities before us will depend primarily upon the degree to which we can continue to make science, business enterprise, economics, and government work effectively together toward a common end. The factors of decisive importance in our future economic growth appear to be not the adequacy of natural resources, or the availability of scientific and inventive genius, but rather the inherent difficulties involved in the over-all operation and management of the complex business, economic, and political system of the modern world.

APPENDIX

ANALYSIS OF CRITICISMS OF BROOKINGS STUDIES OF INCOME DISTRIBUTION AND ECONOMIC PROGRESS

The authorship of the four-volume series of studies published under the general title, *The Distribution of Income in Relation to Economic Progress*, was as follows:

America's Capacity to Produce, by Edwin G. Nourse, Frederick G. Tryon, Horace B. Drury, Maurice Leven, Harold G. Moulton, and Cleona Lewis (1934)
America's Capacity to Consume, by Maurice Leven, Harold G. Moulton, and Clark Warburton (1934)
The Formation of Capital, by Harold G. Moulton (1935)
Income and Economic Progress, by Harold G. Moulton (1935)

As we were reasonably content to allow the trend of events and accumulating evidence to test the validity of the analysis, we seldom replied to current criticisms. It seems desirable, however, at this place to refer briefly to the major objections which were advanced in connection with the several sections of the analysis. The criticisms related in part to the adequacy of the statistical data supporting crucial points, but more largely to the interpretative analysis.

Step 1. Since traditional economic theory held that *normally* all our productive capacity is utilized, it was difficult for many to believe that in a prosperous period such as the twenties there could have been any appreciable industrial slack. Hence efforts were made to cast doubt on the validity of the estimates. It was pointed out that the figures were at best rough approximations; and it was suggested that seasonal factors and other frictional elements were perhaps not given adequate weight.

We ourselves had stated as explicitly as possible that our estimates were, in the nature of the case, merely rough approximations. But we were convinced that while the final estimates might well be off several per cent in either direction, the amount of unutilized capacity certainly ranged somewhere from 15 to 25 per cent.

We had also taken full account of seasonal factors and made allowance for shutdowns essential for periodic repairs and other operating conditions. In short, we sought to arrive at a "practically attainable" capacity rather than a theoretical capacity. Moreover, we checked our findings with technicians connected with the various industries. Finally, after compiling from these results an over-all estimate of productive capacity, we made a further reduction of 5 per cent in order to take account of possible frictional elements not otherwise identified, such as shifts in demand and the dislocations resulting from technological advances.

A directly opposite criticism came from certain writers who had been impressed with the claims of "technocracy" and the potentials of economic planning. Such writers held that we had greatly underestimated the amount of productive capacity by allowing too much for impeding or disturbing factors which could readily be eliminated by a more perfect organization of industrial society. But the question at issue was how well the existing economic organization was performing, not how a more perfect one might function. In short, taking the system as it *is*, how close to capacity was it actually operating?

Steps 2 and 3. Two principal criticisms were made of the analysis of the distribution of income and the allocation of such income as between consumptive spending and saving. The first objection was that the budget samples showing the pattern of expenditures and savings were too meager to warrant positive conclusions. Such reviewers, however, overlooked the fact that all of the budget surveys then available showed closely corresponding results. That is, regardless of the number of families involved, regardless of the geographic area covered, and regardless of the type of occupation in which the families covered were engaged, the division of the income as between the major categories of consumptive goods and as between consumption and savings was very similar. The results shown by this wide variety of samples are as significant as those that might have been obtained from a much larger single sample. (Later and more extensive surveys confirm these patterns. See pages 121-23.)

The second criticism was that the alleged tendency for money savings to increase relatively to spending was not adequately demonstrated. One reviewer sought to destroy the conclusion by showing that there was no *straightline trend* toward greater saving over the whole period under review. We made no such contention, holding merely that the evidence showed an upward tendency over the three decades as a whole, and especially during the period of the twenties, for which the data were more adequate.

A more common criticism was that there was no evidence to show that the *average individual* was becoming more thrifty over the period under review; on the contrary, there was held to be some evidence to show that thrift was presumably declining among the masses. What such traditionalists fail to grasp is that the *thrift habits* of the *average* person, or of the masses, is of very minor importance in aggregate savings. Without *any* change in individual *propensities* to consume, the proportion of the national income that is set aside as savings may, as we showed, rise for two reasons: (1) because a rising level of income has increased the margin for savings, and (2) because the percentage of the aggregate national income accruing to those in the upper-income brackets—where the proportion saved is very high—is progressively increasing. There could be a positive decline in thrift among the masses, and at the same time the percentage of the aggregate national income saved might be rapidly rising.

Step 4. The segment of the analysis pertaining to the relationship between consumption, saving, and capital formation evoked the most vigorous criticism. Adherents of the classical conception that all money savings are automatically spent for capital goods were quick to challenge the validity of our data. They *assumed* that the volume of money savings flowing into investment channels would—apart from bankers' compensations and expenses—necessarily equal the volume of security flotations for purposes of capital construction. Our figures for 1929 which showed roughly 15 billions of individual money savings available for security purchases, as compared with approximately 5 billions of security flotations for purposes of actual capital construction thus appeared to such theorists as obviously erroneous. (*New* security flotations were, in fact, much larger; but compilations by Moody's Investors Service showing the purposes to which the proceeds of corporate issues were devoted indicated that only a fraction of the amounts available was actually used for capital construction. See page 122.)

Critics sought to explain away the disparity between our figures of available savings funds and actual capital formation in two ways:

First, it was pointed out that the savings figures were at best rough estimates, and thus the amount of the savings funds available might be greatly overstated. It was equally possible, however, that such shortcomings as existed in the data might have served to understate the amount of the savings—a contingency that was not mentioned. Recent estimates of individual savings made by the Department of Commerce for 1929 are very close to our estimate—when proper allowance is made for realized capital gains. (See page 365 below.)

Second, it was held that our savings figures were inflated some 6 billion dollars by the inclusion of capital gains as a part of the national money income. This criticism flows from the traditional approach, which fails to recognize the three separate steps of money saving, market investment, and actual capital formation, and which regards money savings as simply identical with capital formation. Since capital gains are derived not from production but from mere enhancement of values, they seemed to be automatically excluded from "savings" as thus conceived.

But realized capital gains do, in fact, provide current funds which the recipients thereof may direct either to consumption channels or savings channels. In 1929, for example, large amounts of goods are known to have been purchased with capital gains; indeed, the flow of funds derived from capital gains into both commodity markets and security markets was a very dynamic—albeit unstabilizing—factor in the business and financial situation of that year. Hence when one is concerned with tracing the flow of *money* income through financial and commercial markets to determine its bearing on the actual functioning of the economic system, there can be no subtraction of realized capital gains. Moreover, if that portion derived from capital gains were to be deducted, it would have to be deducted from *aggregate* money income (including that derived from speculative profits) rather than from the savings portion only. But if this were done, then the disposable income would fall that much short of the aggregate disbursements actually made in consumption and investment channels: the over-all income and outgo accounts simply would not balance. In short, if capital gains be omitted from the aggregate disposable income, then a portion of the goods and securities actually purchased during the current year would also have to be eliminated.[1]

This point may be concretely illustrated by Department of Commerce estimates of savings for the year 1929.[2] The method used by the Department in estimating individual savings was to deduct estimated aggregate consumer expenditures from aggregate income payments to individuals—after allowances for personal taxes, etc. The actual figures are as follows:

	Billions
Income payments to individuals	82.6
Personal taxes, etc.	3.0
Disposable income of individuals	79.6
Consumer expenditures	70.8
Net savings of individuals	8.8

Since aggregate income payments to individuals are obtained by adding up wages, salaries, interest, dividends, etc., it is clear that income derived from capital gains is not included in either "income payments to individuals" or "disposable income of individuals." But, as already noted, individuals actually used money income derived from capital gains in buying commodities as well as in buying securities. Hence the figure from which consumer expenditures must be subtracted is not 79.6 billions, but 79.6 plus 6.2 billions[3] of capital gains—which leaves *money* savings at 15 billions.

It will be noted that this figure is very close to our estimate of individual savings available for investment. The two figures are not, however, altogether comparable because in our figure savings used directly by business enterprisers in capital formation are excluded.

Finally, some reviewers held that our contention that the excess money savings were "absorbed" in bidding up the prices of existing securities involves a fallacy. It was said that "bidding up the price level of existing securities cannot absorb current savings, inasmuch as what the buyer invests the seller disinvests." As others put it, "what the seller gains, the buyer at the higher price loses." This contention is not focused on the issue—which is whether more money savings are required in the purchase of existing assets when their prices are rising. A concrete illustration drawn from a real estate boom situation will perhaps serve best to indicate what is involved.

In the Florida real estate boom of the late twenties the price of land rose rapidly, say, from $1,000 to $5,000 a unit. At the beginning of the boom period a certain property was bought by A for $1,000 out of income. As a result of an abundance of investment money in the hands of B, C, D, and E, together with confident expectations as to future probabilities, the prices at which this land exchanged hands rose at each successive sale. B, C, D, and E, by hypothesis, paid for the land out of current income (money savings). With each successive transfer a greater volume of money savings was required to buy the given plot of land; each new buyer had to write a larger check against his bank account. Money savings to the extent of $5,000 were finally required to purchase land which at the beginning was bought for $1,000. Money savings were thus clearly absorbed in bidding up the price of existing land; and meanwhile no new assets were being created. In this process neither A, nor B, nor C, nor D lost anything. Whether E, the final buyer *to date*, loses will depend upon the price at which he may sell—possibly several years later. All that can be said is that during the *current time period* there were no losses offsetting the realized capital gains.

It was also pointed out that our estimates of capital formation for 1929 were very much lower than those of the National Bureau of Economic Research, the latter running as high as 12 billion dollars. The explanation of this difference, of which we were of course fully aware, is found in the fact that the two sets of figures do not attempt to measure the same things. Our figure of 5 billions related to the amount of new capital financed *through the sale of securities*, including mortgages, and did not pretend to measure the total amount of capital formation. Much new construction is, in fact, financed in other ways, concretely by: (1) direct use of corporate surplus and retained profits of individual business enterprisers; (2) direct business outlays charged to expense or against special reserve funds; (3) bank loans; and (4) direct use of savings by individuals for home construction.

In contrast, the National Bureau was seeking to determine the aggregate volume of actual capital formation, by studying the data pertaining to the production and sale of capital goods. In the Bureau's compilations there would automatically be included not only such capital formation as is financed through the security markets but also that financed by the various other methods just mentioned. In addition, the Bureau's figures also include some durable consumer goods paid for with funds which we classify as consumer expenditures rather than savings. It should be understood that to the extent such goods are classified as capital there is, by definition, a corresponding increase in the *money* income allocated to savings.

Our figures are readily reconcilable with the National Bureau's data by the addition of the items mentioned above. We excluded them simply because they were not pertinent to our analysis—which was focused on the question whether all of the *money savings available for investment through the security markets* was withdrawn from such markets by business enterprisers for the purpose of capital expansion.

Step 5. Criticisms of the final step in the analysis, namely, alternative methods of broadening the distribution of income, were of two types. The first proceeded from the assumption that price reductions in line with increasing productivity are incompatible with large-scale business organization. It was held that to make the plan effective it would be necessary either to break up all large aggregations or consolidations of capital and return to small-scale "atomistic" competition, or to subject the price and profit system to rigid government regulation. Since a general return to small-scale business was a manifest impossibility, those who accepted the conclusion to which the analysis thus far had led regretted that we had not suggested some form of government control. Others, recognizing the inherent administrative difficulties involved in government regulation of prices and profits, simply dismissed the price reduction method as visionary.

This general point of view ignores the fact that the most noteworthy price reductions in recent decades have been made by competing giant corporations. Moreover, it is assumed that it is always good policy for companies which are in a position to "administer" prices to charge at all times all that the traffic will bear. Such an assumption overlooks the importance of competing products and also the significance of expanding markets in the interest of long-run profits.[4]

It is of interest in this connection that in recent years many heads of large industrial corporations have gone on record in favor of reducing prices as a means of expanding markets and sustaining economic progress. Leading business associations have also taken the same position, notably the National Manufacturers Association, the Chamber of Commerce of the United States, and the Committee for Economic Development. The chief deterrent to positive reductions of prices has been the rapid advance in wage rates—which at times has run ahead of technological progress.

The second type of criticism denied that a price reduction policy, even if followed, would be an effective means of broadening the distribution of income. Some held that a reduction in prices would inevitably reduce profits because "marginal costs will tend to rise as output expands." This, of course, ignores the advantages of full-capacity operation, and fails to see that new plant and equipment of improved quality and increased efficiency, would mean progressively lower, rather than higher, costs.

Others admitted that aggregate profits might be increased through price reductions, but contended that this would only make the concentration of income greater. The remedy was thus held to be inconsistent with the requirements. Those who held this point of view failed to differentiate between *aggregate* profits and *relative* profits. It is readily possible for *aggregate* profits to be increasing while at the same time the *relative proportion* of the total income going to profits is declining. For example, if as a result of price reductions in 1929 the slack in the economic system had all been taken up, the aggregate national income would have increased by roughly 15 billion dollars. If 14 billions of this had accrued to workers hitherto unemployed or working but part time, and 1 billion had accrued as profits to the owners of capital, the *proportion* of the new aggregate income going to profits would have been appreciably reduced. Profits, in fact, constitute so small a fraction of the aggregate national income that a substantial increase in the proportion going to wages may occur even when aggregate profits are expanding.

A final criticism—not related to any specific step in the analysis—was that we had not recognized that the entire process of capital formation is automatically regulated by the interest rate. Our point of view with respect to the interest rate may be briefly stated as follows: If the interest rate did in fact automatically regulate the savings process, then no maladjustment between the volume of money savings entering investment channels and the flow of new security issues for purposes of expansion would ever occur. Since the facts clearly show that there was a wide discrepancy, the interest rate was evidently not an effective regulator. It may be noted in this connection that the theory that interest rates are an automatic regulator of the volume of savings and investment was an *assumption only* and had never been inductively verified. As the present writer has pointed out on many occasions, the interest rate is of negligible importance in the calculations of businessmen with respect to capital expansion.[5] The significance of interest is discussed at several places in the present volume.

The reader is here referred to the evidence of later years, presented on pages 121-25, which confirms the major conclusions reached in the four volume series.

NOTES

CHAPTER I

PAGE

8 [1] John Stuart Mill, *Principles of Political Economy* (1848), Ashley ed., p. 751.

9 [2] Although both these lines of reasoning were commonly advanced, the apparent dilemma to which such analysis led was seldom stated as sharply as we have put it in the text above. Indeed, later writers became beguiled with the variations between the rate of interest required to induce additional savings and the productivity of additional capital goods as an automatic regulatory mechanism. If savings should increase, the productivity of the additional physical capital would decline—thus lessening the incentive to save. Conversely, if savings should decline, the high productivity of physical capital would, through raising the return on capital, encourage saving. Thus the money rate of interest and the rate of return on new capital would tend to an equilibrium. This process became a central feature of the automatic mechanism by which the capitalistic, free enterprise system was supposed to be maintained in a state of balance. In contemplating this automatic mechanism of adjustment, there was a tendency to lose sight of the comparatively static conditions to which the analysis led. For further consideration of this problem. See Chap. 4.

9 [3] Mill, *Principles of Political Economy*, pp. 731ff.

10 [4] *Report of the 68th Meeting of the British Association for the Advancement of Science* (1899), pp. 4, 12-13.

13 [5] In truth, the apparent surpluses were a reflection of inadequate buying power rather than satiated appetites. By contrast the increase in purchasing capacity in the United States in the 1940's together with food relief requirements abroad had again produced a condition of "scarcity" for many important food products. This situation may be expected to change as world conditions become more stable and agricultural production increases. See Chap. 5 for agricultural production potentialities over the century ahead.

13 [6] See Harold G. Moulton, *Japan: An Economic and Financial Appraisal* (1931).

16 [7] See National Resources Committee, *Technological Trends and National Policy* (1937), Pt. 3, sec. 1.

17 [8] These estimates are from the Bureau of Agricultural Eco-

PAGE

nomics, *A Chronology of American Agriculture, 1790-1940* (1941).

17 [9] See H. W. Quaintance, *The Influence of Farm Machinery on Production and Labor*, publication of the American Economic Association, 3d Series, Vol. 5 (November 1904) based on investigations published in the *Thirteenth Annual Report of the Commissioner of Labor, 1898*, Vol. 2.

17 [10] The same.

17 [11] Harold Barger and Hans H. Landsberg, *American Agriculture, 1899-1939, A Study of Output, Employment and Productivity* (1942), p. 253, National Bureau of Economic Research. Between 1939 and 1945 the product per worker showed a further remarkable increase of about 30 per cent. (See Martin R. Cooper, Glen T. Barton, and Albert P. Brodell, *Progress of Farm Mechanization*, U. S. Department of Agriculture Miscellaneous Publication No. 630, October 1947.) This increase was, however, in no small part due to longer hours and unusually favorable crop conditions.

19 [12] Adapted from John W. Finch, director of the U. S. Bureau of Mines, in an address before the American Association for the Advancement of Science, Dec. 28, 1937.

20 [13] Harold Barger and Sam H. Schurr, *The Mining Industry, 1899-1939; A Study of Output, Employment and Productivity*, National Bureau of Economic Research (1944), p. 77.

22 [14] Joseph E. Pogue, *Oil and the Americas* (1944).

28 [15] Data from the *Thirteenth Annual Report of the Commissioner of Labor, 1898*, Vol. 1, pp. 28-29, 40-41.

29 [16] See Solomon Fabricant, *Employment in Manufacturing, 1899-1939* (1942), pp. 59-63, 304-05, 325, 331-32; *Labor Savings in American Industry, 1899-1939*, National Bureau of Economic Research, Occasional Paper 23 (1945), pp. 23, 26, 39, 43-51; *Measuring Labor's Productivity*, National Industrial Conference Board, Studies in Business Policy (February 1946) No. 15, pp. 2-3.

29 [17] Spurgeon Bell, *Productivity, Wages, and National Income* (1940), p. 167.

31 [18] Harold G. Moulton, Commercial Banking and Capital Formation, *Journal of Political Economy* (June 1918), pp. 656-68.

32 [19] Traditional theory held that an expansion of bank credit would merely serve to raise prices and could not affect appreciably the volume of production. This reasoning assumed, it will be observed, that the new capital had no effect on production. But in a dynamic industrial society the new capital may be expected both to increase output and lower unit costs, and thus to permit price reductions. Meanwhile the resulting expansion of production

PAGE

serves to generate increased income and thus to make possible the eventual liquidation of the credit. It should be noted that although each particular credit advance has to be liquidated in due course out of savings, the continuous creation of new credits serves to provide a constantly expanding total supply of funds for business purposes—funds which would not other wise be *immediately* available.

36 [20] Alfred Marshall, *Principles of Economics*, 8th ed. (1920), pp. 318-20.

37 [21] F. W. Taussig, *Principles of Economics* (1921), Vol. 1, p. 188.

37 [22] See Chap. 4.

37 [23] Marx's full analysis did not appear until the publication of his monumental work *Das Kapital* in 1867. Nevertheless, the essence of his philosophy was contained in the *Communist Manifesto*. Accordingly, 1848 is commonly regarded as the birth year of communism. Friedrich Engels, an English businessman, was a disciple and financial supporter of Marx, as well as a literary collaborator.

CHAPTER II

40 [1] This summary of American and foreign depressions is based chiefly on Willard L. Thorp, *Business Annals*, National Bureau of Economic Research (1926).

46 [2] For discussion of the efficacy of this mechanism, see pp. 303ff.

CHAPTER III

69 [1] Isador Lubin, *The Absorption of the Unemployed by American Industry* (1929).

70 [2] Edwin G. Nourse, *America's Capacity to Produce* (1934), Chap. 19.

70 [3] For supporting data, see Maurice Leven, Harold G. Moulton, and Clark Warburton, *America's Capacity to Consume* (1934), especially pp. 28 and 102-03.

71 [4] For fuller discussion of this phenomenon, see Harold G. Moulton, *The Formation of Capital* (1935), Chap. 10.

75 [5] Based on composite series of statistical indexes compiled by the League of Nations Secretariat. For original charts, see League of Nations, *World Economic Survey, 1931-32*, p. 64; the same for *1933-34*, p. 320.

76 [6] The Brookings Institution, *The Recovery Problem in the United States* (1937), p. 39.

PAGE

85 [7] Annual Indexes of Industrial Production in Selected Countries, 1930-1938[a]
(1929 = 100)

Country	1930	1931	1932	1933	1934	1935	1936	1937	1938
United States	81	68	54	64	66	76	88	92	72
Germany[b]	88	72	58	65	83	95	106	116	124
Canada	85	71	58	60	73	81	90	100	90
Czechoslovakia	89	81	64	60	67	70	80	96	86
Austria	85	70	61	63	70	80	86	103	...
Poland	88	77	63	69	77	83	93	109	118
Italy	92	78	67	74	80	94	87	100	98
Belgium	89	81	69	72	73	82	87	96	80
France	100	89	77	83	78	76	80	83	79
Estonia	99	91	78	82	96	106	120	139	145
Norway	101	78	93	94	98	108	118	130	127
Chile	101	78	87	96	105	120	124	132	137
Finland	91	80	83	96	117	125	139	156	156
Hungary	95	87	82	88	99	107	118	130	126
United Kingdom	92	84	83	88	99	106	116	124	116
Netherlands	102	96	84	91	93	90	91	103	104
Sweden	102	96	89	91	110	123	135	149	146
Rumania	97	102	89	103	124	122	130	132	132
Denmark	108	100	91	105	117	125	130	136	135
Japan	95	92	98	113	128	142	151	171	173

[a] League of Nations, *World Production and Prices, 1938-1939*, p. 39; *Monthly Bulletin of Statistics* (September 1939), p. 428.
[b] Since March 1935 including the Saar, and since the middle of March 1938 including Austria.

87 [8] For a more detailed statement of recovery measures, see The Brookings Institution, *The Recovery Problem* (1937), App. B.

93 [9] Data from League of Nations, *Statistical Yearbook* and *Monthly Bulletin of Statistics.*

CHAPTER IV

98 [1] Thomas Nixon Carver, *Principles of National Economy* (1921), p. 165.

99 [2] Myron W. Watkins, "Commercial Banking and Capital Formation," *Journal of Poliitcal Economy* Vol. 27 (July 1919), pp. 584-85.

99 [3] See pp. 2-5, Chap. 1.

100 [4] Carroll D. Wright, *First Annual Report of the Commissioner of Labor* (1886), p. 257.

100 [5] David A. Wells, "The Great Depression of Trade," *Contemporary Review* (August 1887), pp. 291-92.

100 [6] Harold G. Moulton, "Commercial Banking and Capital Formation," *Journal of Political Economy* (May, June, July, and November 1918, and July 1919).

106 [7] See for example J. Laurence Laughlin, "Large Fortunes," *Atlantic Monthly* (July 1905); and G. P. Watkins, *The Growth of Large Fortunes: A Study of Economic Causes Affecting the Acquisition and Distribution of Property*, Publications of the

PAGE

American Economic Association (November 1907). In a survey published by the American Statistical Association (March 1908), G. P. Watkins submits statistical evidence which suggests that the tendency toward income concentration occurred in the United States more or less throughout the nineteenth century and that it was also characteristic of other western countries. Indeed such a development is to be expected in rapidly developing economies in which abundant opportunity exists for expanding the scale of business enterprise.

113 [8] Moulton, *Journal of Political Economy* (June 1918), p. 729.

114 [9] This analysis of the relation of consumption and capital formation was focused on long-term trends rather than on cyclical fluctuations. We did not contend that fluctuations in business activity might not sometimes begin with changes in the capital goods industries. A survey of business oscillations in the United States, however, indicated that "in most cases changes in business conditions appear to have originated in forces affecting the output of goods destined for consumption. . . . With reference to capital goods the most that can be said is that in some cases a recession or a pick-up in the construction of such goods has been a supplementary factor in bringing about business fluctuations," while "fluctuations in the amount of residential construction have been an important factor in initiating changes in general business conditions."

Many writers have pointed to the wider fluctuations in capital construction in periods of boom and depression as evidence that the capital goods industries are the pivot around which the economic system revolves. This conclusion does not, however, necessarily follow. The moment demand for consumption goods declines—for whatever reason—the demand for new capital goods declines also, *and in much greater proportion.* A slight shrinkage at the base of the pyramid very nearly eliminates the top. As the amount of unutilized plant and equipment increases as a result of the curtailment of consumptive demand, the production of new plant almost entirely ceases. Conversely, in a boom period a moderate rate of expansion in consumption may call forth a much more rapid rate of expansion in the construction of new capital. But the fact that a dog's tail oscillates more widely than the dog's body does not prove that the tail is wagging the dog.

114 [10] This was, for example, the thesis of the British economist, John A. Hobson.

116 [11] The extent to which proceeds have been used for purposes other than physical capital formation is revealed by compilations made by Moody's *Investors Service* for the period 1921 to 1945 inclusive. See following footnote.

122 [12] Moody's *Investors Service* has compiled estimates of New Domestic "Productive" Capital Issues for the period as far back as

PAGE

1921. From the lists of new domestic issues published by the *Commercial and Financial Chronicle*, a selection of "productive" issues is made. An issue is regarded as "productive" only when it results in new construction, betterments, or purchase of new equipment. It is not considered "productive" when its sole effect is a purely financial change, such as refunding, raising new capital for mergers or acquisitions of old plant or equipment. Funds raised to provide additional working capital are not included.

In applying these general concepts to actual classifications of specific individual issues, a number of cases arise where the purposes of the issue are too vaguely defined to permit complete accuracy. Therefore, the total of "productive" issues is published as a reasonably satisfactory estimate, rather than as an exact figure.

It should be noted here that funds raised to provide additional working capital are not included. Such funds may properly be regarded as "productive" when they are used to purchase additional *quantities* of inventory or to employ a larger labor force; but when they are used merely to finance high-priced inventory or to pay higher wages they clearly add nothing to real production. Over much of the period covered by Moody's figures, ordinary working capital requirements were met almost entirely from internal sources. But since 1945 the great rise in material prices and wage rates has necessitated large flotations to finance the higher cost level.

New "productive" issues for the years 1921-45 are shown below in millions of dollars.

Year	Productive Issues			Total Domestic Less Refunding	Ratio of Productive to Total Domestic Less Refund (Per cent)
	Corporate	Municipal	Total		
1921	864	1,199	2,063	2,900	71
1922	1,335	1,077	2,412	3,287	73
1923	1,624	1,043	2,667	3,678	73
1924	1,941	1,380	3,321	4,409	75
1925	1,824	1,352	3,176	4,956	64
1926	1,801	1,344	3,145	5,098	62
1927	1,781	1,475	3,256	6,132	53
1928	1,495	1,379	2,874	6,725	43
1929	1,787	1,418	3,205	9,420	34
1930	1,939	1,434	3,373	5,917	57
1931	796	1,235	2,031	2,786	73
1932	203	610	813	1,087	75
1933	106	156	262	644	41
1934	63	381	444	981	45
1935	94	430	524	1,258	42

PAGE

1936 ...	379	392	771	1,926	40
1937 ...	635	424	1,059	1,937	55
1938 ...	428	647	1,075	1,842	58
1939 ...	191	506	697	1,321	53
1940 ...	489	478	967	1,475	66
1941 ...	741	381	1,122	1,536	73
1942 ...	292	225	517	964	54
1943 ...	139	125	264	560	47
1944 ...	303	169	472	867	54
1945 ...	693	423	1,116	1,716	65

122 [13] It was this constant excess of available investment money, as compared with the demand therefor, which was responsible for the general downward trend of interest rates both long-term and short-term. For a discussion of the combination of factors responsible for the great fluctuations in interest rates, both long-term and short-term, from 1916 to 1945, see Willard E. Atkins, George W. Edwards, and Harold G. Moulton, *The Regulation of the Security Markets* (1946). This analysis also shows why a substantial new advance in interest rates after the war appeared inevitable.

123 [14] See *Consumer Expeditures in the United States 1933-36*, by Bureau of Labor Statistics and Bureau of Home Economics, published by National Resources Board; *Family Spending and Savings in Wartime* (1941) by the same, published by Bureau of Labor Statistics. For postwar surveys, see Federal Reserve Bulletin (August 1946) and (August 1948).

123 [15] Computed from data in *Survey of Current Business* (July 1948).

123 [16] In 1945 the amounts saved in the lower-income brackets were of course enlarged by the wartime increase in wages, patriotic appeals for saving, and the unavailability of many types of consumer goods.

124 [17] The 1929 figures are from *America's Capacity to Consume* (1934); for 1941 and 1946 data, see *Federal Reserve Bulletin* (August 1947), p. 961.

124 [18] The savings data here used are derived from Department of Commerce data on national income. However the savings figures differ somewhat from the "personal" savings figures of the Department. The Department's method of computing "personal" savings is to subtract aggregate consumption from aggregate personal income. Since both the income and the consumption estimates include numerous non-monetary items, the savings figures do not accurately measure individual *money* savings. We have therefore excluded the non-monetary items from both the income and the consumption estimates.

PAGE

125 [19] Data from U. S. Department of Commerce, *National Income and Product Statistics of the United States, 1929-1946* (July 1947), pp. 19, 44, 45; *Survey of Current Business* (February 1948), pp. 5, S5.

125 [20] John Maynard Keynes, *A General Theory of Employment, Interest and Money* (1936). It should be noted here that some phases of this analysis had been touched upon by Keynes in his *Treatise on Money* published in 1930, especially the point that savings might at times exceed real investment.

126 [21] The same, pp. 27-28.

127 [22] The same, p. 211.

128 [23] The same, p. 96.

128 [24] The same, p. 91.

130 [25] Since Keynes assumed that the marginal productivity of the additional capital would be less than that of existing capital, there would appear to be no possibility that the consumer goods produced by new capital could find a market by selling at lower prices. See the same, pp. 31-32.

132 [26] The same, p. 164.

132 [27] The same, p. 220.

135 [28] The same, p. 106.

137 [29] Alvin H. Hansen, *Fiscal Policy and Business Cycles* (1941), p. 306. Italics added.

137 [30] The same, p. 249. Hansen cited as evidence that in the late twenties consumption was 88 per cent of national income and that it was still 88 per cent in the late thirties, even though the distribution of income had been greatly changed. He implied that the remaining 12 per cent in each case represented funds available for private investment. This, however, left the very sharp increase in taxes out of account. In terms of disposable income, the percentage consumed rose from 88 to about 92.5.

13 [31] Lest Manchuria be regarded as an exception, it should be noted that its settlement was almost entirely on the basis of very small-scale subsistence agriculture.

CHAPTER VI

150 [1] It is of interest to note here that Karl Marx was not concerned with the issue of democracy versus totalitarianism. He was preoccupied with historical processes and revolution, and gave little thought to the organization of economic life once the capitalistic system had been overthrown. After the Russian revolution, events quickly showed the necessity of centralized dictatorship.

161 [2] For a thorough discussion of the evolution of the Russian program, see Alexander Baykov, *The Development of the Soviet Economic System: An Essay on the Experience and Planning in the U.S.S.R.*, (1946), p. 1.

PAGE

179 [3] *The Economist* (Aug. 2, 1947), pp. 177-79.

184 [4] The only toll-collecting and self-supporting water route today is the Panama Canal. Funds were raised by bond issues for the construction of this canal, and the tolls cover interest and amortization charges. However, a part of the cost is properly charged to the government because of the military significance of this route.

194 [5] There are some exceptions to this generalization, chiefly roads handling coal and iron ore. These can be effectively controlled through enforcement of nondiscriminatory standards.

196 [6] Statement of President Roosevelt recommending the act to Congress.

196 [7] See Willard E. Atkins, George W. Edwards, and Harold G. Moulton, *The Regulation of the Security Markets* (1946), pp. 95-99.

198 [8] See for example, consent decree judgment entered on July 2, 1948 in District Court of the United States for the Southern District of New York, *United States of America* v. *International Nickel Co. of Canada, Ltd. and the International Nickel Co., Inc.*

198 [9] See for example, Supreme Court of the United States, October Term, 1947, No. 464, *Federal Trade Commission*, petitioner v. *Morton Salt Company* (setting maximum discounts on carload lots).

199 [10] See for example, Supreme Court of the United States, October Term, 1947, *Federal Trade Commission*, petitioner v. *Cement Institute, et al.*

199 [11] Supreme Court of the United States, October Term, 1945, *American Tobacco Co.* v. *United States.*

201 [12] In the cement case referred to in footnote 10, the Circuit Court of Appeals of the Seventh District, which had original jurisdistion and which decided in favor of the defendants, contended in effect that the Federal Trade Commission apparently fails to understand that a uniform price for a standard product in a given market does not necessarily imply any collusion, but it would be a natural result of free competition. It also charged the Commission with bias and misleading use of language. The Commission "invariably employs the word 'match' for 'meet.' The importance which the Commission attaches to this 'matching of prices' rather than the 'meeting of prices' is illustrated by the fact that in its brief it uses the former phrase not fewer than thirty-seven times. . . . [The meeting of prices implies competition, while the matching of prices implies collusion.] Another favorite word is 'shrink.' It seldom speaks of 'absorbing' freight in order to meet an equally low price of a competitor but invariably talks about 'shrinking' the mill nets. It always speaks of a 'system' or 'formula' and never a 'method' of pricing, and the

PAGE

prices at the point of destination are always described as 'identical' rather than 'uniform.'" See *Federal Reporter*, Vol. 157, 2d Series (1947), p. 554.

CHAPTER VII

204 [1] The assumptions in this chapter about the increase in population and productive power were not derived from any projection of current trends with respect to population growth or man-hour output. The sole purpose was to test the adequacy of basic resources by setting a very high goal. It may be of interest, however, to compare the rate of expansion assumed with the rate of advance that occurred between 1900 and 1940. This may be indicated both by the increase in man-hour output and total national production of goods and services.

Various estimates have been made of the increase in output per man-hour for the American economy in recent decades. The best known of these range from 1.9 per cent to 2.5 per cent per annum. (See Solomon Fabricant, *Labor Savings in American Industry 1899-1939*, National Bureau of Economic Research, Occasional Paper 23, November 1945, pp. 34-40; and S. Morris Livingston, "Post-War Manpower and Its Capacity to Produce," *Survey of Current Business*, April 1943, p. 16). At such rates of increase, compounded, productive power would multiply somewhere from 6½ to 12 times in a hundred years. These rates are for the economy as a whole. The rates of advance for agriculture, mining, manufacturing, and public utilities taken together are somewhat higher than for trade and service activities.

Over the first four decades of the twentieth century population increased 75 per cent, and the length of the working day was meanwhile shortened approximately one third. These factors, as well as man-hour output, of course have a bearing upon the total national production. During these 40 years national product, figured at constant prices, trebled.

The rate of population increase assumed here is thus very much less than that which has actually occurred since 1900. The assumed rate of increase in output per capita is, however, close to that which took place in recent decades.

We made the assumption of a doubling of the population, arbitrarily. It should be observed here, however, that with so small an increase in population relative to the projected increase in output there might well occur important shortages of labor which would restrict the possibilties of expanding output. This seems the more possible in view of the fact that some of the largest increases in indicated consumption would be in lines where the service element, and hence the labor requirement, would be great-

PAGE

est. On the other hand, it should also be observed that if we remove danger of labor shortage by assuming a much larger increase in population with a somewhat smaller increase in total production, greater difficulties might be encountered in obtaining the enlarged requirements of such fundamental products as food and minerals.

However, as already indicated, we are not concerned in any way with prophesying the rate of population increase or the rate of productivity increase, or just where we might be a century hence with respect to either population or per-capita income. Our purpose is solely to answer the fundamental question whether the law of diminishing returns is likely in any near future to become again of such controlling importance as to prevent a vast rise in living standards in the century ahead.

204 [2] Data covering private expenditures are from U. S. Department of Commerce, *National Income and Product Statistics of the United States, 1929-46* (July 1947), pp. 41-44.

The education and health figure, however, includes both private and public expenditures. Private expenditures, shown by Department of Commerce figures, aggregated roughly 8 billions. Public expenditures for these express purposes, amounted in the fiscal year 1946 to approximately 4 billion dollars. Another half billion for education and health are included under the category of public assistance. It may be noted also that health programs conducted by industrial companies are not included in either the public or private categories. These have been estimated at over 100 million dollars a year. See J. Frederic Dewhurst and Associates, *America's Needs and Resources* (1947), p. 259.

The figures for educational expenditures are from statistical summaries of the U. S. Office of Education. The health totals are based upon figures published in U. S. Federal Security Agency, *Social Security Yearbook.*

Recreation and travel expenditures also include government outlays financed through public treasuries. In 1945-46 government outlays for transportation—federal, state, and local—aggregate 2,297 millions, and for recreation facilities 223 millions. Thus we have added 2.5 billions to the private outlay in this category. See Lewis H. Kimmel, *Governmental Costs and Tax Levels* (1948).

205 [3] See National Resources Committee, *Consumer Expenditures in the United States, Estimates for 1935-36* (1939), p. 85; Maurice Leven, Harold G. Moulton and Clark Warburton, *America's Capacity to Consume* (1934), Chap. 6.

205 [4] See National Resources Committee, *Consumer Expenditures in the United States,* p. 84.

205 [5] Miscellaneous expenditures include a wide range of minor

PAGE

items. The most important are: (1) those connected with churches and other religious activities, social welfare agencies, museums and libraries, and philanthropic foundations; and (2) a multitude of personal outlays, covering the charges of financial institutions for services rendered, legal fees, interest on personal debts, and dues to labor unions, business organizations, and professional societies. Since the great bulk of these outlays are for services and involve the consumption of negligible quantities of materials, they may be passed by here without special comment.

207 [6] The method employed in making this estimate was, in brief, as follows: Food consumption in the good year 1941, in quantity terms, by urban families having incomes of $5,000 and over has been estimated by the principal food groups. (See Willard W. Cochrane, *High-Level Food Consumption in the United States*, U. S. Department of Agriculture, Miscellaneous Publication No. 581, December 1945.) It is here assumed that, except that milk consumption might well be raised to a nutritionally adequate level, the quantity of food consumed at this income level would not be greatly increased as incomes rose further. On the other hand, it may be reasonably assumed that all those whose incomes are now much below this level would increase consumption of all kinds of foods, and would enlarge their use of concentrated high-value foods very substantially. It may safely be assumed that all those now having incomes below $5,000 would increase their consumption to the level of those now having incomes of $5,000 or more. Therefore we multiply the per-capita food consumption of the $5,000 and above group in 1941 by the assumed population a century hence.

209 [7] Charles M. A. Stine (the du Pont Company), "Molders of a Better Destiny," *Chemical and Engineering News* (Sept. 10, 1942), p. 1087.

211 [8] There are many individual cows whose production is over 1,000 pounds of butter fat, and the record is above 1,400. While such records are made under special conditions of forced feeding and suspended breeding, and are for 365 days as against the normal 305 days, they nevertheless suggest the range of possibilities.

212 [9] See p. 245 below.

214 [10] See "Uses for Vegetable Wastes" in poultry feeding, U. S. Department of Agriculture, *Science in Farming, Yearbook of Agriculture 1943-47*, pp. 739-43; various publications of the Department of Agriculture dealing with experiments in the use of brewers' and distillers' by-products and yeast in livestock feeding; utilizing garbage as feed for hogs, the feeding of cottonseed products to livestock, and the processing of vegetable wastes to produce high-protein and high-vitamin leaf meals; also Anna M. Wilson, *Fish Meal and Its Uses*, Service Bulletin No. 11, De-

INDEX

INDEX